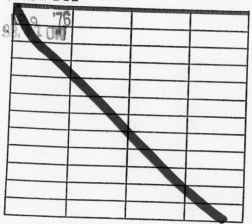

The Government of Republican Italy

THIRD EDITION

JOHN CLARKE ADAMS
SYRACUSE UNIVERSITY

PAOLO BARILE
UNIVERSITY OF FLORENCE

HOUGHTON MIFFLIN COMPANY · BOSTON

NEW YORK · ATLANTA · GENEVA, ILLINOIS · DALLAS · PALO ALTO

The authors, who consider his friendship their

greatest honor, dedicate this book to the memory of

PIERO CALAMANDREI

who epitomizes as no other can the humanistic

tradition of Italy's culture and the aspirations

for Italy's future as expressed in her liberal

democratic constitution

CONTENTS

PREFACE   v

GLOSSARY   vii

1. Introduction   1

2. Fascism   32

3. The Constitution   52

4. Parliament   59

5. The President of the Republic   77

6. The Council of Ministers   88

7. The Constitutional Court   95

8. The Administration   100

9. Local Government   118

10. The Judicial System   134

11. The Party System   152

12. Elections   171

13. The Economy   188

14. Labor and Social Security   203

15. Italy as a Liberal Democracy   214

BIBLIOGRAPHY   239

INDEX   241

PREFACE

The third edition of *The Government of Republican Italy* has been thoroughly revised and brought up-to-date as of June, 1971. An additional chapter has been added on the Constitutional Court.

Florence, Italy

J. C. A.
P. B.

PREFACE

The words in which this book is written are those of John Clarke Adams. It was his task to present the theory and practice of the Italian republic in the English language and to students accustomed to the theory and practice of Anglo-American democracies.

The expert knowledge on which the value of the book primarily rests is that of Paolo Barile.

The political philosophy of liberal democracy that permeates the book and the interpretation of the Italian scene that it presents are shared by the two authors.

The authors thank their many colleagues and friends of whose time and good nature they have unabashedly availed themselves. Professor Giorgio Spini, Professor William C. Fleming and Signora Franca Toraldo di Francia all read the first chapter and made useful suggestions. Dr. Enzo Enriques Agnoletti performed the same services for the chapter on Fascism. Prof. E. A. Bayne consented to read and comment on most of the subsequent manuscript, the Hon. Fernando Santi and the Hon. Vittorio Foa, deputies to parliament and secretaries of the Italian Confederation of Labor (CGIL), kindly made available valuable economic and labor materials to the authors. Senator Leopoldo Rubinacci, the Hon. Tristano Codignola, the Hon. Ludovico

Camangi, Giovanni Canini, Italo Viglianesi and Enzo Dalla Chiesa kindly gave their advice on various details of the political, administrative, and labor scene.

And finally the authors express their gratitude to Dr. Gian Paolo Biasin, to Helen Adams, to Dr. Dayton D. McKean and to the staff of Houghton Mifflin for their valuable assistance in the editing and polishing of the manuscript.

J. C. A.
P. B.

Florence, Italy

GLOSSARY

DC	Christian Democracy (*Democrazia cristiana*)
MSI	Italian Social Movement (*Movimento sociale italiano*)
PCI	Communist Party (*Partito comunista italiano*)
P d'A	Action Party (*Partito d'azione*), disbanded in 1946
PDIUM	Italian Democratic Party of Monarchist Unity (*Partito democratico italiano di unità monarchica*)
PDL	Labor Democrat Party (*Partito democratico del lavoro*), deceased circa 1950
PLI	Liberal Party (*Partito liberale italiano*)
PR	Radical Party (*Partito radicale*)
PRI	Republican Party (*Partito repubblicano italiano*)
PSDI	Democratic Socialist Party (*Partito socialista democratico italiano*). Name of right wing Socialist party 1952–68 and 1970 to date.
PSI	Italian Socialist Party (*Partito socialista italiano*). Name of the major Socialist party 1892–1930 and 1947 to date (except for brief period in 1968).
PSIUP	Italian Socialist Party of Proletarian Unity (*Partito socialista di unità proletaria*). Name of the major Socialist party 1943–47. Name of left wing Socialist party 1964 to date.
PSLI	Italian Workers' Socialist Party (*Partito socialista dei lavoratori italiani*). Name of right wing Socialist party 1926–30 and 1947–51.
PS(SIIS)	Socialist Party (Italian Section of the Socialist International) (*Partito socialista [Sezione italiana dell'internazionale socialista]*). Name of the major Socialist party 1930–43. Name of right wing Socialist party 1951–52.
PSU	Unitary Socialist Party (*Partito socialista unitario*). Name of right wing Socialist party from 1922 to its dissolution by the Fascists after one of its members, Zaniboni, attempted to assassinate Mussolini (November, 1925). Name of second right wing Socialist party 1949–51. Name of the major Socialist party briefly in 1968, after unification with right wing party (PSDI).
SV	South Tirol People's Party (*Südtiroler Volkspartei*)
UV	Val d'Aosta Union (*Union valdôtaine*)

1

Introduction

Area and population

Of the four major powers in western Europe, three — Great Britain, Italy, and West Germany — are approximately equal in population (c. 50,000,000) and in area (c. 100,000 square miles). The fourth, France, is almost twice as large in area and has a population of some 5,000,000 fewer citizens. No fifth power in western Europe can be compared with these states. Spain, Sweden, Finland, Norway, Poland, and Yugoslavia are larger in area than the smallest of the big four, but none has as many as 30,000,000 inhabitants.

Table 1

Country	Area (square miles)	Population (in thousands)	Population Density (number per square kilometer)
France	212,659	49,750	91
West Germany	95,918	57,640	232
Italy	117,471	53,648	178
United Kingdom	94,279	54,744	224

In spite of this evidence of virtual equality among these four major powers, in the opinion of the world at large and of her own citizens as well, Italy has long held the position of *ultima inter pares,* an opinion which has some historical justification but is no longer consonant with reality.

Of these four leading western European powers only one, Great Britain, is a well-established liberal democracy. Great Britain shares with western Europe's lesser powers, notably Belgium, Denmark, the

The Regions and Provinces of

ITALY

International boundaries
Regional boundaries
Provincial boundaries

KEY TO THE PROVINCES OF ITALY

PIEMONTE
1 Alessandria
2 Asti
3 Cuneo
4 Novara
5 Torino
6 Vercelli

VAL D'AOSTA
7 Aosta

LIGURIA
8 Genova
9 Imperia
10 La Spezia
11 Savona

LOMBARDIA
12 Bergamo
13 Brescia
14 Como
15 Cremona
16 Mantova
17 Milano
18 Pavia
19 Sondrio
20 Varese

TRENTINO–ALTO ADIGE
21 Bolzano
22 Trento

VENETO
23 Belluno
24 Padova
25 Rovigo
26 Treviso
27 Venezia
28 Verona
29 Vicenza

FRIULI–VENEZIA GIULIA
30 Gorizia

31 Trieste
32 Udine
93 Pordenone

EMILIA–ROMAGNA
33 Bologna
34 Ferrara
35 Forlì
36 Modena
37 Parma
38 Piacenza
39 Ravenna
40 Reggio Emilia

TOSCANA
41 Arezzo
42 Firenze
43 Grosseto
44 Livorno
45 Lucca
46 Massa
47 Pisa
48 Pistoia
49 Siena

MARCHE
50 Ancona
51 Ascoli Piceno
52 Macerata
53 Pesaro

UMBRIA
54 Perugia
55 Terni

LAZIO
56 Frosinone
57 Latina
58 Rieti
59 Roma
60 Viterbo

MOLISE
61 Campobasso

ABRUZZI
62 Chieti
63 L'Aquila
64 Pescara
65 Teramo

CAMPANIA
66 Avellino
67 Benevento
68 Caserta
69 Napoli
70 Salerno

PUGLIE
71 Bari
72 Brindisi
73 Foggia
74 Lecce
75 Taranto

BASILICATA
76 Matera
77 Potenza

CALABRIA
78 Catanzaro
79 Cosenza
80 Reggio Calabria

SICILIA
81 Agrigento
82 Caltanissetta
83 Catania
84 Enna
85 Messina
86 Palermo
87 Ragusa
88 Siracusa
89 Trapani

SARDEGNA
90 Cagliari
91 Nuoro
92 Sassari

Netherlands, Norway, Sweden, and Switzerland, a tradition of efficient and effective liberal democratic government, a blessing that has been denied to France, Germany, and Italy. The governments of these countries are each the expression of an unachieved democracy; they are each operating under constitutions written after the last war. Of these constitutions, Italy's, which took effect on January 1, 1948, is the oldest and the most democratic.

Geography

The territory of Italy comprises 117,471 square miles, situated in the south of Europe, and jutting deep into the Mediterranean Sea. This territory is divided geographically into three major units: continental Italy, an integral part of the European continent lying between the southern ranges of the Alps and the river Po; peninsular Italy, which protrudes southeastward from the main body of Europe and which is itself transversed by the range of the Apennines, from the west coast near Genoa to the east coast at Ancona; and insular Italy, composed of a series of islands to the south and west of the Italian peninsula, of which Sicily and Sardinia are much the largest. Among the lesser islands the better known, from south to north, are Pantelleria, where the Allies first landed from Africa on the way to Sicily in 1943; Lipari, where the Fascists kept political prisoners; Capri and Ischia, both in the Bay of Naples; Monte Cristo, whose fabulous fictitious count is in good part responsible for the fame of Alexandre Dumas *père;* and Elba, off the coast of Tuscany, where Napoleon was first exiled.

During the twentieth century Italy built a colonial empire and extended her continental frontiers beyond the ethnic limits of the Italian people. Most of these gains were lost after her defeat in the Second World War. The countries annexed by Italy in the Fascist period — Ethiopia in 1936 and Albania in 1939 — were liberated, and their independence was recognized by the peace treaty. At the same time the Dodecanese Islands, taken by Italy during the Italo-Turkish war in 1912, were ceded to Greece. The Italians also renounced their concession in Tientsin and all special privileges and benefits in China. By later United Nations action Libya, comprising Cyrenaica, Tripolitania, and Fezzan, became an independent sovereign state. Eritrea was united with Ethiopia, and Italy's other former colony, Italian Somaliland, pending her independence, was placed under the international trusteeship system with Italy as the administering authority. With the independence of Somalia in 1960 Italy ceased in any sense to be a colonial power.

Political history

Italy, Prince Metternich is alleged to have said, is merely a geographical expression. This half-truth was a useful excuse for the resplintering of Italy at the Congress of Vienna in 1815 and the reestablishment of the petty principalities into which it was formerly divided. Thus after 1815 in the territory that is now Italy there were two native kingdoms at the northern and southern extremes of this geographical expression, Piedmont and Naples (the former also known as the Kingdom of Sardinia and the latter as the Kingdom of the Two Sicilies). Sandwiched between were one grand duchy (Tuscany), three duchies (Modena, Lucca, and Parma) and a Papal State. The former maritime republics of Genoa and Venice were denied their independence by the monarchist and legitimist Congress of Vienna; and the former was given to Piedmont and the latter, along with the Lombard plain north of the Po, including Milan, became a kingdom within the Austro-Hungarian Empire, under the name of the Regno Lombardo-Veneto.

In 1815 considerable evidence substantiated Metternich's statement. Italy had been politically divided since the Middle Ages. The population of the various sections of the country had markedly different racial and cultural origins and histories. Only a small number of educated people could be said to have in common the language of Dante Alighieri and the aspiration for political unity of Niccolò Machiavelli.

What Metternich failed to realize or was at any rate careful not to say was that Italy was nevertheless a political necessity. The petty principalities reestablished by the Congress of Vienna were anachronisms that were almost certainly doomed to failure. They maintained their unstable equilibrium for as long as they did in part because of the lassitude of a Europe exhausted by Bonaparte's destructive dynamism and in part because it was in the interest of the great powers, particularly Austria, to keep them standing; but the respite was not long enough to give most of them time to consolidate their position.

Of the seven Italian states, only four, Tuscany, the Papal States, Naples, and Piedmont, had any real consistency. The three duchies, Lucca, Modena, and Parma, were artificial units. Lucca consisted mainly of the present Tuscan province of Lucca. Parma and Modena consisted primarily of the Emilian provinces of Piacenza, Parma, Reggio, Ferrara, and Modena, lying across the Apennines, to the north of Tuscany. The Duchy of Parma, however, extended west across the Apennines to the present province of Massa on the Tyrrhenian Sea. Of these Lucca was the first to go, expiring with its childless duchess Maria Luisa in 1847. Modena and Parma collapsed a dozen years later, when their protector, Austria, went down in defeat in the first of a series of four consecutive wars that she lost between 1859 and 1945.

The governments of these improvised duchies were reasonably enlightened. Living conditions were not significantly different from those in other parts of northern Italy (Piedmont, Regno Lombardo-Veneto, and Tuscany), but one could hardly expect these unnatural little agglomerations to elicit loyalty or sacrifice from their subjects.

The Grand Duchy of Tuscany was a more rational entity. It was twice as large as the three duchies together, and it was a geographical, historical, and cultural unit. Its first Grand Duke, Pietro Leopoldo, was one of the most enlightened and competent of the eighteenth-century despots. He was among other things an efficient and far-seeing administrator, and he had the respect and loyalty of most of his subjects.

To the south were the Papal States, with their capital in Rome, and the Kingdom of the Two Sicilies, with its capital in Naples. The Papal States were larger than the duchies and grand duchy combined, and the Kingdom of the Two Sicilies was more than twice as large as the papal territories.

These governments had the advantage of being both traditional and indigenous, and had they shown even a small part of the efficiency and concern for the public weal of the Tuscan and Piedmontese governments, they might have evolved like many of the monarchies of the European continent toward representative democracy. Such an evolution, however, was not within the intentions or the capabilities of the southern Italian despots. William Gladstone described the government of Naples of his day with essential truthfulness beneath oratorical embellishment when he called it "the negation of God erected into a system of government." Although the Roman Popes of the nineteenth century were men of greater culture than the incredible kings of Naples, their government, except for a moment on the accession of Pius IX, was no better.

Until 1848, that year of revolution throughout Europe, the prestige of Tuscany, like that of the Papacy, had been high in Italy, but after the revolutions both the Grand Duke Leopoldo and the formerly liberal Pope, Pius IX, reacted in such a way that they lost all chance of leading the movement for a united Italy. After the Florentine revolt had been put down by a coalition of the great families of the landed aristocracy who invited the Grand Duke back, he stupidly offended his loyal subjects by returning escorted by Austrian troops.

Pius IX's reaction to the establishment of the Roman republic by Garibaldi and Mazzini was more violent. The "liberal" Pope in whom Gioberti and others hoped to find the leader of the cause of Italian unity turned about-face and became the implacable foe of united Italy and of liberal democracy.

The remaining state, the Kingdom of Piedmont and Sardinia, was ruled by reasonably enlightened despots. Its king, Carlo Alberto, proved far wiser (or better advised) than Leopoldo and Pius. He refused to rescind the constitution the people wrested from him in 1848, and that document, known as the *Statuto,* remained the basic formal law of Piedmont and later of Italy, until 1948. With the rise of nationalism the anachronistic duchies were doomed to go, and the Italian provinces of Austria were sure to be freed; with the rise of democracy the reactionary governments of Rome and Naples were doomed to failure: plums ripe for picking that fell to the industrious and sober Piedmontese, in part as a result of the statesmanship of Camillo Benso Conte di Cavour and the military victories in most of which the Italians played a secondary role, but also in part by default. In ridding themselves of their tyrants the Italians had nothing to lose. Only Tuscany might have challenged Piedmontese hegemony, but Tuscany was saddled with an unpopular Grand Duke and lacked a Cavour.

Thus with the defeats of Austria in 1859 (with the help of the French) and in 1866 (with the help of Prussia) Lombardy and the Veneto were joined to Piedmont, and continental Italy was united. Parma, Modena, Tuscany, and part of the Papal States joined Piedmont in 1859 and 1860. In 1861 the rest of peninsular Italy (except Rome) and Sicily were incorporated after Garibaldi's campaign. With the fall of Napoleon III as a result of the Franco-Prussian War, the royal forces entered Rome, and for the first time since Roman days Italy was united. At the end of the First World War the northeastern boundaries of continental ·Italy were pushed further into Europe at the expense of Austria, and the provinces of Trento, Bolzano, Trieste, and Istria were added.

At the end of the Second World War further rectifications of Italy's northern frontiers were made, this time to Italy's disadvantage.

The greatest loss was to Yugoslavia, to which was ceded all of the province of Istria and part of the province but not the city of Trieste. The port cities in this ceded territory, which included Fiume and Zara, were overwhelmingly Italian but the hinterland was predominantly Slav. It was a bitter blow to Italy to have these Italian cities made subject to a Balkan Communism, but the Fascist oppression of the Slav minorities in Italy and Mussolini's support of Ante Pavelic's Croatian tyranny during the war, plus the fact that a member of the House of Savoy sat on the Croatian throne,[1] made Italy's case a weak

---

[1] Aimone, Duke of Spoleto, of the Aosta branch of the House of Savoy, and a cousin of the King of Italy, accepted the throne, but never entered his realm.

one. Italy was permitted to keep Trieste, a city of emotional value to Italy and little practical value to anyone.

At the insistence of Charles de Gaulle the Franco-Italian frontier was also rectified, and two hamlets, Briga and Tenda, were ceded to France. De Gaulle's claim, which included the entire region of Aosta, came as a surprise, as no previous French government had made any territorial claims against Italy. In demanding from a defeated Italy in 1945 compensation in territories for Mussolini's stab in the back when he attacked a defeated France in 1940, De Gaulle risked creating a new Alsace-Lorraine for France. The prevailing reaction in Italy has been to consider De Gaulle's act one of petty vindictiveness that belied the myth of *grandeur* which he sought to assume for himself and his beloved country, an act that was hardly worth notice and quite beneath contempt.

Austria also sought, but was denied, a rectification of the Austro-Italian frontier involving the cession of the province of Bolzano, where the majority are German-speaking Tyrolese. The present boundary is a geographic rather than an ethnic one and it is a source of almost constant friction between the Austrian and Italian governments. The Austrian Catholic Party is particularly virulent in its attacks on Italy as with the addition of the votes of the intensely Catholic South Tyrol, it would be in a position to govern Austria by itself, without forming a coalition with the Socialists. Austria's claim carried little weight with the victors, as she was a defeated power.

Political unity

Italy is a united nation in the sense that Italian unity has been the common aspiration of all articulate Italians. Few Italians fought against the unification of Italy. Not even the Pope, armed with his traditional power of excommunication and his newly recognized (July 18, 1870) attribute of infallibility, had a single Italian fighting for him when the excommunicated Italian army of Vittorio Emanuele II entered Rome on September 20, 1870.[2]

With the single exception of the Sicilian separatist movement after World War II, which sought to make Sicily instead of Alaska the forty-ninth united state of America, there have been no Italian secessionist movements, and no wars of secession like those that Switzerland and the United States endured. The French-speaking population of the Val d'Aosta also expressed dissatisfaction after World War II, but through the efforts of local leaders, such as the region's most famous

[2] Ernesto Rossi, "Il nostro venti settembre," *Il ponte,* XV (1959), pp. 1069–1085 at 1077.

citizen, the historian Federico Chabod, the unrest was quickly overcome by the creation of a semiautonomous region. The Germanic population of the province of Bolzano are continually advocating secession, but they are Italians only in a legal sense.

Cultural disunity

The virtual consensus in Italy favoring political unity, however, neither resulted from nor brought about cultural unity.

The divisive force of regionalism operates in all territorial groups. The distinction between north and south, the city and the country, the right and wrong sides of the railway, are well-known phenomena. As long as they are counterbalanced by a sufficient basis of consensus these distinctions do not weaken the state. In Italy, however, in spite of a well-established political unity, the cultural divisions are great. Although these differences exist from region to region and even from province to province (and there are ninety-three provinces in Italy), the one radical difference which splits Italy in two is that between the north and the south. This difference has geographic, historical, and economic causes.

Cultural geography

In spite of the barrier of the mountains to the north, the position of Italy is quite different from that of Spain and Portugal. The Iberian peninsula is almost completely cut off from the rest of Europe by the Pyrenees mountains, and consequently Spain and Portugal have been only sporadically in contact with western European culture. The Alps have formed no such barrier against Italy. They protect the central part of Italy's northern frontier, but leave free access to the east and the west. Accordingly, northern Italy, comprising continental Italy and the northern part of peninsular Italy, instead of developing in relative isolation from Europe has long been an integral element in Western civilization. Southern Italy, which comprises the southern part of peninsular Italy and all of insular Italy, still remains, on the other hand, attached to the Mediterranean culture more than to the Western tradition.

Because of her geographical position, then, Italy is the crossroads of two important world cultures. Southern Italy is essentially Mediterranean in its culture pattern, while northern Italy forms an integral part of Western civilization. The dividing line between these two regions can be drawn roughly from Rome north and slightly east to Ancona on the opposite shore. The Apennines, unlike the Pyrenees, are not rugged enough to create a culture frontier, and all of Tuscany is culturally a part of the West. Rome belongs to both cultures. By the nature of its inhabitants it is more Mediterranean than Western, but a long line of European popes and its hundred years of experience as capital of an important European state have brought much of Western culture to this ancient Mediterranean city.

Cultural history

It was in northern, European Italy, during the late middle ages, that the city-states emerged. By the twelfth century these city-states, linked together in the *Lega lombarda* or, more loosely, under papal aegis in the Guelph faction, were able to stand off the Hohenstaufen emperors. City-states had arisen in the south of Italy as well; Amalfi particularly had been an important maritime power. The Hohenstaufens, however, were successful in curbing the city-states in the south and in setting up a centralized monarchy, while the ensuing Norman conquest imposed feudalism on Mediterranean Italy.

With a consistency that would almost suggest a conscious will, history has continued to keep these two cultures apart. The three most glorious movements of Italy's past — the *Rinascimento* (Renaissance), the *Risorgimento,* and the *Resistenza,* as well as her most shameful episode, Fascism — were all products of European Italy.

The Renaissance occurred in the hill towns of Tuscany and Umbria and in the *Val padana* (the Po Valley). From there it passed northward to France and England, where it took root and flourished. Although the Renaissance was a lay rather than a religious movement, it happened that the great Renaissance popes came from the merchant and banking families of the northern Italian cities. These popes gave the Renaissance their blessing and in so doing they encouraged and greatly hastened its growth. Had the new architects built no churches, had the painters and sculptors not adorned them, had the scholars not enjoyed the benevolent interest of the high ecclesiastic authorities, the Renaissance might never have reached fruition.[3] Thus these north Italian popes brought the products of the Renaissance to Rome as to a lesser degree the kings of Naples introduced them to Naples, but in the south the Renaissance tended to remain an exotic foreign plant.

The Renaissance itself would not have developed when and where it did had not the existence of the city-states in European Italy prepared its way. By the late Middle Ages these city-states had achieved a considerable degree of political independence and democracy. Their

[3] Giorgio Spini, *Storia dell'età moderna dall'impero di Carlo V all'illuminismo* (Rome: Cremonese, 1960), pp. 20–22.

presence in north and central Italy and their absence in the south were important factors in the division of Italian culture.

The *Risorgimento,* the nationalist movement of the nineteenth century that strove for Italy's unification, was also a primarily northern movement. Cavour, Gioberti, Balbo, D'Azeglio, and Vittorio Emanuele were Piedmontese. Garibaldi was from Nice and Mazzini from Genoa. Cattaneo and Iacini were Milanese, Manin and Tommaseo, Venetians, and Ricasoli, Tuscan. The poets Alfieri, Leopardi, and Foscolo, the composer Verdi, the novelists Manzoni, Nievo, and Fogazzaro, were all of the north. The few voices of liberty arising in the south, such as those of Silvio Spaventa and Carlo Poerio, were silenced by reactionary and tyrannous governments.

Not only in Italy's glorious moments have the north and the south been separated. Fascism was also a divisive force and a product of the north, or more particularly of the Po Valley and Tuscany. (Piedmont, which contributed heavily to the *Risorgimento* and the *Resistenza,* played a minor role in the Renaissance and Fascism.) Of the Fascist leaders Mussolini, Balbo, Grandi, and Arpinati were from Emilia-Romagna; Farinacci was a Lombard; the Cianos and Pavolini were Tuscan. The south took Fascism as it has most other governments during the past centuries, without enthusiasm but without revolt. Only in reactionary Puglie did it grow strong native roots.

The *Resistenza* again was a northern phenomenon. Southern Italy passed quickly from Fascist occupation to Allied occupation in a basically negative fashion without the chance or the necessity of making a moral choice. Naples itself chose and chose for the best, driving the Germans out of the city before the Allies arrived; but it was all over in a week, and, if we can go by the postwar election results, soon forgotten. Fate decreed that the Allied advance was to stop soon after the fall of Rome just about on the vaguely defined boundary between southern and northern Italy. It was north of that line that the *Resistenza* was formed.

For a year and a half north Italy was under the domination of a ruthless enemy and a despised coterie of traitors, who supported Mussolini's puppet republican government at Salò, a resort town on Lake Garda, conveniently near the main road of retreat to Germany through the Brenner Pass. The resistance movement was made up of the efforts of individual Italians to fight against the foreign and the native enemy. The fight was cruel, and there came for every man and woman, as in the Lowell poem,

> the moment to decide
> In the strife of truth with falsehood
> For the good or evil side.

Seldom in history has the choice between good and evil been so simple intellectually and the choice of right so dangerous. Evil was in command, powerful, cunning, unscrupulous. The right was only in men's hearts; the king and the legal government headed by General Badoglio had fled to Brindisi and then to Salerno. Their flight was a virtual abdication, as in their haste to flee they prepared no adequate plans for continuing the struggle, and left behind them a condition of anarchy. It was necessary not only to choose the right side but to organize it. The north Italians rose to this challenge. The resistance movement directed a partisan army formed of 200,000 fighting men and an organization at least as large that was actively engaged in their support. Spontaneous assistance in the form of food, shelter, clothing, and information was given by millions of others although the price of this aid, if discovered by the Germans and the Fascists, was possibly torture and certainly death. More than 100,000 partisans and civilian supporters gave their lives in choosing justice and liberty. These losses were heavier than the Allied losses for the entire Italian campaign.[4] The resistance movement, in short, was the moral purging that gave Italy once more the right to her place in the civilized world.

In a sense the *Resistenza* was the reincarnation and the fulfillment of the *Risorgimento*. Participation in either was a voluntary act of courage and sacrifice in the interest of liberty and justice. But whereas the *Risorgimento* was an élite movement that hardly concerned the great mass of the population, who accorded it little more than the benevolent interest of sympathetic spectators, the *Resistenza* brought together for the first time all classes of Italians, who deliberately banded together and risked their lives for an ideal, the creation of a new Italy where justice and liberty would reign.

Economic factors in the cultural dichotomy of Italy

A later chapter is devoted to the Italian economy. Two economic factors, however, have strengthened Italy's cultural dichotomy. The abundance of hydroelectric power and vast supplies of methane gas in the north give that section of Italy relatively inexpensive fuel. This advantage, in addition to the basic one that derives from northern Italy's proximity to the European market and the European sources of supply, has helped to attach European Italy to European culture and to leave Mediterranean Italy still further isolated.

[4] Massimo Salvadori, *Storia della resistenza italiana* (Venice: Neri Pozza, 1955), p. 165. See also Charles F. Delzell, *Mussolini's Enemies, the Italian Antifascist Resistance* (Princeton: Princeton University Press, 1961).

Mediterranean Italy

Description of a culture type necessitates creating an abstraction as unreal as the economist's economic man or the jurist's reasonable man. Only a few individuals in any culture fit the culture type perfectly, and individuals can always be found who are the antithesis of the culture pattern in which they live. The culture type is a composite less of the individuals than of their aspirations. It is a pattern to which they are encouraged to conform, but they succeed only to the degree that their individual personalities are compatible with it.

The Mediterranean culture is native to insular Italy and to peninsular Italy up to and including Rome. This culture extends around the Mediterranean basin from Spain to North Africa, to Asia Minor, to Greece and Italy. The Mediterranean Italians are a subgroup and are themselves again divided into distinct small groups, Sards, Sicilians, Calabresi, Neapolitans, Pugliesi, Abruzzesi, and Romans. The culture of Mediterrean Italy is more foreign and more exotic to Americans than is that of European Italy; it therefore appears easier to generalize about it.

Among the main characteristics of the Mediterranean culture are the following:

1. *A deficient sense of social responsibility.* Southern Italians are as loving fathers and mothers, as good husbands and wives, as devoted children, and as loyal friends as anyone else. Their private morality is not in the least inferior to that of any other group, but they feel little moral obligation to the community, to pay taxes, to cooperate with the police, or in any way to serve the public interest.[5]

2. *An inordinate desire to be a "furbo" coupled with an obsessive fear of being "fesso."* The man whose word is sacrosanct in private dealings will not hesitate to cheat the state or the man in the street who is not his friend. In so doing, in fact, he is likely to gain status in his own eyes and in those of his society. Everyone wants to be a

---

[5] Prof. Banfield calls this type of social behavior "amoral familism." One cannot read his description of a society of amoral familists such as he found in southern Italian communities without despairing of establishing liberal democracy there. (See Edward C. Banfield, *The Moral Basis of a Backward Society* [Glencoe: The Free Press, 1958], particularly chapter 5. This chapter has been abstracted in Mattei Dogan and Richard Rose, eds., *European Politics* [Boston: Little, Brown, 1971], pp. 78–87.) As Alessandro Pizzorno ("Amoral Familism and Historical Marginality," *International Review of Community Development,* XV [1966], pp. 55–66; also in Dogan and Rose, *op. cit.,* pp. 87–98) points out, amoral familism is virtually a negation of democratic society in that it produces almost complete alienation from the constituted authority.

furbo, an untranslatable word that describes the character of Renard the Fox in the medieval French stories and of Jeha in the Arab tales, and that refers to skill in employing ruses that are usually, but not necessarily, dishonest.

In Italian literature it was the Florentines who first made the *furbo* famous. Dante described Gianni Schicchi, Boccaccio invented Calandrino, and Machiavelli extolled the *furbizia* of Cesar Borja, one of history's most complete failures, who, having become lord of vast domains in central Italy through trickery, treachery, and the power of his father, Pope Alexander VI, lost them all soon after his father's death.

The cult of the *furbo,* no longer popular in European Italy, is still admired in Mediterranean Italy. In *Cristo si è fermato a Eboli* Carlo Levi tells of a highly respected man in a hamlet in southern Italy whose prestige came from the fact that he was living off a pension acquired dishonestly from the United States government. The basis of the prestige was not his relative wealth but that he was *furbo* enough to cheat so powerful an institution as the United States government. In order to publicize his claims as a *furbo* a southern Italian will boast to his guests of how he has his shoes mailed to him from abroad one at a time because no one steals one shoe, and of how he got an electrician friend to tinker with his meter so he has to pay for only a fraction of the electricity he uses. A *furbo* often gets more satisfaction out of taking an unfair advantage in a single business deal than from making an honest profit in a series of deals with the same man.

Along with the desire to be a *furbo* there is the fear of being a *fesso,* the person the *furbo* cheats. This not ungrounded fear leads to an inordinate amount of mutual suspicion and naturally makes amicable or honest relations between the civilian and the government agent exceptional. Professor Rossi goes so far as to say that Switzerland is richer than Italy only because it is better administered, and that it is better administered because the Swiss are less *furbi* than the Italians.[6]

The Mediterranean Italian is likely to consider himself well qualified to be a *furbo* because he is confident he comes from a particularly intelligent race. The culture does seem to favor the development of quick, alert, and original minds that may, however, be better at comprehension than accomplishment.

3. *A preoccupation with sex.* An obsession with sex on the part of males, called *gallismo,* has been a dominant feature of Mediterranean life since Roman times, both on the Arab south and the Latin north of the Sea. In no other major culture, unless perhaps that of India,

---

[6] Ernesto Rossi, *Il malgoverno* (Bari: Laterza, 1955), p. viii.

is sex such a central theme. This has led to the cloistering of women and the almost continual frustration of men, as a result of an inordinate concentration of their thoughts and energies on a single phase of human experience. Given this attitude, it is natural that the highest achievement of the *furbo* is to seduce the *fesso's* wife or daughter. This does not happen often, but the possibility adds to the general distrust. The Sicilian novelist Vitaliano Brancati spent most of his life analyzing, describing, and satirizing this aspect of his culture. *Paolo il caldo* (Paul the Hot), the novel that was intended to culminate his study of this problem, was unfinished at his death. *Don Giovanni in Sicilia* (Don Juan in Sicily) and *Il bell'Antonio* (Pretty Tony) treat this problem more cheerfully and more superficially. The Piedmontese novelist Sibilla Aleramo, who had been married to a southerner, wrote on the same subject from the woman's point of view in *Una donna*.

4. *A keen interest in people as individuals and a respect for individual idiosyncracies.* Another aspect of the Mediterranean culture is its personalness. There is little attachment to institutions and great interest in individuals. Whereas about 90 per cent of the northern Italians, like many other Europeans, vote for the party ticket without casting a preference vote for an individual candidate, in some parts of the south over half the voters for the constitutional parties cast preference votes for a specific candidate. The Mediterranean world is centered on people to a higher degree than is twentieth-century Western civilization.

5. *A democratic attitude in social (but not political) relations.* Because of the importance of people there is a high degree of social (as contrasted with political) democracy in southern Italy. There is tolerance for others' weaknesses and a strong feeling that all are brothers under the skin. This also leads to a high degree of compassion and a willingness to help others, at least momentarily, even at a sacrifice and danger to self, without, however, more than temporarily inhibiting the logically incompatible desire to play the *furbo*.

It would be unfair to Mediterranean Italy to leave the impression that it constitutes a united culture. To be Abruzzese or Pugliese, Sardinian or Calabrese, Sicilian or Roman or Neapolitan, suggests even to the outsider the possession of distinct and different culture traits, and the southern Italian himself is likely to recognize or to impute significant culture differences from valley to valley within the same region.

There is a gentleness about the Abruzzese and an amenity to discipline that distinguishes him from the other Mediterraneans. The Abruzzesi who have migrated to the United States have used these traits to create for themselves a stronghold in the construction business as masons, bricklayers, and carpenters. The region is strongly Catholic in politics. Although it is approximately in the center of Italy, it is mountainous, relatively inaccessible, and therefore infrequently visited.

Puglie, the heel of Italy, has a three-class system peculiar to itself. It is the only part of the south where much of the land is both flat and rich, but this land is held for the most part in large parcels by wealthy and often absentee owners. There is also a large class of independent farmers who till their own small plots of land. The social position of these farmers lies between that of the wealthy landlords and the sub-proletariat of the semiemployed *braccianti* (farm day laborers). The poverty and ignorance of these small landowners whose farms are often submarginal is little less than that of the *braccianti*. The independent farmers work from twelve to fourteen hours a day to eke out a living and often cannot afford to send their children to school, while the *braccianti* are lucky to find work as often as 100 days a year. The two groups are mutually antagonistic, the former having fascist and the latter communist political leanings. Thus Puglie is the only region in the south where a local fascist movement flourished and its principal city, Bari, was the most fascist community south of Rome.

The land of the island of Sardinia is poor. Its subsoil contains inferior coal that not even the Italians want now that they have found methane gas. The poor soil is used largely for grazing. Until recently the island was infested with malaria-bearing mosquitoes.

Sardinia's poverty and its remoteness from the mainland of Italy and from the rest of the world have left it in isolation. The island has lagged in both economic and cultural development. For instance, the local dialects are said to be the only Romance language dialects that have preserved the Latin hard *c* before *e* and *i*. The dialects also make use of strange consonants that mainlanders find difficulty in both hearing and reproducing. As a result of this backwardness Sardinia has had to make rapid and major adjustments in its traditions in the past quarter century in order to assimilate itself into the modern world. The process has been painful and has led to a wave of kidnappings and assassinations, doubtless caused in part by the unsettling influence of accelerated social change.

The Sardinians, like the Abruzzesi, lack the high degree of anarchic individualism typical of the rest of Mediterranean Italy. Perhaps the fact that they have been adequately governed (by the Piedmontese and then by Italy) for a considerable number of years explains the relative lack of antigovernment feeling in comparison to that found further south.

Calabria, like Sardinia, is one of the poorest and most prolific parts of southern Italy. It is also one of the most beautiful. There is in

Calabrian culture a sobriety and a rudimentary sense of honor similar to that found in equally backward and remote Sardinia and that is lacking in the more sophisticated and more corrupt environments of Sicily or of Naples.

Sicily is the largest Italian region in territory and is second to Lombardy in population. It is first in the headaches it has caused itself and the rest of Italy.

Like Puglie and Naples, Sicily is a land of contrasts, with great wealth for the few and utter poverty for the many. Its climate is significantly hotter and drier than that of the mainland, and this means it is too hot and too dry for comfort or for good crops.

The Sicilians themselves, however, and not their land, are their own worst enemies. Their most notable cultural achievement over the centuries has been the development of the worst system of government known to mankind. This is the government of the *mafia*.

The *mafia* is an illegal association of gangsters who exact tribute primarily for abstaining from criminal activities (i.e., who sell protection from themselves) and who resort to hints of murder and actual murder when their privileged position or their profits are threatened.

The *mafia* is both less and more than it is normally considered to be outside of Sicily. It is less in that there is probably no single coordinated and centralized *mafia* organization from whose headquarters orders filter down to the lower echelons. Such an organization would be almost inconceivable in Sicily or anywhere else in the Mediterranean. Were the *mafia* so unified and centralized it would be much easier to eradicate than it actually is.

On the other hand, the *mafia* is more than it appears to be because it is not merely a way of government; it is unfortunately a way of life that permeates Sicilian culture. A peculiar aspect of the *mafia* that distinguishes it from the typical *banditismo* common to the deep south and Sardinia is its relationship to the state. The bandits are against the state, and the state is seriously trying to eradicate them; but the *mafia* is with the state, and the state does little to interfere with its collections.

In recent years the *mafia* has undergone a metamorphosis. Its center of activity once was the countryside, where it was often used by the landlords to maintain their position. With the decline of agriculture and the increased importance of industry and commerce, the *mafia* has become urbanized without, however, losing any of its power. The *mafia* normally is allied with the political party in power.

Although the *mafia* has given all Sicily a bad name, the phenomenon is actually limited to the western half of the island, to the provinces of Palermo, Agrigento, Trapani, and part of the province of

Caltanissetta. The principal city of the eastern section, Catania, is called the Milan of the South. In Messina, Siracusa, Ragusa, and even in the poor internal province of Enna, this peculiar Sicilian plague is virtually unknown. In fact, the only place where the *mafia* system has been successfully exported is to the United States, where Al Capone was the first major *mafia* figure.

The Neapolitans are distinguishable from other southern Italians by an unusual degree of gentleness and superficial cheerfulness. They have fooled generations of the British into believing the myth of the happy, carefree "wop," lazing and singing in the sun, and generally indulging in *dolce far niente*. The picture is false but in the long run more profitable in courting favor from rulers and tips from tourists than the sadder truth. Although there are now murderous gangs in the wholesale food business, gangsterism is not typically Neapolitan, and honor, that abused, pathetic, but noble anachronism of much of Italy's south, is not a major motivation of Neapolitan behavior. The Neapolitans are world famous for their popular songs, of which *O Sole Mio* and *Santa Lucia* are the best known in the United States.

The Neapolitans are also the least isolated and in a sense the most sophisticated of southern Italians. Naples is the only major seaport in Mediterranean Italy, and the former capital city of all the south. Neapolitans thus for centuries have been aware of many things undreamed of (at least until modern times) in the philosophies of most southern Italians.

Rome occupies a unique place in Mediterranean Italy. Its position as capital of Italy and of the Roman Catholic Church and as a wealthy international metropolis gives it a veneer of Europeanism, and for centuries the culture of Europe has been brought to this "Eternal City." The roots of Rome and the Romans, of the poor quarters of Trastevere as well as of the traditional papal nobility, belong to the old Mediterranean culture. Some of the great splendors of Europe have been grafted on the roots, particularly at the Vatican, but the grafting has produced little native-grown fruit.

As Italy grows more united, however, Rome, as the capital city, tends to attract a greater number of artists and intellectuals. The University of Rome, a relatively late comer among Italian universities, is assuming a leading position in Italian education. Rome and Milan in a certain sense are now emerging as national centers while the other culture centers are at best maintaining themselves as provincial centers, attracting little talent from beyond their traditional borders. In this sense Rome is becoming a center of European culture in spite of its Mediterranean foundation and the continued immigration of Mediterranean Italians in the lower economic groups.

The term "culture" is used in two rather distinct senses. To the sociologists it generally signifies the patterns of behavior common to a society, and it has been used in this sense up to the present in this chapter. To others, however, culture may signify the intellectual, esthetic, creative aspects of a society. If we look at the culture of Mediterranean Italy in this sense we shall find that there are only two centers of importance: Rome and Naples.

The cultural value of Rome in this narrow sense, other than the historical value of the monuments of ancient Rome, is mainly due to the importation of creative artists and cultural products by the Popes. Rome's major native contributions are the Early Christian churches, which in some instances date back to the fourth century after Christ, the music of Pierluigi da Palestrina, whose polyphony was the culmination of the period of medieval and Renaissance music, and the baroque architecture beginning with Michelangelo and reaching a climax in Bernini, a Neapolitan by birth. Rome has had a long theatrical tradition; it was the birthplace of the *commedia dell'arte,* of the famous poet and librettist, Pietro Metastasio, as well as of the great comedian, Ettore Petrolini. In the postwar period Rome has made notable contributions to the films with Anna Magnani, Vittorio De Sica, and Roberto Rossellini.

Naples alone of the Mediterranean cities maintained a philosophical, judicial, literary, and musical tradition. The philosophers Giovambattista Vico and Benedetto Croce both lived and wrote in Naples, and there was a continuous flow of philosophical, historical and political writing through the centuries that separate them. There have been virtual dynasties of distinguished Neapolitan jurists, of whom the Arangio Ruiz, the Azzaritis, the Scialoias, and the Bianchi d'Espinoza are outstanding. The long Neapolitan literary tradition reached its apex with the critic, Francesco De Sanctis.

It should be remembered, however, that all these men were culturally (in the second sense) Europeans. They wrote in Italian (i.e., Tuscan dialect), not in Neapolitan, and they were contributing to European culture. In these literary fields, however, the Neapolitan contributions were all peripheral to the mainstream, which for the most part went along its course much as it would have without the presence of the Neapolitans.

Such would not have been the case, however, if the West had been deprived of the Neapolitan contribution to music. From Alessandro Scarlatti (1659?–1725) to Pergolesi (1710–1736), the Neapolitan school of music was a major influence. Scarlatti, a Sicilian by birth, was instrumental in setting the form of the operatic aria, which until the late nineteenth century was the foundation and the *raison d'être* of opera. Pergolesi developed the comic opera *intermezzo* that was the springboard for Mozart (*Le nozze di Figaro* and *Così fan tutte*) and Verdi (*Falstaff*).

Southern Italy's most important contribution to painting was Antonello da Messina, who was instrumental in bringing Flemish painting to Italy.

Even in this cavalier and superficial survey of the contributions of Mediterranean Italy to Italian culture, mention must be made of certain recent contributions of the south that are not connected with the major schools of Rome and Naples.

Sicily has produced noted scholars who are not associated with Naples, including the jurist Santi Romano, the political theorist Gaetano Mosca, and the critic Giuseppe Antonio Borgese. There is one distinguished publishing house in the south, that of Laterza in Bari.

Although the south has produced few singers, several outstanding artists have come from the south, including the greatest of the *castrati,* Farinelli (Puglie), as well as Enrico Caruso (Naples), Giuseppe De Luca (Rome), Tito Schipa (Lecce), and Mariano Stabile (Sicily).

Southern Italian politicians have come in good part from Sicily, including the strong man of the late nineteenth century, Francesco Crispi, the chief Italian representative at Versailles, Vittorio Emanuele Orlando, and the founder of the Catholic *Partito populare,* Don Luigi Sturzo. Basilicata has also made a distinguished contribution with Emanuele Gianturco, Francesco Saverio Nitti, and Emilio Colombo. Republican Italy's first southern Presidents of the Council have been the Sicilian Mario Scelba, the Sardinian Antonio Segni, and the Pugliese Aldo Moro. Southern Italy's contribution to the anti-Fascist movement was headed by the historian Gaetano Salvemini from Molfetta (Puglie), the political leader Giovanni Amendola from Salerno, near Naples, and the Communist Giuseppe Di Vittorio from Foggia (Puglie). Naples has contributed the eminent jurists who became the first and second presidents of the Constitutional Court, Enrico De Nicola and Gaetano Azzariti. Two of the outstanding personalities of the present democratic left, Ugo La Malfa (Republican) and Riccardo Lombardi (Socialist), are of Sicilian origin but have lived and operated primarily in Rome and in the north and are completely Europeanized in their outlook.

Finally, Mediterranean Italy has contributed heavily to Italian literature. The foreign student can learn much vicariously about the south and its various regions. The Sicilian Giovanni Verga describes lower and middle class life of Sicily in *I Malavoglia* and *Mastro Don Gesualdo,* as does Luigi Pirandello in his numerous short stories, *Novelle per un anno.* Giuseppe Tomasi di Lampedusa's *Il gattopardo* is a masterful historical novel deating primarily with Sicily's upper classes. Leonardo Sciascia's *Il giorno della civetta* is a remarkable study of the *mafia* in the form of a novel. The description of Sardinian culture was the life work of the Nobel prize-winner Grazia Deledda. Corrado Alvaro, author of *Gente in Aspromonte,* is perhaps the best known literary spokesman for Calabria. Perhaps the most typical and traditional Naples is that of the poetry of Salvatore Di Giacomo and of the many plays by the dean of Neapolitan actors, Eduardo De Filippo. The anti-Fascist novels of Ignazio Silone, of which *Fontamara* and *Pane e vino (Bread and Wine)* are best known, are laid in the Abruzzi. Traditional Rome is found in the sonnets of Giuseppe Gioachino Belli. A more than half Europeanized Rome is described in the novels of Alberto Moravia. The poets Gabriele D'Annunzio (Abruzzi) and Salvatore Quasimodo (Sicily) are expatriate southerners who lived and worked mainly in the north. D'Annunzio, however, wrote some short stories and plays laid in the Abruzzi.

European Italians and foreigners have also contributed significantly to the literature about the south. Carlo Levi's autobiographical *Cristo si è fermato a Eboli* tells of his internment in Basilicata as a political prisoner. The life of the poor in Sicily has been relentlessly documented by the Triestino Danilo Dolci in *Inchiesta a Palermo* and in *Fate presto (e bene) perché si muore.* The British journalist Gavin Maxwell describes the same *ambiente* somewhat more luridly in *The Ten Pains of Death.* The prizewinning French novel of Roger Vailland, *La loi,* depicts the Mediterranean aspects of life in Puglie. Postwar Naples is described sentimentally by the American John Horne Burns in *The Gallery.* Ottiero Ottieri's *Donnarumma all'assalto* is a fictionalized study of the setting up of a branch factory near Naples by the Olivetti Typewriter Company. The pagan aspects of the South are portrayed in Norman Douglas' *South Wind.*

Some of Italy's best films have dealt with aspects of southern culture; notable among them are Pietro Germi's *Divorzio all'italiana* and Luchino Visconti's *Rocco e i suoi fratelli.*

European Italy

European culture (Western civilization) is the large culture group to which the American culture belongs. European Italy, its birthplace, which has contributed greatly to its development, is divided culturally into five major regions, Piedmont, Lombardy, the Veneto, Emilia-Romagna, and Tuscany, each of which has its own contribution to make to the common culture. Each of the smaller regions can be treated as a cultural appendage to one of the five major regions.

Piedmont, in the northwest with its elegant capital Torino (Turin), is the least Mediterranean — some would say the least Italian — part of Italy. It is a sober, orderly, efficient, courteous, and unimaginative society. Piedmont gave Italy its greatest statesman, Cavour; its perennial Premier, Giovanni Giolitti; the first and fourth Presidents of the Republic, Luigi Einaudi and Giuseppe Saragat. It has also contributed many leading Communist politicians. The region has produced outstanding scholars, most of whom taught or teach at the University of Torino. The publishing house of Giulio Einaudi has brought Torino back to prominence in the publishing field, and the newspaper *La Stampa* has kept it at the top in journalism. Piedmont alone in Italy has a military tradition, and the higher ranks in the army still contain a high percentage of upper-class Piedmontese. Piedmont's large contribution to liberal anti-Fascism was in the main inspired by Piero Gobetti, the first great anti-Fascist of the younger generation.

Piedmont, however, can be considered Italian only for the last few hundred years. During the period of the Italian Renaissance it was a borderland between France and Italy, more French than Italian both linguistically and culturally, and still living in the Middle Ages. The social system was feudal, based on serfdom, which had disappeared from Italy centuries earlier. The merchant class that created cities had yet to appear. The fortunes of Piedmont began to rise in the sixteenth century, when much of Italy fell under the stultifying hand of the Hapsburgs, who greedily took possession of Milan and Naples, but had little interest in subduing the backward subjects of Emanuele Filiberto, Duke of Savoy. The modernization instigated by Emanuele Filiberto and his heirs, however, was directed toward the elimination of feudalism and the establishment of a centralized authoritarianism on the model of the French monarchy.

Perhaps because of Piedmont's lack of Italian tradition its contribution to Italian culture, at least until the present century, has been meager. Vittorio Alfieri, a contemporary and admirer of George Washington, is Piedmont's most famous poet. By far its most respected literary figure, however, is Cesare Pavese.

The Waldensians, the only Christian religious minority of importance in Italy, are found mainly in this region. The Roman Catholic kings of Piedmont established religious tolerance before the unification of Italy.

Genoa is the capital city of the coastal region of Liguria. Like Venice, Genoa used to be a great maritime power, but unlike that of her sister city on the Adriatic, her commercial expansion was not accompanied by a corresponding cultural growth. Genoa too has had her great men, Giuseppe Mazzini and the poet Eugenio Montale, but has contributed little to art, architecture, or music.

To the east of Piedmont lies Lombardy with its capital Milan, which in a sense is the capital of all northern Italy. Lombardy is not a closely knit region. The intensely Catholic provinces to the east, Bergamo, Brescia, and Como, are centers of the textile industry. The southern provinces are Pavia, the ancient capital of the Lombards, Cremona, home of the Stradivarius and Guarnerius families, and Mantova (Mantua), former seat of the Gonzagas, leading patrons of the arts. Most of the rest is Milan, one of the great modern cities of the world, which, like Brussels and Rotterdam, and unlike any other Italian city, has been virtually remodeled since World War II. Milan is the business center and one of the culture centers of Italy. It is also the major publishing center and the home of Italy's other leading newspaper, *Il corriere della sera.* Lombardy has contributed its share to Italian culture from the Renaissance on. Among its greatest figures are the composers Claudio Monteverdi (Cremona) and Gaetano Donizetti (Bergamo), the penologist and reformer Cesare Beccaria (Milan), and the novelist Alessandro Manzoni (Milan). Milan's opera house, the *Teatro alla Scala,* has since the eighteenth century been the acknowledged world center of Italian opera. Milan's most famous artist is the Tuscan Leonardo da Vinci, who lived and worked for much of his mature life in Milan for the Sforza family and who left a profound impression on the Milanese school of painting. Three of the last four popes are Lombards — Pius XI (Milan), John XXIII (Bergamo), and Paul VI (Brescia).

To the east of Lombardy lie the Veneto and its unique sea capital, Venice. During the millenium of freedom of their island republic (c. 800–1798) the Venetians developed one of Europe's major subcultures. As Venice prospered and the descendants of her fishermen founders became seafaring traders, the city began to incorporate part of the mainland into her domain until finally it had spread to the gates of Milan. Among the contributions to Western civilization said to have been invented or introduced by Venice are family names, glass windows, mirrors, chandeliers, table forks, licensed prostitution, modern diplomacy, pianos, public libraries, and double-entry bookkeeping. Today the people from the entire region speak similar dialects and share a common culture, a notable feature of which is the gracious manners of the people, which are superior to those of their neighbors in and out of Italy.

Of the mainland cities of the Veneto, Padova has made the greatest contribution to culture, through its university (one of the oldest and most important in Europe) and through its art and architecture. Verona is another city of the Veneto with a long and glorious history. Vicenza produced the architect Antonio Palladio.

Venice's most famous dialect writer is the dramatist Carlo Goldoni. The Venetian tradition in painting extends from the Bellinis and Giorgione in the Renaissance to the Ferrarese De Pisis in the twentieth century, through such other masters as Titian, Tintoretto, Veronese, and Tiepolo. Her architecture as exemplified by the Doge's Palace and the *Teatro La Fenice* is of a unique and supreme beauty. Opera, after its start in Florence, made its first popular success in Venice, where the Lombards Monteverdi and Francesco Cavalli wrote and produced. Antonio Vivaldi, perhaps Italy's greatest composer for orchestra, was Venetian. The Veneto's contribution to the lyric theater includes three of this century's most eminent singers, Toti Dal Monte (Venice), Giovanni Martinelli (Padova), and Tito Gobbi (Verona). One of Italy's finest novelists, Ippolito Nievo, and her greatest actresses, Adelaide Ristori and Eleonora Duse, were also from the Veneto, as well as Italy's most famous traveler, Marco Polo, and her most famous adventurer, Casanova.

Politically the Veneto is Italy's most Catholic region; it normally returns a clear Catholic majority to Parliament.

The Veneto is primarily an agricultural area, although the textile industry is important in the western provinces of Verona and Vicenza. The Veneto is the only region in Italy's north from which there is significant emigration. The *Veneti* who have come to the United States have usually settled in California, where they raise the grapes for the best American wine.

When one crosses the Po one steps into peninsular Italy. There are two important subcultures in the European part of peninsular Italy, which are divided geographically by the Apennines. To the north and east of these mountains, in the lower Po Valley, lies the rich region of Emilia-Romagna; to the south and west lies Tuscany. The Marche and Umbria, two small, hilly regions contiguous to Emilia-Romagna and Tuscany, will be treated here as parts of these two major regions.

Peninsular Italy is less Nordic than continental Italy. It can be argued, in fact, that the full Italian flavor is only found south of the Po. A remarkable feature of the culture of this part of Italy is its *campanilismo* (roughly, provincialism). Each *campanile* (bell tower) is itself a culture center, and loyalties remain local. Here people think of themselves as citizens of the teeming and prosperous provincial capitals, most of which have their own glorious traditions and independent histories. These local traditions have been nourished and expanded through the centuries by contributions from the new generations of citizens, and sometimes from citizens of a nearby province temporarily in eclipse. Although Emilia-Romagna is less of a culture unit than the regions already described, there is an effulgence, a warmth, a cordiality, and a pagan materialism about the whole region that creates a sort of unity in spite of the intense provincial loyalties. Perhaps this is because in the main the stock has been the same for over a thousand years, as there has been remarkably little immigration. The southern Italians who go north to seek their fortune rarely seem to settle in these close-knit and basically self-sufficient societies, but instead pass on to the more highly industrialized north.

Another distinguishing aspect of the culture of this part of Italy is the degree to which the highest esthetic achievements are based on and remain folk art. Dante and Ariosto are still recited at length from memory by semiliterate peasants. The patrons of the gallery of Parma's opera house constitute the most feared (and among the most vociferous) music critics in Italy. Here man-made beauty is neither esoteric nor exotic; it is as much a part of life as the wind, the sea, and the stars.

This region has contributed much of the finest in Italian art, particularly in its more exuberant aspects. Ravenna offers its medieval architecture and mosaics. Ferrara contributes its early Renaissance art and late Renaissance music, and the poetry of Ludovico Ariosto, born in Reggio, contributions which were made possible in the main by the largesse of the D'Este family. Parma offers its Renaissance painters, headed by Antonio Allegri (Correggio), and Italy's greatest creative and interpretive musicians, Giuseppi Verdi and Arturo Toscanini. Modena's major contribution is its Romanesque cathedral.

Bologna has the richest heritage of all. Its university, the oldest in Europe, made of Bologna a medieval center of learning. Accursio, Irnerio, Bartolo, its major medieval scholars, started this lovable rather than lovely city in its democratic and lay tradition. Although an active center of art and particularly instrumental music through the Renaissance (the sonata and the concerto grosso took form there under Arcangelo Corelli), Bologna did not maintain the preeminence she had gained in the late Middle Ages, and after her subjection to Rome she went into eclipse. In the twentieth century the most famous person from the province of Bologna so far is the physicist Guglielmo Marconi. In the nineteenth and twentieth centuries many of Italy's major actors and singers have come from this region. Among the greatest names are those of the actor Ermete Zacconi and of Giulietta Simionato and Ezio Pinza, two of the supreme artists of the operatic stage. The same effulgence and exuberance that is typical of the art and the cuisine of the region have given the women of Emilia-Romagna an international reputation normally expressed in laudatory superlatives.

The politics of Emilia-Romagna tend to be extreme. Mussolini came from this region, as did Balbo and Grandi, and it was the scene of much Fascist violence. Now it is the most Communist region of Italy, and three of its principal cities, Bologna, Modena, and Reggio, have had Communist mayors continuously since the first postwar elections. The reasons for this seem to be a tradition of intense anticlericalism and the sharecropping that prevailed in agriculture. Sharecropping, until recently the normal method of farming in the northern part of peninsular Italy, and rare further north and in the south, was particularly conducive to reiterated feuding between the farmers and landowners, and to the consequent strengthening of extremist and intransigent political parties. The leading politician of the region in the present period is the Socialist leader Pietro Nenni.

The Marche, to the south of Emilia, is the home of the composer Gioacchino Rossini (Pesaro), of Italy's leading romantic poet, Giacomo Leopardi (Recanati), and of her famous actor, Ruggero Ruggeri (Fano).

The hill towns that comprise Tuscany and Umbria were the birthplace of the Italian Renaissance. The Tuscans Dante Alighieri, Francesco Petrarca, and Giovanni Boccaccio created the Italian language there some six hundred fifty years ago, almost three centuries before Shakespeare and the King James version of the Bible gave modern English its cast. The Tuscans have never relinquished their place of preeminence in Italian literature and have consistently contributed more than their share to its development. Tuscany and Umbria are the only regions of Italy where Italian is the native spoken language. Elsewhere Italian has been superimposed on local dialects.

In painting only Venice rivals the home of Giotto, of Masaccio, of Piero della Francesca, of Botticelli, of Leonardo, and of Michelangelo. Its Renaissance architects and sculptors, Brunelleschi, Donatello, Ghiberti, and Cellini, are unsurpassed. Opera was born in Florence, the work of Iacopo Peri and the *Camerata,* but in the field of music Tuscany has not lived up to this early achievement. The Pisan, Ruffo Titta (generally known as Titta Ruffo), is the outstanding Tuscan contribution to the lyric stage.

The intellectual achievement of Tuscany almost equals her esthetic achievement. Niccolò Machiavelli and Galileo Galilei are outstanding among her Renaissance figures. In the twentieth century the jurist, statesman, and essayist Piero Calamandrei best epitomizes the glorious Tuscan tradition.

There is a sobriety about Tuscan art that the superficial critic of Italian culture may feel is anti-Italian and that is certainly in contrast to the richness, vivacity, and warmth of Emilia. This austere Tuscan simplicity is found in the poetry of Dante and the prose of Boccaccio and in most aspects of subsequent Tuscan culture. Even in her cuisine Tuscany eschews the supererogatory and highly caloric fare that is the pride of Emilia.

In politics, however, the Tuscan is often an extremist. The hill towns that were once hotbeds of the most virulent Fascism now teem with Communists. This political extremism of the Tuscans can be partially explained by their traditional anticlericalism. The proximity of Tuscany to the former Papal States and the historical rivalries between the two governments have had their effect. As long as the clerical party remains nominally a center party, there is nothing for the Tuscan to do except go right or left. Lucca, however, with its independent history, is a Catholic stronghold. The most famous Tuscan politicians, on the other hand, have been of the center. Baron Bettino Ricasoli (Cavour's successor), Count Carlo Sforza (Italy's leading anti-Fascist diplomat), Giovanni Gronchi (Italy's second President), and Amintore Fanfani (four times to date [1970] the President of the Council of Ministers) are all Tuscans. .

No Tuscan worth his salt, however, would admit there was a single Tuscan type. He would be willing to expatiate on the differences among the citizens of Siena, of Pisa, of Livorno (sometimes called Leghorn in English), of Lucca, and of Florence, and as for those anarchists the *Lunigiani* who live in the province of Massa, he would probably refuse them even the honor of being classed as real Tuscans. Local pride of this kind goes to lengths that it is difficult for Americans to understand.

There are few important industries in the region, although marble comes from Carrara and wool cloth is manufactured at Prato. The crops of Tuscany are diversified, and little that is grown elsewhere in Italy need be imported. Exports to other parts of Italy and abroad include the oil of Lucca and Chianti, one of the few of Italy's famous wines that ship well and compete favorably on the foreign market. The artisans of Tuscany are among the most famous in Italy, and Tuscan linens, leather goods, and pottery are honored by those who know them.

Umbria, whose cultural life has been closely associated with that of Tuscany, was the home of St. Francis and of the painters Perugino and Raphael. Giotto left us, there in Assisi, the masterpieces with which he adorned the church dedicated to Italy's most beloved saint. The hill towns of Umbria, clustered in the Apennines, are somewhat higher and more remote than those of Tuscany.

A partial synthesis

In spite of all the differences among the many little Italies, both in the north and in the south, there are significant similarities over Italy as a whole.

We suggest that there are at least three common qualities that deserve mention here. Italian culture, for instance, is essentially feminine. The fatherland, the *patria* of the Romans, becomes the *madre patria* (mother fatherland). Regardless of the orthodoxy of the Roman Catholic Church regarding the relative position of the Trinity and of the Virgin Mary, there is no question that the Madonna is in Italy the most loved and prayed-to heavenly being. In the human sphere mothers are the most loved and respected persons, and neither boys nor men are ashamed to be tied to their mothers' apron strings. Feminine qualities that Italians of all parts of the land admire and that abound in Italy are patience and compassion. Italians know how to suffer and endure, not stoically but with dignity, bending but not breaking, and they are quick to comprehend and succor the suffering of others.

Students who begin to read Italian political and social history may be surprised to discover the predilection the Italians seem to have for choosing political leaders whose characters are either so saintly or so devilish that they are not very successful in handling public affairs. The prototype of the saint is Francis of Assisi, that of the devil Niccolò Machiavelli. The saintly type is too pure for compromise and too naïve to face the sordid facts of politics; the devil is too cynical, or too *furbo,* which is often the same thing, to realize that you cannot fool all the people all the time. The resultant plethora of saints and devils on the Italian political stage has tended to increase Italy's political difficulties, for many Italians out of respect for the saints and appreciation for the beauty of their concept of society continue to elect saints to public office, and many other Italians, feeling that it is a sign of true *furbizia* to select a *furbo,* have often supported cynics and crooks.[7] After twenty years of Mussolini the *furbi* went out of style in the north, although the popularity of some Sicilian leaders seems to rest on the traditional respect for the *furbo,* and the immense local popularity of the former mayor of Naples, Achille Lauro, seemed to be related to the commonly held opinion that his fortune had been accumulated through *furbizia.* The saints, however, are still in high favor all over Italy. The former mayor of Florence, Giorgio La Pira, a lay Franciscan, is the most likely of the lot actually to become a saint, but his former political antagonist, the Florentine anticlerical Piero Calamandrei, inspired no less admiration for his idealism and devotion to public service.[8] Other important saints on the recent Italian political scene include the *Risorgimento* leaders Giuseppe Mazzini and Giuseppe Garibaldi; the Socialists of the early twentieth century Filippo Turati and Camillo Prampolini; and in the present day, Fer-

---

[7] See Elisabeth Wiskeman, *Italy* (Oxford: Oxford University Press, 1947).
[8] Carlo Galante Garrone, "Un ingenuo in parlamento," *Il ponte,* supplement to Vol. XIV (1958), pp. 114–141.

ruccio Parri and Danilo Dolci. Even the Communists have their saint in Antonio Gramsci.

Another Italian characteristic of importance to historians and political scientists is the tradition of the citizenry expressing their dissatisfaction with the government through parading and oratory in the central squares (*piazze*), a sort of tumultuous pressure that stops short of actual revolution. These manifestations, which are Italy's compromise between the ballots of the liberal democracies and the bullets of most of the rest of the world (there is a great temptation to call them ballets — using the British pronunciation) are discussed in the following chapter, which deals with Fascism.

Conclusion

The synthesis, however, is only partial. The Mediterranean and the European cultures have not fused, and there is little reason to suppose they will do so in the future; thus Italy's cultural dichotomy continues to be a source of bewilderment for the foreigner and of mutual distrust and misunderstanding for Italians.

Foreigners are confused because the migrating Italian they know is generally the Mediterranean Italian, hard-working, hot-headed, uneducated, "foreign" looking — and what is more, "foreign" acting and "foreign" feeling. What has this immigrant to do, they wonder, with the Italy of Dante Alighieri, of St. Francis, of Galileo, of Leonardo, of Verdi? Which is the real Italy, his or theirs, and the answer is that Italy is both these things: she is the child of the Mediterranean and the mother of Europe.

The distrust and misunderstanding created among Italians by this dichotomy keep regional animosities alive and give Italy in the minds of many Italians an ambiguous position, both a part of and alien to western Europe.

Massimo D'Azeglio, one of the leaders of the *Risorgimento,* made an often quoted and apt remark: *"Fatta l'Italia, bisogna fare gli italiani"* (Having made Italy, we must make Italians). The impetus of the *Risorgimento,* however, was spent creating the modern democratic state of Italy and of aligning Italy with the progressive elements of western Europe; the second task proved to be one that could only be accomplished gradually over the centuries.

It may seem strange that two cultures would exist side by side for so long without having one tend to absorb the other or without some other kind of amalgamation. Although Italy is not a very big country it is a very long and mountainous one. Until recently it took more time to go from Palermo to Milan by train than to go from Milan to Copenhagen. Contacts between the European Italians and the lower classes in the south have in the past been mainly through the miserable barracks life of the conscript soldier.

The process of making Italians, then, is still going on. It is less one of fusion than of adaptation of the south to the north. The process is greatly slowed down, however, by the fact that the individuals who are ready to make this adaptation are often the ones who migrate from the south to the Americas or to Europe, including European Italy. Emigration is in itself, therefore, only another divisive force in that it tends to deprive the south of its European-minded personalities.

2

Fascism

The march on Rome

Benito Mussolini organized but did not lead the March on Rome of October 28, 1922, which brought Fascism to power.

According to Fascist propaganda the March on Rome was the culmination of the Fascist revolution, but in the military sense, at least, there was no revolution.[1]

The government at Rome at that time was headed by Luigi Facta, who was ready to meet the Fascist threat with a decree of martial law. Had King Vittorio Emanuele III signed this decree, as he was bound to do in his capacity of constitutional monarch, it is quite possible that Mussolini's advent to power would have been permanently prevented. The king, however, an ill-informed and suspicious reactionary, refused to sign the decree and accepted the resignation of the government. The king's action was not only an error in judgment; it was also the act of a morally corrupt man who was willing to break his pledge to uphold the Constitution.

Although neither a military victory nor a constitutional method for assuming power, the March on Rome was in a sense quite in the Italian tradition. From the Renaissance on, the Italian people have been wont to express dissatisfaction with their government by milling around the central squares of their cities, making and listening to speeches. If the demonstration appears to represent the "general will" and not merely factional opposition, it is the custom of the government either to resign or to alter its course and personnel in accordance with the wishes of the demonstrators.

[1] Gaetano Salvemini, "Anniversario, che cosa fu la Marcia su Roma," *Il ponte,* IV (1948), pp. 982–995. For an excellent short account of fascism see Alan Cassels, *Fascist Italy* (New York: Thomas Y. Crowell, 1968).

The *Risorgimento* used the general technique of a public demonstration, or "row in piazza," to use Professor Trevelyan's expression,[2] as a principal means of achieving its ends, and the despotic rule of the various petty tyrants was ended in 1859 and 1860 by inspirational speeches, spontaneous uprisings, and general confusion, rather than by a coordinated military campaign. The March on Rome was in a sense merely an iteration of this Italian tradition, to which the king, in acquiescing, reacted in the traditional manner.

Although the methods by which Mussolini reached power were traditional, his advent to power marked the return to the Western world of a form of government that historians must brand as the worst this century has so far provided. Something much like it was known to the Greeks over 2000 years ago, and condemned by virtually all the Greek political philosophers. Plato and Aristotle referred to it as democracy, but what they meant was the rule of a demagogue through mob intolerance and mob violence. The Greek demagogue, however, pernicious as he was, could not gain effective control over a territory substantially greater than that which he could bawl at. Modern means of communication and the superiority of offensive over defensive weapons, and the ease with which the former may be obtained, have brought back the demagogue and democratic tyranny, dormant and impotent for two millennia, in a more terrible metamorphosis. Dictatorships are known to many societies and to all ages, but popular dictatorships, those backed by the active support of mobs, are a twentieth-century recrudescence of an ancient evil from which the world had long been free.[3]

Historical background

From 1860 to the close of the First World War, that is, for a period of two generations, Italy had been governed by a series of liberal coali-

[2] George Macaulay Trevelyan, *The Historical Causes of the Present State of Affairs in Italy* (Oxford: Oxford University Press, 1925). A recent example of this practice was the rioting in Genoa in June, 1960, that led to the fall of the clerical-Fascist government of Fernando Tambroni. For a brilliant Fascist apology stressing the traditional aspects of Fascism, see Curzio Malaparte, *Italia barbara* (Turin: Gobetti, 1925). The political strikes (i.e., strikes against the state) that became an everyday occurrence in Italy in the late 1960's seem to be a variant of the row in piazza. They are the Italian equivalent of much of the work done by pressure groups in Great Britain and the United States.

[3] See Curzio Malaparte, *La technique du coup d'état* (Paris, 1931), later in English and Italian translations. Malaparte believes the Fascist technique was first used by Leon Trotsky.

tions. The Liberal Party had been the party of the *Risorgimento,* the party of Camillo Benso Conte di Cavour. Its origins were glorious and its principles those of liberal democracy, but it never became a political party in the modern sense; it remained (until after World War II, when Giovanni Malagodi turned it into a small, coherent, conservative pressure group) a coterie of mutually antagonistic factions, divided roughly into a liberal right and a liberal left.

In the historical period of laissez faire, when state intervention was normally at a minimum, this large amorphous group was able to govern by temporizing with day-to-day events and by postponing action on the long-range problems, which might have assured a positive prognosis for the future of liberal democracy in Italy. When Italy, perhaps mistakenly, entered the First World War in 1915 she embarked upon an enterprise that was far beyond her means. The end of the war found the Italian nation nearly bankrupt economically and so badly divided against itself politically as to become virtually impotent. Hindsight, the historian's sixth sense, reveals many causes for the liberal's failure. Most of these causes are but aspects of a single fundamental cause. Neither in 1919 nor earlier had the Italian state represented all the Italian nation; it merely represented the Liberal Party and the other smaller constitutional parties, of which none had numerical significance.

The most powerful and the traditional enemy of the Italian liberal state was the Vatican. Roman Catholic opposition to the Italian state was based on both philosophical and material grounds. The attitude toward liberalism, the philosophy of the Italian state, was succinctly expressed by Pope Pius IX in Art. 80 of the *Syllabus of Errors* (8 December, 1864). [It is an error to believe that] "the Roman Pope can or should come to terms with liberalism." Papal pretensions to temporal power, furthermore, made the church consider any Italian state, particularly with its capital in Rome, a usurper. The attitude of the church hierarchy toward the state was that of a virulent but not violent hostility to be expressed in noncooperation.[4]

In the closing period of the nineteenth century the Italian workers, following those of other European countries, became aware of their political and economic power and formed a Socialist party, which in Italy's case was her first modern political party. The policy of this party was Marxist and revolutionary, but generally nonviolent. In spite of its normal distaste for violence, however, it was consistently an anti-constitutional party unwilling to cooperate in parliament with the representatives of "bourgeois capitalism."

[4] See Arturo Carlo Jemolo, *Chiesa e stato in Italia negli ultimi cento anni* (Turin: Giulio Einaudi, 1948); Luigi Salvatorelli, *Chiesa e stato dalla rivoluzione francese ad oggi* (Florence: Nuova Italia, 1955); Ernesto Rossi, *Il sillabo e dopo* (Rome: Edizioni Riunite, 4th ed., 1965).

The policy of the church, however, took another turn with the creation of the *Partito populare* by Don Luigi Sturzo in 1919. A major purpose of this party was to win the workers' allegiance away from the Marxist parties, and to give the Vatican a voice, perhaps a deciding voice, in the temporal affairs of Italy.

This party was not a constitutional party. Like the Socialists and Communists on its left and the Nationalists on its right, it was bent on destroying liberalism. In January, 1922, Luigi Sturzo proclaimed the impotence of the bourgeois liberal democratic state, praised the Fascists for having spurned the proffered friendship of Giolitti and the democrats and commented on the violent extralegal exploits of the Fascists "without a sign of moral reprobation."[5]

The South presented the governing class in Italy with a colonial problem with which it was unable to cope. The *laissez faire* economic policy of the liberals mitigated few of the south's economic ills, and the liberals' faith in the virtual certainty of social progress, once irrational and illiberal restraints were eliminated, led them erroneously to conclude that no more needed to be done in order to transform the numerous subproletariat of the south, as well as the narrow-minded petty bourgeoisie, which was fearful of the masses and jealous of its own slight superiority, into responsible and dedicated citizens of a liberal democracy. Woodrow Wilson, it should be remembered, made the same mistake in 1919 when he thought that the elimination of existing tyrannies would make the whole world safe for democracy.[6]

Liberalism's failure with the south led to a double standard in Italian politics. Elections in the north were probably no more corrupt and no less democratic than those of other liberal democratic states. Many of the southern constituencies, however, were little more than rotten boroughs. Giovanni Giolitti should perhaps be as infamous for his manipulation of this rotten borough system in the south as he is commendable for his wisdom and skills as a practical politician in helping the north.[7]

[5] Luigi Salvatorelli and Giovanni Mira, *Storia dell'Italia nel periodo fascista* (Turin: Giulio Einaudi, 1956), p. 195. See also Richard Webster, *The Cross and the Fasces* (Palo Alto: Stanford University Press, 1960).

[6] See for this view Massimo L. Salvadori, *Il mito del buongoverno* (Torino: Einaudi, 1960), particularly the introduction. The body of this informative book presents the proffered solutions to the southern problem by many leading liberals of the period, including Pasquale Villari, Giorgio Sidney Sonnino, Leopoldo Franchetti, Giustino Fortunato, Napoleone Colaianni, and Francesco Saverio Nitti.

[7] Gaetano Salvemini expressed this view succinctly and picturesquely: "The difference between Giolitti and Mussolini was quantitative rather than qualitative. Giolitti was for Mussolini what John the Baptist was for Jesus." (Gaetano Salvemini, "Fu l'Italia prefascista una democrazia?" *Il ponte,* VIII [1952], p. 285.) This view would explain the acquiescent apathy of south-

These powerful enemy groups were flanked to the right and the left respectively by weaker but more violent enemies of the liberal state. On the extreme right there were the Nationalists and various groups of more or less disreputable adventurers. On the left were many of the young Socialist leaders straining under the moderation of the great old men of the movement, and at the extreme left were the anarchists and the members of the newly formed Communist party.

These enemies of the liberal state were not new. The church's position had been known from the beginning, and the Socialists had been in operation for over a quarter-century. Although the extreme groups were newer, they had had precursors not notably different from them, or rather from what they appeared to be. It is not improbable that the liberal state could have continued to weather these attacks had it not been for the failures of the liberals themselves. The failure of their foreign policy, the failure to maintain public order, and the failure to cooperate among themselves must each be weighed heavily in assessing the causes of the death of liberalism in Italy.

Italians were disillusioned by the failures of Italy's foreign policy after the war. Although Italy was the fourth major victorious power at the peace conferences in Paris, the representatives of Great Britain, France, and the United States — David Lloyd George, Georges Clemenceau, and Woodrow Wilson — showed little sympathy with or understanding of the Italian point of view, and Italy's then premier, the distinguished Sicilian jurist Vittorio Emanuele Orlando, was quite inadequate to the task of gaining sympathy and understanding. These conferences were probably the first international meetings to settle the affairs of Europe in which the common language of the inner circle was English and not French (Wilson, like most Americans, was no linguist; Clemenceau had lived in the United States); Orlando knew no English. It was the first major conference for the settlement of European affairs in which the colossus from the Western Hemisphere clumsily, but with the best intentions in the world, threw its weight around. This weight was thrown against Italy.

The spirit with which Italy entered the First World War, the spirit of *irredentismo,* was fed by the desire to win from Austria the essentially Italian cities of Trento and Trieste. A secret treaty was signed in London in 1915 between Great Britain, France, and Italy granting Italy these cities and adjacent territory, as well as a good part of the Dalmatian coast. Wilson refused to recognize the treaty because it was not

---

ern Italians to fascism, which was just another tyranny to them, both a bit more burdensome and a bit more productive than most. See Salvadori, *op. cit.,* pp. 362–366.

an open covenant openly arrived at. Wilson's stubbornness and Orlando's consequent failure led to the sentiment in Italy that Italy had won the war and lost the peace. This sentiment greatly weakened the prestige of the liberal state and exacerbated the animosities between the neutralist forces in Italy that had opposed Italy's intervention in the war in 1915 and the interventionists who had demanded it.

Another equally bitter struggle undermined Italy's unity and the prestige of the state. This was the reciprocal animosity between unionized labor and the returning soldiers. Both sides were guilty of intolerance, of violence, of criminal acts. The liberal state lost general esteem when it failed to keep order or to redress grievances brought on by the disorder.

The situation of liberal democracy would not have been hopeless, however, if there had been unity among the liberal forces and comprehension of the gravity of the dangers ahead. For sixty years the liberals had been governing Italy more or less successfully without seriously considering the inarticulate and impotent antiliberal forces. Politics for them was an intraparty rather than an interparty game. This blindness on the part of the liberals was aided by the fact that the great issues of the immediate postwar period divided the liberals as well as the antiliberal opposition.

The basic cleavage in the liberals and in the nation during and after World War I was that between the neutralists and the interventionists. The neutralists, headed by the Piedmontese Giovanni Giolitti, opposed Italy's almost disastrous participation in the war. They were supported by the antiliberal left and by one of Italy's major newspapers, *La stampa* of Turin. The interventionists had no single outstanding leader, but they were supported by much of the antiliberal right, and another major newspaper, *Il corriere della sera* of Milan, was their spokesman. The animosities between these groups continued into the Fascist period.

Another cleavage hardly less disastrous to the liberal cause was the personal rivalry between Giolitti and Francesco Saverio Nitti, the leading southern liberal politician. These men were not able to work together even in the face of threats from Fascist hoodlums or revolutionary Marxism.

The man who appears to have been best qualified to save the Italian liberal state was Giovanni Giolitti. He alone advocated a long-term program that offered a reasonable chance to reestablish political and economic stability. He was, however, beset by many enemies. The right hated him for having been a neutralist in 1915. Business interests resented his conciliatory policy toward the rash of political and economic strikes that plagued Italy during his last previous ministry, a policy that in the long run had been successful and had saved much bloodshed. The left would not cooperate with a bourgeois government. The Catholic *Partito popolare* was eager to knife a liberal who wished to maintain the clear distinction between church and state (which is a fundamental principle of the American government); its antagonism was further whetted by Giolitti's insistence that bearer shares in corporations be discontinued. Giolitti wanted this so that the large stockholders might be known to the government and taxed on their profits; the Vatican was eager to hide the financial involvements of the various religious orders.[8]

It was perhaps inevitable that after the success of his conciliatory policy toward the Socialists, Giolitti should follow a similar policy with the Fascists; by giving them flattery and political responsibility he hoped and expected to induce them to turn to legal rather than violent methods. Giolitti was a wily and experienced politician, but he was too old to realize that Fascism was something new, something more virulent than anything he had previously dealt with, that the violence, which represented "the epiphenomenon of the Socialist movement, was the very substance of Fascism."[9]

The question still to be answered is why it was Fascism that took over as the liberal state was dying. Liberal democracy in Italy had traditional enemies that might appear to have been more powerful and more popular. Where were the Socialists, where were the Vatican and the *Partito popolare* in 1922? What about the other anticonstitutional groups, the Communists, the Anarchists, the Nationalists, the Futurists, the followers of D'Annunzio?

The left was singularly inept in that fateful year. The Marxist movement was divided into three parties, and in the major central party there was little contact or comprehension between the old guard of intellectual leaders and the new generation of postwar followers. With the advent of universal suffrage in 1919 the Socialist Party grew at such a rate that the old leadership, consisting of such intellectuals as Filippo Turati, Claudio Treves, Giovanni Emanuele Modigliani, and Camillo Prampolini, despite their great prestige, lost effective control of the party to a group of newly elected postwar deputies, who lacked experience in leadership and showed little or no capacity for learning. On the left the Communists broke away in 1921 and on the right was a small constitutional social-democratic party (*Unione socialista*) under Ivanoe Bonomi and Leonida Bissolati that contributed its meager help to the support of the liberal state. The irresponsible speeches for a

[8] See Salvatorelli e Mira, *op. cit.,* p. 199.

[9] *Ibid.,* p. 168. See also Harold Dwight Lasswell and Renzo Sereno, "Governmental and Party Leaders in Fascist Italy," *American Political Science Review,* XIII (1937), pp. 914–929.

revolution and the half-baked plans for carrying it out made by the postwar batch of Socialist incompetents led to sporadic strikes and violence in 1920. By 1922 there was little fight left in Socialism, and the movement's leaders and followers hardly spoke the same language.

The Catholic position was considerably stronger, but unlike the Socialists, the Catholics had nothing in particular against Mussolini. In destroying the liberal state he was working for them. Pius XI had favored the Fascists since their early days when he was Archbishop of Milan. He eulogized Mussolini many times after the March on Rome.

The deathblow to the liberal state, however, was a gratuitous act of the Fascists. By October, 1922, the month of the Fascist March on Rome, the Italian state with little help from anybody had succeeded in muddling through the worst of its postwar crisis. Labor unrest was dwindling; the great and essentially amorphous Socialist Party no longer thought of revolution. Materially Italy would have been on the road to recovery, had it not been for the Fascists.

Components of the Fascist Party

The Fascists in this period were the major and virtually the sole disturbers of the peace. Many of them were sadists and cowards whose pleasure it was to beat up or murder unarmed persons, to commit robbery and arson. The greatest crime of the liberal state was that it took no effective measures against these Fascist marauders, many of whose arms came from the police and the army. There is no evidence that the government actually supported the Fascists, but it utterly failed to protect peaceful unarmed citizens against armed brigands and, what is worse, it did not even seriously attempt to take action or to admit its moral responsibility to do so.

It is easy now to point out that the rise of Fascism was evitable, that in October, 1922, the Communist menace had waned, and that had the King been willing to sign the decree for martial law the army could have crushed and disgraced the Fascist upstarts. All this was not so obvious in 1922. Then Italy was recovering from a victorious but disastrous war. Her government and her governors were generally discredited, for in the long run men who cannot gain the confidence of parliament cannot hope to have the confidence of the people. Italian nerves were suffering from shell shock. Italian minds were not in a sufficiently contemplative mood to perceive that Italy's vacillating politicians were in the main successfully muddling through. In short, Italians needed something to unite on, to rally around, and the Fascist movement, which appealed vaguely to their better sentiments, was at once the most attractive and the most blatant of available symbols.

Fascism was a complex movement composed of several basically distinct elements. The most important of these were the *squadristi,* the *ben pensanti,* the *idealisti,* the *fiancheggiatori,* and *il Duce.*

The *squadristi,* already described, were the armed brigands who created the disorder that served as an excuse for the March on Rome, the extralegal force that frightened many anti-Fascists into silence or acquiescence, the means through which the Fascist leaders could exercise effective control without the necessity of operating through democratic or legal channels. The *squadristi* were for the most part criminals, motivated by criminal instincts.

The *ben pensanti* (the well-thinking persons) were of a conservative disposition and were able to close their eyes to the violence, the sadism, and illegalities perpetrated by the *squadristi.* It was particularly easy to accept this point of view if there were some specific personal gain derived from the movement. Italian capitalists, for instance, could the more easily overlook the negative side of Fascism when they thought of Fascism's work in crushing trade unions. The *ben pensanti* were above all afraid of communism. The Russian revolution had occurred only five years previously, and many people on both the right and the left believed the same kind of revolution was imminent in Italy. Historians now tell us that there was no real danger of any such thing.

To understand what Fascism was to the *idealisti* one need only consider what Americanism means to the Americans who supported the Un-American Activities Committee, and who want Americanism taught in our public schools. The great majority of these men are neither nefarious nor stupid. They are convinced that Americanism is the finest thing in the world, and they contemplate it with hearts beating a little faster and eyes moist with tears. Pressed for the meaning of Americanism, however, they can only say that it is the American way of life; they may add that it is anti-Communist, and that it follows the Constitution, but they have only a foggy and distorted recollection of constitutional principles. Italian Fascists had the same difficulty in defining Fascism. It is probable that most of the *squadristi* and of the *ben pensanti* enjoyed sporadic or occasional emotional binges in the morass of this idealistic sentimentality.

The *fiancheggiatori,* a term that means approximately fellow travelers, made up perhaps the great mass of Italians. They did not believe deeply in Fascism, but they had no desire to disturb their peace by fighting it; they would pay lip service to Fascism, even admire it for its successes no matter how obtained. Perhaps the best description of them is to say they had a high toleration for Fascism and tried to derive what personal benefit they could from this outward acquiescence.

The final element was Benito Mussolini, *Duce* of Fascism. (*Duce* is the Italian form of the Latin *dux,* leader, from which are also derived *Duke* and *Doge.*) A great deal has been written about Mussolini's essentially simple character, much of which is sheer fantasy.[10] Mussolini was egocentric, ambitious, unprincipled, and clever. With no scruples and interested exclusively in his own well being, he could devote his talents to this end with a singleness of purpose denied to a greater man. Mussolini does not fit in any of the usual categories. He was not interested in the personal use of violence, as were the *squadristi;* he was too shrewd to be a *ben pensante,* too cynical to be an idealist, and too involved to be a *fiancheggiatore.*[11]

Pre-Fascist leaders

Before Mussolini there had been pre-fascist leaders, in some ways more original and more remarkable men than the Duce himself, who had appealed to some of the same forces and fancies that later formed Fascism. Two of these were the poets Filippo Tommaso Marinetti and Gabriele D'Annunzio.

Marinetti (1876–1944), who was born in Egypt and educated in France, was the founder of the politico-artistic movement called Futurism, an aesthetic school whose value lay in its startling and hyperbolic denunciation of the conformist decadence that was common in aesthetic circles in 1909, when Marinetti launched his Futurist Manifesto in Paris. The Futurists attacked the medical profession; sick people, they thought, were weaklings and deserved to die. They advocated the abolition of the police force on the grounds that people should be

---

[10] Mussolini the great lover is described in Margherita Sarfatti, *Dux,* translated as *The Life of Benito Mussolini* (New York: Stokes, 1925, and London: Butterworth, 1925). The superman is set forth in Yvon de Begnac, *Vita di Benito Mussolini,* Vols. I, II, III (Milan: Mondadori, 1936–40). Mussolini the ascetic is portrayed in Dante Germino, *The Italian Fascist Party* (Minneapolis: University of Minnesota Press, 1959). More accurate descriptions are found in Giuseppe Antonio Borgese, *Goliath* (New York: Viking Press, 1937), in George Seldes, *Sawdust Caesar* (New York: Harpers, 1935), and in Anzhelika Balabanova, *My Life as a Rebel* (New York: Harpers, 1938). See also Laura Fermi, *Mussolini* (Chicago: University of Chicago Press, 1961), and Christopher Hibbert, *Benito Mussolini* (London: Longmans, 1962). Perhaps the greatest insight into this man is found in the film "The Great Dictator," written and directed by Charlie Chaplin, in which Jack Oakie gives the performance of his life as Mussolini.

[11] See also H. R. Trevor-Roper, "The Phenomenon of Fascism," in S. J. Woolf, ed., *European Fascism* (London: Weidenfeld & Nicolson, 1968), pp. 18–38. Trevor-Roper finds two magic ingredients in fascism: clerical conservatism and dynamic fascism. The present authors prefer to use the term fascism exclusively to designate the latter.

able to defend themselves. They were against moonlight, romantic love, tenors, and spaghetti, considering them decadent. They extolled war, violence, modern science, particularly airplanes, and all ultra-modern and "unbeautiful" art.

In the immediate postwar period, before it fused with Fascism, Marinetti's Futurist Party ran in the Italian elections, and Marinetti even succeeded in getting himself elected to Parliament on the following platform:

1. Sell all the art treasures of Italy abroad.
2. Fill the art galleries with Futurist art.
3. Abolish all taxes and live off the proceeds of the sale of the art.
4. Build the largest navy in the world.
5. Conquer the world.
6. Regain the art treasures.[12]

This program seems silly until one compares it with Hermann Goering's policy: "Guns instead of butter." A country which produces armaments instead of food must use the armaments to rob others of their food or else it will starve to death. The only difference, and it is a fatal one, between Marinetti's theory and that of Goering is that the latter was taken in deadly earnest by the vast majority of the German nation whereas the former merely amused the Italians.

The important point, however, is that this kind of movement responded to a political as well as to an aesthetic need. It showed the way to more serious movements that played successfully on the same basic dissatisfactions that Futurism titillated.

Gabriele D'Annunzio, Principe di Montenevoso (Gabriel of the Annunciation, Prince of Snowy Mountain) exemplified another of the dying gasps of the Romantic movement. He was a sensuous roué ever seeking a new thrill for his sated spirit. Like Marinetti, D'Annunzio found the bounds of the literary world too narrow to satisfy his inordinate demands for self-expression, and turned to politics. Marinetti, D'Annunzio, and Mussolini met first on common ground, when each began to advocate war against Germany. At that time, however, D'Annunzio was of the three by far the most important figure. He had the greatest influence in getting Italy into the war, and he certainly had the most fun during the war.

> Meanwhile D'Annunzio, amidst Our War, fought His War. He had a rank in the Italian army and before the end was a colonel.

[12] Much of Marinetti's political writing is assembled in F. T. Marinetti, *Teoria e invenzione futurista* (Milano: Mondadori, 1968). One of the several variants of this program is given on pp. 373–377.

There was nothing to do, in the trenches of mud and stone, for the cavalry, to which he naturally belonged. So he lived in whatever princely hotel or villa he chose, mostly in Venice; and from time to time he went on whatever gallant enterprise he pleased, in the spirit of those Ariostean paladins whose whereabouts remained unknown to the Emperor Charlemagne. Often he was driven in his car by his chauffeur, along the front; sometimes he would embrace a fallen hero; but he delighted especially in a kind of individual venture, largely advertised, as when he, with some Ulyssean companions on a motorboat, glided into a well-protected Austrian harbour just to make fun of the enemy, then safely sneaked back home; or as when he, also with Ulyssean companions, flew over Vienna, an angel Gabriel, dropping instead of high explosives, leaflets of high sounding prose. He was in the Army, he was in the Navy, he was in the Air Force: ubiquitous. But though he was officially registered as a commissioned officer in the Army, he preferred, and adopted on his own authority, a title of the Navy: comandante; commander.[13]

The war had been fun for D'Annunzio, and he was not happy when it ended. His period of boredom and inactivity, however, was short. After the war Italy sought territorial aggrandizement in Dalmatia, the eastern coast of the Adriatic. This territory had once belonged to Venice, much as England had once belonged to Rome, and many of the fisherfolk still spoke or understood Venetian dialect. The mainland, however, was solidly Slavic. The Allies were willing to grant many of Italy's claims, but they did not sate the rabid chauvinists, and so D'Annunzio led a march on Fiume, which turned out to be the twentieth century's closest approximation to a comic-opera libretto.

Fiume, like Trieste, was a seaport of the Austro-Hungarian Empire on the Adriatic coast. The city itself was predominantly Italian, but it was surrounded by a purely Slavic people. Although it had been declared a free city at Paris, D'Annunzio did not hesitate to seize it and hold it almost a year and a half. The occupation was able to continue for so long a time unmolested by reason of a set of fortuitous circumstances and its own preposterousness, which stunned the world. During this time D'Annunzio developed much of the pageantry of Fascism.

The people and the soldiers convened in the square beneath the palace of the government. The poet, in his over-medalled military

13 Borgese, *op. cit.*, pp. 112–113.

uniform, appeared, conveniently flanked by some of the staff, on the balcony. . . . There he delivered an elaborate harangue. . . . At the end he bolstered up as best he could his penetrating but rather effeminate voice, and asked the people for consent.

The people raised their right hands and arms, and answered: Yes. The gesture of the raised right arm, which was sooner or later the Roman, and, unbelievable but true, the German salute, had been picked up at random from classical museums, from gestures of Graeco-Roman orators and rulers. . . . In antiquity it had occasionally been an attitude of oratorical vehemence. . . . It never had been the ordinary salute in the streets of Greece and Rome.[14]

D'Annunzio, however, did more than talk. He also wrote the constitution of the Regency of Carnaro, which was the name he gave Fiume. The constitution is a rare and wonderful document, based on the ancient *corporazioni,* the medieval guilds.[15]

The bell tolled for D'Annunzio when Giovanni Giolitti, Italy's perennial premier, returned to office and brought with him as his Foreign Minister a young career diplomat, Carlo Sforza. Sforza saw the necessity of peace with the Slavs and the removal of D'Annunzio. First he negotiated the Treaty of Rapallo, and then he was ready to tackle the poet. D'Annunzio was verbally adamant. Again in the words of Borgese, "He swore with . . . the most powerful impact of his biblical eloquence that he never would abandon the holy city . . . and that the cowardly henchmen of Giolitti and Sforza should have to tread on his bleeding corpse before violating Fiume."[16] The Battle of Fiume, however, was short and virtually bloodless. A shell burst on the façade of the government palace and D'Annunzio left. "It is easy to say that the poet was too much of a poet to become a real Caesar; it would probably be mean to investigate the supposed crisis of his personal courage. Much fairer it is to grant that when confronted with the necessity of irretrievable decisions, he loathed bloodshed, and his delicate artist's hands withheld the gesture."[17]

[14] *Ibid.,* pp. 158–159.

[15] For an English translation of the constitution see Odon Por, *Fascism* (London, 1923); for the original and for D'Annunzio's major speeches at Fiume, see Gabriele D'Annunzio, *Per la più grande Italia* (Milan: Istituto nazionale per l'edizione di tutte le opere di Gabriele D'Annunzio, 1932).

[16] Borgese, *op. cit.,* p. 168.

[17] *Ibid.* For the entire Fiume incident see also Pentad, *The Remaking of Italy* (Harmondsworth: Penguin Press, 1941), pp. 195–199, 202.

Benito Mussolini's war experience was short but not exotic. It consisted primarily of a series of wounds in the rump. Mussolini was no genial daring playboy like Marinetti, whose poetic effulgence could burst forth in lines like "Thou reservest alone for me thy gasoline kisses, o pipe line," nor was he an effete erotic like D'Annunzio, who erected an altar to Artemis, the Greek goddess of chastity, in his garden and weekly had his love letters burnt before it.[18] He appealed, however, to the same emotions that Marinetti and D'Annunzio had aroused and that had attracted to Fascism many Futurists and many participants in the Fiume expedition. At the same time he vulgarized the movement and attracted to it greater and more diverse forces, thus turning an extravaganza in bad taste into a sordid reality.

And so Italy, which in the past had frequently and dolorously felt the scourge of foreign tyrants, placed herself at the mercy of a home-grown tyrant, who before he fell revealed traits in his own character and those of his cohorts which previously Italians had thought were inherent in Teutonic barbarians and Spaniards but were bred out of civilized peoples.

First Fascist period, 1922–1926

Mussolini's first cabinet was an ordinary coalition government in which most parties from the Catholic center to the right were willing to participate. Neither Italian nor world opinion was ready to assert that the King had acted unwisely in avoiding the danger of civil war in making the colorful and popular leader of the Fascists responsible for public order instead of allowing him to continue to flout it.

The dictatorship advanced by easy stages, as if the government were testing out the people to see how much they would take. As they took more and more, the people were increasingly despised by the ruling Fascist clique, and before their twenty-odd years of disgrace were over they were forced to suffer indignities to which not even the Germans were ever subject.

Mussolini's verbal lashings were the first indication of the things that were to come. His speech to Parliament when he was seeking his first vote of confidence was of a signal arrogance. In this speech Mussolini boasted that if Parliament refused him the vote of confidence he would seize power anyway and so much the worse for Parliament. Instead of reacting with dignity to this insolence, Parliament seemed to be swept by a wave of masochism and submitted. This was the beginning of the end of the free Italian Parliament.

[18] The source of this anecdote is a lecture by Professor Walter Starkie.

Two years later Mussolini held an election. Not seeing a majority in sight for his party, he had a new electoral law written giving the party that received the plurality three-fourths of the seats in the Chamber. The Fascists, by forming a coalition with the right, guaranteed themselves this plurality. After this artificial majority was gained, there was no way to stop the Fascists as the *Statuto* of Carlo Alberto did not require any special amendment process and left Parliament legally free to alter it at will.

Shortly after these elections the Fascists suffered their most serious setback. This was the result of the reaction against the murder of the Socialist deputy Giacomo Matteotti in June, 1924. High Fascists, not excluding Mussolini, were implicated, and Italian public opinion was deeply shocked. Had it been necessary to hold an election after the murder, possibly the Italian people would have thrown Mussolini out of office. Instead, the murder occurred after the Fascists were well entrenched in power and able to withstand the waves of protest and indignation.

The next basic change made by the government after the electoral law was the gag law, taking away freedom of the press. This law was issued in decree form July 15, 1924, and later, at the leisure of Parliament, turned into a regular law. The next major step occurred in 1926, when the much publicized corporate system was put into operation.

Second Fascist period, 1926–1936:
The corporate system and the Lateran Pacts

The corporate system was not a Fascist idea; it was a contribution of one of the Nationalist leaders, Alfredo Rocco, who took the idea from the French Catholic theorists, particularly from René Charles Humbert, Marquis de la Tour du Pin Chambly de la Charce, who in turn gave credit for it to the then pretender to the French throne, the Comte de Chambord.[19] The corporate system had become the classical Catholic suggestion of the way to insure economic coordination and labor peace. The theory was that economic self-interest should be subject to controls in the interest of the community as a whole in the same way that individual interests were controlled, and that economic groups as well as territorial groups should be bases of the state and should be represented in its institutions. To carry out this system it was neces-

[19] René Charles Humbert, Marquis de la Tour du Pin Chambly de la Charce, *Vers un ordre social chrétien. Jalons de route* 1882–1907, 5th ed. (Paris, 1929). The major essay on the corporate system was first published in 1883.

sary to create a series of institutions to represent all possible economic and labor groups and to give each worker a vote in one of the groups and at the same time to set up a series of special courts within the regular judicial system to handle collective and individual labor disputes. Since all labor disputes that could not be conciliated would be settled in court, strikes, lockouts, and other means of economic warfare were outlawed, and the state and the general public would be free from the menace of internecine economic strife.

The theory of the corporate system sounds good, but its practice, in Italy as elsewhere, left much to be desired. There is nothing basically undemocratic about the idea in theory, but the practice in Italy certainly made but little pretense at democracy.[20] Most corporate representatives in the unions, the corporations and the parliament were, in law, and all of them in fact appointed from above and not elected from below.

The institution of the corporate system served two purposes for the Fascists. For the first time they could claim to be making an innovation of social importance and consequently had something to ballyhoo. It also gave them a strangle hold on the economic life of the country and permitted them to create thousands of additional soft jobs for deserving Fascists.

The corporate system went into effect with the law of April 3, 1926, No. 563, but it was not fully implemented until the creation of the corporations many years later. (The term *corporation* is a misnomer, perhaps resulting from the carelessness of a journalist. The Italian word *corporazione* should have been translated *guild* when used in this sense.) It was expected that the corporations, institutions in which capital and labor collaborated for the realization of common ends under the tutelage of the state, would be formed spontaneously by the professional associations of workers and management to which the corporate system gave legal recognition in 1926, but there was little spontaneity in Fascist Italy. Since, by 1934 only one corporation had been established "spontaneously," the remaining corporations were instituted forthwith by decree.

[20] Alfredo Rocco, "Crisi dello stato e sindacati," *Politica,* VII (1920), pp. 1–14, *La trasformazione dello stato* (Rome, 1927), and "Politica e diritto nelle vecchie e nuove concezioni dello stato," *Nuova antologia,* CCCLVIII (1931), pp. 356–390. Contra, Gaëtan Pirou, *Essais sur le corporatisme* (Paris: Félix Alcan, 1938) who holds the corporate system is intrinsically undemocratic. For accounts in English of the pre-Fascist corporate theories see John Clarke Adams, "Some Antecedents of the Theory of the Corporate System," *Journal of the History of Ideas,* III (1942), pp. 182–189, and Svend Ranulf, "Scholarly Forerunners of Fascism," *Ethics,* L. (1939), pp. 16–34.

The year 1926 was a big one for the Fascists; they took over not only the economic system but the judicial system as well, with the establishment of the Special Tribunal for the Defense of the State. This court, which was not bound even by the inferior Italian codes of procedure, tried persons who were accused of crimes against the state. It was given retroactive jurisdiction and its judges needed no law degree, provided they were good Fascists.[21]

By the law of April 3, 1926, No. 660, promulgated the same day the corporate system was instituted, the prefects were given a strangle hold over local government. With this law the power of the Fascists was secure, opposition was stifled, and the Fascists were in control of everything that mattered. Previously their control had been *de facto,* based on their illegal use of violence; now it was legalized.

Then for nine years the dictatorship functioned quietly. Mussolini had talent as an administrator. The majority of the Italians undoubtedly were reasonably content. Much was done to make the citizen grateful to the ubiquitous government. Real wages were slashed, but government services increased. There was pageantry galore to amuse the crowds. None of the old symbols was destroyed; one could and was encouraged to revere the King, the Pope, Italian heroes of the past, many of whom would have been nauseated at Mussolini. But although bearers of all the old symbols of power were still around, standing nearby was a Fascist to control their actions. In no other European country was there such a difference between law and practice. Reading the *Statuto* and even the various laws, an unobservant man would hardly realize a revolution had occurred. Here there was none of that mania to destroy the old and build anew that ravaged Germany under Hitler. The key word of the Fascist government was *duplicità,* which means both duplicity and duplication. For every official of the regular government there was a Fascist official, representing the unofficial government, and often it was the latter who held the real power. By the side of the legislature there was the Great Council (*Gran consiglio*) of the Fascist Party. By the side of the regular courts there was the Tribunal for the Defense of the State. By the side of the army there was the Fascist militia. By the side of the prefect was the provincial head of the party. Even the conductors on the railroad trains were flanked by armed Fascists. But this was duplicity also in the English sense, for it made of the real government a façade, behind which the Fascist Party intrigued, more for its own good than for the good of the country.[22]

---

[21] Herman Finer, *Mussolini's Italy* (New York, 1935), p. 242.
[22] Piero Calamandrei, *La funzione parlamentare sotto il fascismo* (Rome: Camera dei deputati, 1948).

During this hiatus, in February, 1929, the Lateran Treaties were signed, making peace and an alliance with the Vatican, on terms highly favorable to the latter. It was at this time that Pius XI called the Duce a man sent by Providence.

Third Fascist period, 1936–1945: The nazification of Italy

The third phase of Fascist tyranny started after the successful Ethiopian war. By this time Mussolini had lost touch with the people. Needlessly he copied many of the worst aspects of Hitlerism and then instituted further indignities of his own contrivance. The anti-Jewish legislation in Italy was particularly stupid. There are few Jews in Italy, and no Jewish problem had ever existed there.

The Fascist anti-Jewish legislation was irritating and humiliating rather than savage. Jews were forbidden to attend the universities, to enter certain professions, to belong to various social and professional organizations, to employ Christian servants, to marry Christians, and to have listed telephone numbers. Many were exiled to remote villages by police order and without trial and placed under police surveillance. No Jew *qua* Jew, however, was sentenced to death in Italy, and there were no concentration camps or gas chambers.

The public did not accept this policy with enthusiasm, and often government officials enforced it with apologies, but it excited no rebellion. With the coming of the war and the Nazis the Fascist government began ordering the deportation of Jews to Germany. This action was the beginning of the end of Fascism. The essentially liberal and humanistic Italian tradition revolted at such gross immorality and inhumanity, and with increasing frequency the army and the civil servants refused to obey these orders and, along with many priests and the people at large, all at the risk of their own lives, helped the Jews to hide and to escape. At that very moment when the German officer or civil servant absolved himself of all responsibility for the abominations he was committing with the facile apology that he was merely carrying out the orders of his superiors, the Italian on the whole was sufficiently realistic to admit his personal responsibility and sufficiently moral to refuse to obey an immoral order. The first popular resistance to Fascism in Italy was the spontaneous reaction to the deportation orders against the Jews.

Fascism made its own contributions to tyranny. Two examples will suffice as illustrations. In the Italian language and in some of the dialects the form of polite address is the third person singular, *lei,* instead of the second person plural, *voi,* common to French and English. One day Mussolini made it a misdemeanor to use *lei* and required everyone to use *voi*. This was as if the President of the United States should make it a crime to use *you* in addressing a single person and should require the use of *thou*.

If by this bit of grammatical tyranny Mussolini showed his scorn of the rights and feelings of the people in general, another of his whims demeaned the very Fascists who had put him in power. Fascists, he decided, should be athletes, and consequently he held sporting events in Rome in which pot-bellied party hierarchs had to run and jump through burning hoops. These feats were duly filmed and shown in all of Italy's movie theaters, where they were particularly popular with the then growing number of Italy's anti-Fascists.

A phase of Fascist despotism little known abroad was the virtual reestablishment of serfdom in Italy. A law of the early thirties made it illegal for a farm family to leave its province of origin in seach of work without a police permit and subjected the employer to a fine to be paid to the police official who had refused the permit. In 1939 a more detailed and radical law was enacted that among other things: (1) forbade anyone to migrate to a provincial capital or to seek work there without a police permit; (2) made it a crime to let a house, apartment, or room in a provincial capital to persons from another commune who lacked a permit; (3) made it a crime to buy a house in another commune and live in it without a permit; (4) forbade farm laborers to register in employment agencies for nonagricultural labor; (5) made it a crime to employ anyone who should have had such a permit and did not.[23]

In June, 1940, Mussolini made the fatal decision to stab France in the back, and Italy was embarked in a disastrous, immoral, and unpopular war. On July 25, 1943, Mussolini was deposed and arrested. On September 11 of the same year he was rescued by German parachute troops and taken to north Italy to set up the Republican government of Salò. In April, 1945, as he was fleeing to Switzerland with his mistress, Clara Petacci, he was again arrested. His captors were Communist partisans, and both he and Petacci were shot. Mussolini's body was taken to Milan and hung upside down in Piazza Loreto for some time, where it was subjected to indignities. The Communist newspaper *Unità* printed an obituary for Petacci called "Homage to Claretta," pointing out that she would not have been harmed had she consented to be separated from Mussolini and suggesting that she was the

---

[23] For a fuller account see Luigi Einaudi, "Servitù della gleba in Italia," in *Lo scrittoio del presidente* (Turin: Giulio Einaudi, 1956), pp. 561–589.

only prominent Fascist or Fascist sympathizer who, having the choice, had the courage to die at her post.

And so Italy, on the wreck of twenty years of moral degradation and of material waste and destruction, with the talents of a generation in great part destroyed by murder, miseducation, and intimidation, set out to improvise a democratic republic. For this task she called on her oldest and wisest men, those who had withstood Fascism either in exile or at home, and on that part of her youth that had fought the partisan war for justice and liberty, and they met to write a constitution.

3

The Constitution

Constituent Assembly

On June 2, 1946, the Italian people elected 556 deputies to their first Constituent Assembly. The most important act of this body was the drafting of the Constitution, which it ratified on December 22, 1947. The Constitution was then promulgated by the provisional President of Italy, Enrico De Nicola, on December 27 and took effect on January 1, 1948.

For the previous hundred years Italy, or such of her territory as was under the house of Savoy, was governed under the *Statuto*, the Constitution which the Piedmontese obtained from Carlo Alberto in that year of popular rebellion throughout Europe: 1848. This Constitution was of the type called flexible, however, in that it could be amended by simple legislative action. It therefore could not stand up before the onslaught of the Fascist tyranny which, although never abrogating it, defaced and distorted its principles beyond recognition.

The members of the Constituent Assembly were on the whole of high caliber. They included distinguished scholars such as the philosopher Benedetto Croce, the economist Luigi Einaudi, the Latinist Concetto Marchesi, the mathematician Gustavo Colonnetti, and the law professors Piero Calamandrei, Tomaso Perassi, Costantino Mortati, Giuseppe Dossetti, Egidio Tosato, and Giuseppe Grassi; prominent pre-Fascist statesmen, including former Prime Ministers Vittorio Emanuele Orlando, Francesco Saverio Nitti, and Ivanoe Bonomi; former Foreign Minister Count Carlo Sforza; outstanding partisan leaders, such as Ferruccio Parri and Luigi Longo; and almost all of the post-Fascist political leaders.

The Constituent Assembly was dominated by three parties, the Christian Democrats (Catholic), the Communists, and the Socialists. Four other parties, the Liberal, the Labor Democratic, the Republican, and

the Action parties, which were also anti-Fascist and basically democratic, were active in drafting the Constitution. Owing to the prestige
of their leaders, these four parties had, in fact, greater influence than
their numbers merited. The other minor parties were mostly of a
reactionary nature and had little influence in forming the Constitution.
No single party had a majority in the Assembly, and no stable coalition
was formed that could impose a unified program. Therefore a separate
majority was formed on each major issue. The Christian Democrats
were usually the nucleus of this majority, but its other component parts
varied according to the issue at stake.

The Committee of Seventy-Five

A body of over 500 persons is not well adapted to constitution-mak-
ing. The Assembly was therefore wise in delegating, on July 15, 1946,
the task of drafting the Constitution to a committee of seventy-five of
its members, chosen to represent the parties in proportion to their
strength in the Assembly. In general, the parties were represented on
the committee by their abler men.

The Seventy-Five elected as its president the respected jurist and pre-
Fascist deputy Meuccio Ruini, a member of the Labor Democrat Party.
The Committee then divided itself into three subcommittees, charged
respectively with drafting the parts of the constitution dealing with
(1) rights and duties of citizens, (2) the constitutional organization of
the state and (3) social and economic rights and duties. These subcommittees elected as their presidents respectively the Christian Democrat Umberto Tupini, the Communist Umberto Terracini, and the Socialist Gustavo Ghidini. The second subcommittee, which was the
largest, was again subdivided. Terracini himself headed the subsection
dealing with the executive power, the Republican Giovanni Conti
headed the one dealing with the judiciary, and the Christian Democrat
Gaspare Ambrosini presided over the subsection that dealt with local
government.

The Committee of Eighteen

When the various sections and subcommittees had finished their
work, the Seventy-Five appointed a committee of eighteen to coordinate
the Constitution and put it into final form for presentation to the Constituent Assembly. The Eighteen was composed of the presidents of
the committee and its subdivisions, of outstanding law professors such
as Calamandrei (Action party), Perassi (Republican), Grassi (Liberal), and Tosato, Dossetti, and Mortati (Christian Democrats). Pal-

miro Togliatti, the Communist leader, was also a member. The Seventy-Five adopted the redraft made by the Eighteen with only slight modifications and presented it to the Assembly on January 31, 1947. During the rest of 1947 the Assembly discussed, altered, and after 173 sessions, finally approved the Constitution.

The Constitution was not submitted to the electorate for approval. Thus the Assembly was saved from the possible embarrassment of having the voters reject the Constitution, as had occurred in France shortly before. On the other hand, the Italian Constitution was deprived of the prestige it might have gained through approval by popular vote. All in all, however, Italy was probably well advised not to risk a popular vote that might have split the country geographically, as the vote on the monarchy had done.[1]

The innovations

The most fundamental change that the Constitution effected is in the quality of the Constitution itself. The Albertine *Statuto* of 1848 was susceptible to amendment by ordinary legislative enactment, as is the unwritten constitution of Great Britain. The republican Constitution of 1948 is of the type the jurists call "rigid." Laws are invalid if in the opinion of a judicial authority they conflict with the Constitution, and the Constitution cannot be amended by ordinary legislation. This innovation was intended to be the major bulwark against future tyrannies. By transforming the Albertine *Statuto* into a rigid constitution it sought to place the principles expressed in the Constitution out of the reach of parliamentary caprice. The Constitution has thus demoted the legislature by subjecting its action to review by a judicial body, and so Italy is no longer an example of that early type of democratic state based on a sovereign legislature.

The Constitution provides for five important institutional changes: (1) the abolition of the monarchy and the establishment of a parliamentary republic (Arts. 83–91); (2) the transformation of the Senate from an appointive to an elective body (Arts. 57–60); (3) the establishment of the Constitutional Court (Arts. 134–137); (4) the establishment of regional governments (Arts. 114–133); and (5) the creation of the High Judicial Council (Arts. 104–107). None of these changes can be considered revolutionary. Each is in keeping with mod-

[1] Piero Calamandrei, "Cenni introduttivi sulla Costituente e sui suoi lavori," in Piero Calamandrei and Alessandro Levi, *Commentario sistematico alla costituzione italiana,* 2 vols. (Florence: Barbèra, 1950), Vol. I, pp. lxxxix–cxl. An English version of the Constitution may be found in *Ten Years of Italian Democracy,* 1945–1956 (Rome: Presidency of the Council of Ministers, Information Office, 1956), pp. 5–35.

ern trends and in line with the experience of other Western democracies. The President's powers and functions are similar to those of the French President of the Third and Fourth Republics; the Senate is modeled after the French Senate; the influence of the United States is seen in the Constitutional Court; the doctrine of federalism is behind the establishment of regional governments; and the creation of the High Judicial Council, similar to that of the French Fourth Republic, has the support of a cardinal democratic principle, that of the separation of powers.

Other innovations of note, but of secondary importance relative to those already mentioned, include: (1) provision for initiative and referendum (Arts. 71, 75); (2) the creation of an advisory council on economic and labor problems (Art. 99); (3) the institution of a mild type of presidential veto (Art. 74); (4) a series of provisions aimed at strengthening the government *vis-à-vis* Parliament (Arts. 92, 94); and (5) the abolition of special tribunals (Arts. 102, VI). A description of the new institutions will be found in the following chapters.

In the field of civil and political liberties the Constitution grants the traditional privileges and immunities of the American Bill of Rights and the French *Déclaration des droits* and supplements them with some new rights and privileges, such as the right to an education (Art. 34), the right to work (Art. 4), and the privileges of forming trade unions and of striking (Arts. 39–40). These traditional liberties are not new to Italy, but they are stated more completely in the new Constitution than in the Albertine *Statuto,* and they further benefit from the rigidity of the Constitution, which renders invalid ordinary legislation that is incompatible with them.

The weaknesses

The major weaknesses of the Constitution would appear to be the incompatibilities among its 157 articles.[2] Another weakness, according to some, is the confusing admixture of articles obligating the state (*norme precettive*) and those merely setting goals the state should seek to attain (*norme programmatiche*).

It is convenient to discuss these points in reverse order. The second

---

[2] Of these articles 139 (numbered 1 to 139) are called "permanent articles" and eighteen (numbered from I to XVIII) are called "transitory and final articles." Of these latter some are of only temporary significance, like Article 7 of the United States Constitution, which states the conditions under which the document will begin to have legal effect. Others deal with matters that ideally would not have constitutional relevance, such as the outlawing of the Fascist party, the nonrecognition of titles of nobility, and the exclusion from public office of the Savoia family (the former ruling family), and these articles perhaps are expected in some future state of bliss also to become anachronisms.

point arises from the fact that alongside the articles in the Constitution that confer rights on citizens and subjects and that limit the power of the state are found other articles that express only the intentions of the Constituent Assembly. In a speech before the Assembly, Calamandrei argued[3] that the inclusion of these articles in the Constitution would cause future Italian governments unnecessarily to lose credit in the eyes of the Italian people because it places obligations on the state that it is in no position to fulfill. Article 32, for instance, states, "The Republic protects the health of the individual as his fundamental right and as an interest of the collectivity, and guarantees free medical treatment to the poor." For the present this statement is only a pious wish, as the government is in no financial position to carry it out. Calamandrei pointed out that pious wishes and ethical principles have their place in constitutions, but that place is in a preamble rather than in the corpus, which is supposedly operative. Calamandrei's suggestion that these articles be relegated to a preamble was defeated, however, as others felt that if they were included in the body of the Constitution, the principles they set forth would have a normative value in the sense that they would (1) invalidate any action directly contrary to their provisions, and (2) serve for the interpretation and application of other norms.

The contradictory statements in the Constitution are another obvious weakness. Many of these incompatibilities result from the inclusion of the Lateran Pacts in the Constitution (Art. 7). The Lateran Pacts contain several provisions obnoxious to Western democratic concepts of civil liberties found in the Italian Constitution. An example is the provision that a former priest cannot be employed by the government in a position that puts him in contact with the public — obviously in contrast with the "equal protection" provision of Article 3 of the Constitution. By 1971 it was apparent to both the Italian government and the Vatican that the time had come to renegotiate the Lateran Pacts, and cautious steps in this direction were taken by both parties.

The implementation

It took the Italians less time to write the Constitution than to implement it.[4] Of the major institutional changes, only two were immediately effectuated (the change from monarchy to republic and the

---

[3] *Atti dell'Assemblea Costituente*, 1947, Vol. 49, pp. 1743–1755.

[4] John Clarke Adams and Paolo Barile, "The Implementation of the Italian Constitution," *American Political Science Review*, XLVII (1953), pp. 61–83; and Paolo Barile, *Corso di diritto costituzionale* (Padova: CEDAM, 2nd ed., 1964), pp. 54–67.

creation of an elective Senate). Four regions (Sicilia, Sardegna, Val d'Aosta, Trentino–Alto Adige) were established by 1949, and Friuli–Venezia Giulia was activated in 1964. It took eight years (until 1956) before the Constitutional Court was in operation, and the High Judicial Council was not a going concern until eleven years after the promulgation of the Constitution. As for the fifteen ordinary regions, they existed only on paper until 1970, twenty-two years after the promulgation of the Constitution that formally established them. In that year elections were held for their legislative councils, but by the end of 1971 these regions had not yet begun to function.

Except for those requiring no enabling legislation, the minor innovations have had even rougher sailing (a happier metaphor would have put them in the doldrums). The President's right to ask Parliament to reconsider a bill went into effect automatically, as did the provision empowering him to appoint the new President of the Council of Ministers, rather than merely to designate a candidate for the approval of Parliament, and those requiring the signature of 10 per cent of the members of a house of Parliament for a motion of confidence, as well as a cooling-off period of three days before its discussion. The initiative provision of the Constitution likewise required no parliamentary action to become effective.

The National Economic Council, on the other hand, was not established until 1957, and Italy is scheduled to hold its first referendum (in an effort to abrogate the divorce law) in the spring of 1972, in accordance with enabling legislation enacted only in 1970. Special tribunals are still flourishing, but the jurisdiction of the military tribunals with respect to personnel not on active duty has been curtailed.

A constitution, however, is more than the skeleton of a state. It has a soul as well as a body, and it would be an injustice to the great and good men who wrote the Italian Constitution should we believe that they conceived of their task primarily as that of organizing the state. This technical problem offered little challenge to a body like the Constituent Assembly, replete as it was with eminent jurists. Their real purpose was ethical and political rather than jural; it was to create a liberal democracy, which is less a form of government than an end of government, a way of acting, a procedure.

The organs of government described in the Constitution are at last nearly all in operation. The body is almost complete, not so the soul. Forces inimical to the spirit of the Constitution as well as those ignorant of or impervious to this spirit dominate key points of the Italian administration and important centers of political power, and so the new Italy envisaged by the majority of the Constituent Assembly is only in part realized.

To resist change, reaction has relied on the force of inertia. The very negativeness of this approach, however, leads the reaction to retreat before any firm resolve on the part of the progressive forces that represent the spirit of the Constitution. The future of Italy is thus in the hands of those who understand and support this spirit. If they are to prevail they must remain faithful to the slogan of the Florentine anti-Fascist resistance: *Non mollare* (Don't give in).

4

Parliament

Structure

In liberal democracies parliament is *primus inter pares* among the major institutions of government. It is the voice of the people and the guardian of their rights and privileges, and it is the source of law.

It is a trick of fate that this latter mighty function has been entrusted to parliament; but just as some individuals have had high office thrust upon them far beyond their modest abilities merely because they happened to be at the right place at the right time, so the institution of parliament, which had traditionally been the defender of the people against the abuse of the royal prerogative, received the new legislative power almost by default, as it were, being the only institution readily available when the legislative power was wrested from the king. Unfortunately the legislative function is not one that parliament is well suited to perform, particularly in the present era in which highly technical legislation must be produced *en masse*. Today virtually every country is dissatisfied with its legislature. Indicative of this present discontent is the relegation of parliament to a position of clear inferiority in the French Constitution of 1958. The Italians have as much reason as any and perhaps more than some to complain of the inadequacy of their legislative process. As is the case with most governmental institutions, the present structure of the Italian Parliament is the not very logical result of a series of contending factors. Among other forces it has been influenced by the classical democratic theories on parliamentary supremacy and on the advantages of bicameralism, and above all by the inertia of tradition. To these have been added the efforts of the Constituent Assembly to remodel the former royal parliament. The remodeling, however, was more a work of restoration of an institution destroyed by Fascism than a work of innovation. The

Chamber, for instance, was exhumed virtually in its former state, while most of the undemocratic factors in the composition of the Senate were not revived.

Italy's Parliament is a bicameral body composed of a Senate (*Senato*) and a Chamber of Deputies (*Camera dei deputati*). According to the original constitution the number of members of each house was a function of the population and thus increased as Italy grew in size. A 1963 constitutional amendment,[1] however, fixes the number of elected members at 630 deputies and 315 senators. The amendment has not altered the provision by which (1) the President of the Republic may appoint up to five life senators and (2) ex-presidents become themselves life members of the Senate.

The Chamber of Deputies is an ordinary type of lower chamber. Its members are elected for five-year terms directly by universal suffrage from large electoral districts by the list system of proportional representation. At first senators were elected for six-year terms, but no Senate sat for a full six years, as in 1953, 1958, and again in 1963 the President of Italy dissolved the Senate simultaneously with the Chamber at the end of the latter's five-year mandate for the purpose of holding elections to both houses at the same time. The 1963 constitutional amendment reduced the senatorial term of office to five years.

Italy is one of the few European states with a bicameral legislature in which the two houses have virtually equal power.

Upper houses in Europe have traditionally been of three kinds: (1) houses of peers, as in Great Britain, (2) indirectly elected bodies, as in France, Holland, and Sweden, or (3) bodies representing the constituent parts of the federation, as in Switzerland and since 1949 in Germany.

The Royal Italian Senate was a fourth type of upper house, composed exclusively of members appointed for life by the king from among those of his subjects who had distinguished themselves in politics, government, administration, the arts, the sciences, the armed forces, or for their wealth. Many of these men rarely attended the Senate meetings, and the actual business of the Senate was carried on by a minority of the more politically minded members. This Senate was much the type of body into which the British House of Lords is evolving. Its entire membership was an exclusive club composed of the persons the government wished to honor, but since only a minority of members was active, it was in practice a small debating society where elderly and distinguished statesmen could debate with a certain leisure and informality the political problems of the day.

[1] Constitutional amendment of February 9, 1963, No. 2.

The present Senate is a pallid miniature of the Chamber. Although its powers are equal to those of the Chamber, it tends to attract older and less active politicians, and there is an atmosphere of semiretirement about it. In the first quarter-century of Italy's Republic only one of its twenty-three governments has been headed by a Senator (the Zoli government). The most prestigious and important ministries rarely go to Senators.[2]

Personnel

Italian legislators are like American but atypical of European legislators in that they are for the most part lawyers. Taking the total number of individuals elected to the Constituent Assembly and the first three legislatures we find that 320 out of 1358 (27.25 per cent) were lawyers. The next largest group was professional party workers, teachers, and labor leaders with 189 (13.92 per cent), 139 (10.01 per cent), and 120 (8.84 per cent) respectively. Over half (53.5 per cent) of the total had a law degree.[3] The percentage of lawyers, however, has steadily decreased since 1913 while the professional politicians and the labor leaders reached their highest percentage and the teachers their second highest in 1958. As in France, the number of journalists is high relative to Anglo-American legislatures.[4] The salary of both senators and deputies, including allowances, is slightly under a million lire (about $1600) a month. Each party, however, has also elected second- and third-raters. In this respect the situation in Italy is similar to that in the United States, where there seems to be no common denominator among representatives other than that each was successful in getting himself elected.

Organization

As in France, both houses of Parliament are officially organized into parliamentary groups (*gruppi parlamentari*) by party. Each deputy

[2] See Alberto Spreafico, "Il senato della repubblica: composizione e stratificazione sociale," in Mattei Dogan and Orazio Maria Petracca, *Partiti politici e strutture sociali in Italia* (Milano: Edizioni di Comunità, 1968), pp. 609–643. Spreafico's findings are not belied by the records of the four governments (Rumor I, II, and III, and Colombo I) that have followed the publication of his study.

[3] See S. Somogyi, "Costituente e deputati, 1946–1958. Analisi statistica," in Giovanni Sartori, ed., *Il parlamento italiano* (Napoli: Edizione scientifiche italiane, 1963), pp. 9–140 at 25–26, 35.

[4] See L. Lotti, "Il parlamento italiano, 1909–1963. Raffronto storico," in Sartori, *op. cit.,* pp. 139–200 at 161. The dominance of lawyers continued down through the first Colombo government, which took office on August 6, 1970. Of its twenty-seven ministers, at least twenty had law degrees.

informs the president of his chamber of the group to which he wishes to belong. A parliamentary group must contain at least ten members. Members of small parties who have not elected enough legislators to form an official group of their own may if mutually agreeable join with other parties; all those who are unwilling or unable to avail themselves of this privilege are forcibly included in a single mixed group (*gruppo misto*). Each parliamentary group elects its own officers.

The number of parliamentary groups depends on the number of parties with enough elected candidates. In the first four republican legislatures the number in the Chamber, including the mixed group, has varied from seven to nine, and in the Senate from five to eight.

Each house is also organized into standing committees (*commissioni permanenti*) in such a way that every legislator is usually a member of not more than one committee. There are fourteen committees in the Chamber and eleven in the Senate. The standing committees of the Chamber are selected according to two different procedures. The members of the committees for constitutional matters (*affari costituzionali*), foreign affairs (*affari esteri*), and budget and state-controlled enterprises (*bilancio e partecipazioni statali*) are nominated by the various parliamentary groups to the number of one representative for every twenty members of the group. Fractions of over 50 per cent entitle the group to an extra representative. These committees have memberships in the low thirties. The parliamentary group then assigns the rest of the members in equal numbers (as far as this is possible) to the remaining eleven committees, which are composed of between forty-five and fifty members each. The apparent reason for the smaller size of the three committees is that they have appreciably less work to do. The budget committee is the only house committee that is divided into subcommittees to do its regular work. The eleven Senate committees are appointed in the same manner as the majority of the house committees and are composed of between twenty and twenty-five members each. Whenever a senator or a deputy becomes a minister or under-secretary he is replaced on his committee by another representative of his parliamentary group. This is virtually the only way that a man becomes a member of more than one committee.

The competence of the committees is divided along the lines of the administrative divisions between the ministries. The pairing is not exact, however, as there are nineteen ministries and only fourteen committees, one of which, that on constitutional matters, is not related to any single ministry. The Chamber's standing committees are, besides constitutional matters, foreign affairs, and budget and state-controlled enterprises, (1) internal and religious affairs, (*affari della presidenza del consiglio, affari interni e del culto, enti pubblici*), (2) justice (*gius-*

tizia), (3) finance (*finanze e tesoro*), (4) defense (*difesa*), (5) education (*istruzione e belle arti*), (6) public works (*lavori pubblici*), (7) communications (*trasporti, poste e telecommunicazioni, marina mercantile*), (8) agriculture (*agricoltura e foreste*), (9) commerce (*industria e commercio, artigianato, commercio coll'estero*), (10) labor (*lavoro e previdenza sociale, cooperative*), (11) public health (*igiene e sanità pubblica*). The Senate has no constitutional-matters committee and no budget and state-controlled enterprises committee, and combines public works and communications. The quorum for Chamber committees is one-fourth of the members; for the Senate, one-third.

The membership on the committees follows the experience and alleged competence of the legislators. Ex-ministers are normally on the committees concerned with the subject matter of their former ministry, and they often serve as chairman (*presidente*).

Besides the standing committee, each house has a rules committee, an elections committee, and a library committee.

In accordance with the traditional Italian theory of the separation of powers, no judicial action can be taken against a deputy or a senator without the permission of the body of which he is a member. The Chamber has a special committee to advise it on these matters, while the Senate gives this work to its permanent committee on the judiciary.

Americans may be surprised to learn that in the first ten-year period of Italy's republican parliament the judicial authorities requested permission to initiate proceedings against deputies in 906 cases and that in 110 cases their request was granted, while in 326 it was refused. Final action was not taken in the other cases.[5] It is possible that a considerable number of these requests which were made to the first Parliament and which were not finally acted upon before that Parliament was dissolved were made again to the second Parliament, so that the actual occasions on which the judicial authorities take action may be several hundred less than the total requests. The major crime with which the deputies are charged is libel against public officers. Frequently the charge is based on political speeches. The fifth Legislature, elected in 1968, was faced with requests for authorizations to prosecute deputies for refusal to pay traffic fines, and in the case of one deputy, refusal to pay damages to a seventy-nine-year-old man suffering from serious internal injuries resulting from having been run over by the deputy.[6]

[5] These figures are taken from *I deputati e senatori del terzo parlamento repubblicano* (Rome: La navicella, no date), pp. xv-xviii.

[6] See Eugenio Scalfari, "Processo all'onorevole," *L'espresso,* February 9, 1969, pp. 4–5.

The committees' policy is to refuse permission to initiate legal proceedings against a deputy for political actions. It is, however, difficult to decide just when antigovernment statements are libelous and when they are not, particularly when they have been made by Communists, and the committee passing judgment is dominated by the Christian Democrats.

The Italian Parliament also has two types of special joint committees: the watchdog committee and the investigatory committee.

Some watchdog committees are composed only of members of Parliament, as is the case with the radio and television committee. Others contain top administrative officials along with the legislators. Examples of these mixed watchdog committees are the ones on (a) the issuing and circulation of bank notes, (b) the administration of the public debt, and (c) the deposits and loans of the social security agencies. These committees are not particularly active or useful.

Investigatory committees are special committees set up to gather information on a specific problem, for the purpose of preparing legislation or of examining some inefficiency or dereliction of duty on the part of the administration. So far, Parliament's investigatory committees have accomplished little. Committees have been set up to study such important matters as unemployment and working conditions in the factories. The unemployment committees were headed by prominent political figures, Ezio Vigorelli and Roberto Tremelloni, and that on factory conditions by an intelligent and respected right-wing Catholic, Leopoldo Rubinacci. Both unemployment committees presented detailed reports. Rubinacci's committee, in spite of the conservative bias of its president, disclosed intolerable conditions in thirty-two volumes of reports and documents. Still Parliament did nothing. Another committee investigating a governmental agricultural agency (*Federconsorzi*) and headed by one of Italy's most distinguished and respected agricultural economists, Manlio Rossi-Doria, claimed that the bad judgment (or worse) shown by *Federconsorzi* has cost the state over a million million lire ($1,600,000,000). Again no action.[7]

There have of course been exceptions to this general attitude of Parliament. At times the government has acceded to pressures for reform, and although it has seldom moved with the alacrity and grace that would have helped to win the approval of the progressive forces in Italy, it has finally assented to the enactment of the necessary enabling legislation to set in operation most of the structural reforms prescribed by the Constitution. In only one important case, when it nationalized the

[7] Eugenio Scalfari, "Cosa conta un deputato?" *L'espresso,* February 16, 1969, p. 7.

electrical companies, has it gone further than the Constitution required.

Of greater significance from the point of view of an independent parliament are the rare but important cases in which the Parliament has acted against the ruling majority. On certain occasions individual Socialist deputies have been able to build up sufficient support in and out of Parliament to move the majority from an entrenched position. Typical of these actions have been the Fortuna divorce bill, Eugenio Scalfari's disclosure of a scheme for a rightist *putsch,* Luigi Anderlini's disclosure that the Vatican was not paying Italian income taxes on dividends from Italian investments, Luigi Mariotti's uncovering of scandals in the social security system, and Tristano Codignola's ferreting out of the surreptitious siphoning of additional funds from the state schools to the parochial schools.

Procedure

The Italian Parliament performs the functions normally attributed to parliaments in parliamentary democracies. It is the supreme legislative body, and it also acts as an electoral college for the indirect elections of high state officers. It elects the President of Italy and one-third of the members of both the Constitutional Court and the High Judicial Council.

Legislation

Bills may be introduced by the government, by individual members, by regional councils, by municipal councils (but only for the creation of new provinces or for changes in provincial boundaries), by the Economic and Labor Council (CNEL), or by initiative. Only the first two of these methods are used frequently. (Out of 6771 laws enacted from 1948 to 1968 only twelve were initiated by regional councils, one was presented by initiative, and none was introduced by the CNEL or by a municipal council.[8]) The reason for this state of affairs is that in virtually any situation in which the necessary two-thirds of the membership of the CNEL agree to the bill, or in which a majority of a regional or municipal council supports the bill, or when the signatures of 50,000 voters can be acquired, it will be less effort to get a member of Parliament to introduce the bill.

Initiative proposals in Switzerland and in the American states that permit the procedure are normally submitted directly to the voters, and thus are a method of eliminating the legislature from the legislative

[8] The CNEL did introduce a single bill, but it was never enacted.

process. Initiative proposals in Italy, however, serve only to introduce bills in Parliament.

The Chamber distinguishes between government bills, which it calls *disegni di legge,* and private member bills, which it calls *proposte di legge* (its generic name for bills is *progetti di legge*), and it follows a different procedure with each one. The Senate does not make either the nominal or the procedural distinction; it uses *disegni di legge* for all bills, as, incidentally, does the Constitution.

All government bills and all bills passed by the Senate are sent immediately to the appropriate standing committee by the President of the Chamber. Private member bills may at the request of the sponsors, and must (if they require disbursement of funds), be debated in the Chamber before going to committee. This debate gives the sponsor the opportunity to speak in favor of his bill, but if the Chamber does not approve the bill, it is dead.

Italy is one of the few European countries that place no limit on the right of private members to initiate legislation. The privilege of presenting private member bills is denied by law in Germany and by practice in Switzerland, and is severely curtailed in France and Great Britain. The Italian legislators, however, show little restraint in this matter. More than half the bills discussed in the Italian Parliament are private member bills (1375 private member bills during the first Parliament (1948–53), 2514 in the second (1953–58), and 2910 in the third (1958–63).[9] Few of these bills dealt with significant matters. The main legislative task of a modern parliament should be to criticize constructively the coordinated body of government bills presented for its approval. The right of initiative reserved to private members is a useful democratic device for keeping the government on its toes and particularly for the introduction of nonpolitical legislation not included in the government program (e.g., the Merlin bill closing government-controlled brothels [passed] and the bill forbidding the use of live pigeons in trapshooting [defeated]), but the exaggerated use of the private member bill in Italy leads to confused, fragmentary, and conflicting legislation.

The standing committees may follow three types of procedure in handling bills; they act as an advisory body (*in sede referente*), a legislative body (*in sede deliberante*), or a drafting body (*in sede redigente*). The presiding officer of the house determines in each case in which capacity the committee is to function. In practice only the Chamber committees, and not those of the Senate, meet *in sede referente.*

[9] Alberto Predieri, "La produzione legislativa," in Sartori, *op. cit.,* pp. 203–276 at 213. These bills, however, are rarely presented by a single deputy. The usual practice is for the originator to get as many co-signers as possible.

The advisory function is that which is normally associated with standing committees in other countries. In this guise the committee studies the bill and reports it back to the house. It may propose amendments or consult other committees, either on its own motion or on the request of the President of the house. The committee appoints one of its members to present its view on the bill to the house, and if there is a minority report as well, a specific member is designated to present that opinion. All types of bills may be handled in this manner.

This procedure, however, which is the normal one in other liberal democracies, is the exceptional one in Italy, where the usual procedure is for the standing committee to act *in sede deliberante* and to take final action on the bill. Italy appears to be the only state in the world in which full legislative power is granted to parliamentary committees, and the only precedent for such a grant of power appears to have been offered by the Fascist Chamber of Guilds and Fasces. The practice, however, is specifically sanctioned in the Italian constitution, seemingly as a precaution against giving either house of Parliament the excuse of overwork for delegating legislative power to the executive branch.[10]

When a committee acts *in sede deliberante* any member of the government can appear before the committee and any deputy may come in and have his say. Only members of the committee, however, may vote. This procedure cannot be used for constitutional matters, for the ratification of treaties, for the approval of the budgets, for the delegation of legislative power, or for the enactment of electoral laws. (The Chamber adds taxes to this list.) The bill can be reported back to the Chamber (or the Senate, as the case may be) at any time before the final vote at the request of (1) the government, (2) twenty deputies (10 per cent of the senators), or (3) one-third of the members of the committee.[11]

Although this peculiar Italian procedure has obvious advantages, such as lessening the work load of the individual deputy, and making

[10] See the comments of Costantino Mortati reported in Leopoldo Piccardi, Norberto Bobbio, and Ferruccio Parri, *La sinistra davanti alla crisi del parlamento* (Milano: Giuffrè, 1967), p. 108. For well-reasoned opposition to the bestowal of legislative power on the committees see Luigi Einaudi, *Lo scrittoio del presidente* (Turin: Giulio Einaudi, 1956), pp. 17–19, and Constantino Mortati, *Istituzioni di diritto pubblico,* 8th ed. (Padova: CEDAM, 1969), pp. 696–701.

[11] The Constitutional Court may invalidate a law improperly approved *in sede deliberante,* if the Constitution requires the traditional method for that particular subject. (See Silvio Traversa, "La riserva di legge d'assemblea," *Rivista trimestrale di diritto pubblico,* XX [1970], pp. 271–307.) For a more detailed account of this procedure see Francesco Cosentino, "Parliamentary Committees in the Italian Political System," *Journal of Constitutional and Parliamentary Studies* (New Delhi), Vol. 1, No. 2 (1967).

it possible to discuss proposed legislation in an atmosphere more conducive to reasonable compromise than that of a politically charged house, these assets appear to be outweighed by the weaknesses inherent in the procedure. Each parliamentary committee is composed, for the most part, of the parliamentary experts in the subject matter of the proposed legislation to be brought before the committee. Thus it tends to represent special and vested interests rather than the public or consumer interest in the matter. Furthermore, during the first four legislatures (1948–68) the public and the press were excluded from the committee meetings, thus making impossible the kind of publicity for legislative deliberations that is generally considered an important and perhaps is actually an essential element of the liberal democratic process. A summary of the committee proceedings was published at a later date, but this gave an insufficient guarantee of publicity, as irregularities in procedure, such as a lack of a quorum, could be passed over. Both houses of the fifth legislature elected in 1968 have undertaken a detailed overhauling of their procedures. Among the most significant changes proposed have been the printing of a detailed stenographic report of committee meetings *in sede deliberante* and the televising of such meetings for the benefit of the press and the interested public.[12]

Although minutes of the meetings (*processi verbali*) exist, the President of the Chamber of Deputies, Giovanni Leone, refused to make them available even to the Constitutional Court when this body requested them as evidence. Leone maintained that the procedures through which Parliament chooses to legislate are its own business (are *atti interni*), and that the only official external act is the one in which the President of the Chamber transmits the approved bill to the President of the other chamber or to the President of the Republic.[13]

When a bill has been sent to a committee *in sede referente* and there is virtual unanimity among the committee members on the bill, the committee often requests the President of the house to give it power *in sede deliberante*. This request is normally granted if the subject matter of the bill permits.

The drafting function of the standing committees is not mentioned in the Constitution but is set forth in the rules of the Chamber (Art. 85). Legislation may be referred back to the committee for final drafting and in this case any member of the house may appear before the committee

[12] Amintore Fanfani, President of the Senate, attributed the greater efficiency he discerned in the senate in 1971 in part to the new practice of televising committee meetings. See *La stampa,* August 1, 1971, p. 17.

[13] Decision of March 3, 1959, No. 8, *Giurisprudenza costituzionale,* IV (1959), pp. 237–72 at 257–58. See also the comment of Paolo Barile, "Il crollo di un antico feticcio (gli *interna corporis*) in una storica (ma insoddisfacente) sentenza," *ibid.,* pp. 240–249.

to offer his suggestions. The redraft that the committee reports to the Chamber is voted on without debate. The constitutionality of this procedure is questionable,[14] and it is being used with decreasing frequency.[15]

The standing committees may also serve in a consultative and in a policy-forming capacity. When the committees are acting in their consultative capacity (*in sede consultiva*) they are in effect advising another committee. Normally this advice is not binding, but under certain circumstances the advisory opinions of the Finance and Constitutional committees may be overruled only by the whole house.[16]

When committees act in a policy-forming capacity (*in sede politica*) they are collecting information either for purposes of future legislation or of better controlling the administration. Some of this activity is quite informal, as when committees meet off the record with senior administrators. The use of legislative hearings, however, is relatively new in Italy.[17]

All bills must be approved in both houses before they become laws. There is no particular procedure established when the two houses disagree. The bill goes back and forth from Palazzo Montecitorio (the seat of the Chamber) to Palazzo Madama (the seat of the Senate, formerly the Roman residence of Madama, the daughter of Emperor Charles V, and of the Florentine Popes Giovanni [Leo X] and Giulio [Clement VII] De' Medici) until agreement is reached or until Parliament is dissolved.

Italian parliamentary procedure follows French practice as far as the rules of debate are concerned.[18] Each article of a bill is discussed and voted on, and then a final vote is taken on the entire bill. Discussion may be lengthy, and on occasion dilatory tactics are used by the opposition. The usual method is to present numerous amendments to the bill, but the filibuster has also been tried.[19] Italian voting procedures, however, are somewhat peculiar. The basic procedure is a rising vote. If there is doubt as to the outcome the President of the house may request a division. In the Italian division the ayes and nays congregate

14 Mortati, *op. cit.,* pp. 701–702.

15 See Cosentino, *op. cit.,* pp. 11–12.

16 Cosentino, *op. cit.,* pp. 12–13.

17 See Alberto Predieri, *Contradittorio e testimonianza del cittadino nei procedimenti legislativi* (Milano: Giuffrè, 1964), and Alberto Predieri, "Per l'introduzione delle udienze legislative nel parlamento italiano," *Il ponte,* XXII (1966), pp. 1109–1127.

18 See D. W. S. Lidderdale, *The Parliament of France* (London: The Hansard Society, 1951), and Lord Campion and D. W. S. Lidderdale, *European Parliamentary Procedure* [London: Allen & Unwin, no date (1953?)].

19 See *L'espresso,* February 15, 1962. In this case the longest speech was an eight-hour affair by the neo-Fascist Giorgio Almirante.

in separate corners of the hall. It is thus different from the British division, better known to American students, during which the deputies are counted as they file out of the house by two exits, one exit being for the ayes and the other for the nays. (The division is not provided for in the revised regulations under discussion in the Senate.)

The deputies and senators, if they wish, may ask for one of three other types of vote in place of the rising vote. The request must be made before the vote takes place and must be made by a specific number of legislators. The number is ten for a division, fifteen for a roll call and twenty for a secret vote. A request for a secret vote takes precedence over a roll call and either takes precedence over a division.

Unlike the American roll call that normally begins with the first letter of the alphabet, the first name called on the Italian roll call is determined by lot. The rest of the names are then called in alphabetical sequence continuing from the name drawn by lot, and those legislators who do not respond the first time round are called a second time. The roll call is required for votes of confidence.

The secret vote is an unusual feature of the Italian parliamentary procedure. It was required for all final votes on legislation under the Albertine constitution of 1848, but the present constitution does not mention it. The rules of the Chamber specify its use for the final approval of all legislation, and although not required by Senate rules, it is frequently used in the Senate as well. The procedure is to give each deputy two balls, one white and one black. Two urns are provided, also colored white and black. To vote in favor of a bill, the legislator places the white ball in the white urn and the black ball in the black urn. To vote against it he places the balls in the urns of the opposite color. The secret vote contradicts a basic democratic principle that gives the voter the right to know how his representatives vote in Parliament. Italians, however, see in the secret vote a method of freeing the representatives from the necessity of always voting according to party instructions. This argument is not particularly convincing to foreign observers, who suggest that with the abolition of the secret vote the parties might give greater independence to the deputies and only require strict party voting on issues of major importance to the party line.[20]

Electric voting is proposed in the revised regulations of both houses, under discussion, but provision has been made to permit secret electric

[20] See John Clarke Adams, "Il voto segreto in parlamento," and the reply of Enzo Enriques Agnoletti, in *Il ponte*, XVI (1960), pp. 148–150. For an authoritative attack on the practice see Mortati in Piccardi *et al.*, *op. cit.*, p. 111. For a roundup of authoritative opinion against the secret vote and a brief exposition of the main arguments for and against, see Paolo Barile, "L'ombra dell'urna," *La stampa*, October 30, 1970, p. 2.

voting, that would tabulate the number of votes cast without revealing the names of the legislators who voted for or against.

Constitutional amendments

The procedure for enacting constitutional amendments differs from that of enacting ordinary legislation only in that (1) the proposed amendment must be passed twice by each house, (2) a three-month interval must elapse between the two times, and (3) the amendment must be passed by an absolute majority the second time. Furthermore, if the amendment does not obtain a two-thirds majority of each house on the second vote, it is subject to a referendum at the request of (a) 20 per cent of the members of either house, (b) five regional councils, or (c) 500,000 voters.

Control over government

As in all true parliamentary systems, the government is the creature of the Parliament; it must resign when it fails to maintain the latter's confidence. In Italy it must have the confidence of both houses. A new government must come before Parliament to request approval within ten days of its formation. At any subsequent period a motion of no confidence, signed by 10 per cent of the deputies or senators, will be debated and voted (by roll call) in the house to which it was presented. The Constitution requires a three-day cooling-off period between the presentation of the motion and its discussion. (Constitution, Art. 94). Such, at least, is the theory. In practice it has normally been the parties, acting in an extraparliamentary fashion, that have overturned the government.

Parliament's supervision of the administration is exercised in a variety of ways. Through its legislative power it can curtail or abolish the greater part of the government organization. Through the power of the purse it can reward or penalize particular agencies. It is also free to set up investigating commissions and to put more teeth into existing regulatory legislation. Little effective use, however, is made of these powers.

The question period is a control device common to most parliamentary systems but not found in the United States model. It is an important part of British parliamentary practice, but in Great Britain no formal distinction is made between the two types of questions the Italians call *interrogazioni* and *interpellanze*.

Members of the Italian Parliament may make *interrogazioni, interpellanze,* and motions. An *interrogazione* is a question put to the government or an individual minister that merely asks whether or not an alleged fact is true. When making an *interrogazione* the questioner normally states whether he wishes an oral or a written answer.

An *interpellanza* is a question concerning the motives or the intentions of the government and obviously requires more time and thought on the part of the government. It may lead to the presentation of a motion, which is normally a type of censure of the government. A motion, however, may be presented without a question having been asked first. The most serious type of motion is the motion of no confidence, mentioned above. From 1948 to 1958, 235 motions were presented to the Chamber and 101 to the Senate.

During the first two legislatures (1948–58) an average of 5545 *interrogazioni* were presented in the Chamber of Deputies each year. The same period produced a total of 1885 *interpellanze* and 235 motions in the Chamber, and 801 and 101 respectively in the Senate.[21] Only about a quarter of the *interpellanze*, however, were actually discussed on the floor of either house.[22] The following decade brought forth an increase in the curiosity of members of Parliament, resulting in a significant increase in *interrogazioni* and *interpellanze*.[23]

Parliamentary deportment

From the Anglo-American standpoint, the deportment of Italian legislators is deplorable. Verbal and even physical violence is not uncommon, and sessions are frequently suspended for brief cooling-off periods when the speaker can no longer be heard. American readers in attempting to picture the Italian Parliament in operation should think of something halfway between the deportment of the American House of Representatives and the American national political convention.

The disciplinary power of the presiding officers is virtually limited to calling members to order and suspending sessions. More serious measures may be proposed by the president, but they must be approved by the Chamber or the Senate, as the case may be.[24]

[21] *I deputati e senatori,* p. ix.

[22] *Ibid.*

[23] See Piccardi *et al, op. cit.,* p. 94. For examples of questions asked in Parliament see Alessandro Prefetti, "I curiosi in parlamento," for many years a regular feature in the Florentine magazine *Il ponte.*

[24] For an example of unmannerly conduct in Parliament on the part of a minister, see *Atti della Camera dei deputati, prima legislatura, Discussioni, Resoconto,* pp. 5380 ff. See also Carlo Galante Garrone, "Un 'ingenuo' in Parlamento," *Il ponte* (numero straordinario dedicato a Piero Calamandrei), XIV (1958), p. 125.

Parliament as an electoral college

For election to Italian offices. The two houses of the Italian Parliament normally meet together when that body acts as an electoral college. The elections held in this manner are those for the election of the President of Italy, for five of the judges of the Constitutional Court, and for seven of the members of the High Judicial Council (*Consiglio superiore per la magistratura*).

The electoral college for electing the President of Italy consists of all members of Parliament and three delegates from each of the regional assemblies except that of Aosta, which has one, the delegates to be elected by the respective assemblies. Election is by secret ballot, and a two-thirds majority is required on the first three ballots. Thereafter a simple majority suffices. (Constitution, Art. 83.)

The five judges of the Constitutional Court elected by Parliament serve for nine years and are chosen by a secret ballot. A three-fifths majority is necessary for election. On the first ballot 60 per cent of the Parliament must vote in favor of the nominee. On subsequent ballots 60 per cent of those voting suffices. (Constitution, Art. 135, Law of March 11, 1953, No. 87, Art 3.) Parliament also elects a panel from which the additional sixteen judges who serve with the Constitutional Court judges in impeachment trials are selected by lot.

The seven members of the High Judicial Council elected by Parliament serve four-year terms. The same qualified majorities pertain to these elections as to those of the Constitutional Court judges (Constitution, Art. 104, Law of March 24, 1958, No. 195, Arts. 1 and 22).

For election to international bodies. The Italian Parliament elects a total of seventy-two members of three international bodies. Eighteen Italian representatives sit on the Consultative Assembly of the Council of Europe. Eighteen more are members of the Western European Union. The remaining thirty-six are part of the European Parliament. The first of these bodies represents fifteen western European countries and was established in 1949 in London. The second represents seven of these countries, Belgium, France, Great Britain, Luxembourg, the Netherlands, Italy, West Germany, and was established in 1954. The last of the bodies represents the six countries of the European Community (Belgium, France, Italy, Luxembourg, the Netherlands, West Germany) and was established in 1958. In each of these cases each house of Parliament elects half of Italy's representatives from among its own members.

Conclusion

The Italian Parliament has never been an outstanding success. In the pre-Fascist period an amorphous liberal party won a majority at every election and the frequent turnover of governments, due to factional rivalries, only illustrated the saying *"Plus ça change, plus c'est la même chose."* It was in part his first-hand experience as a deputy and senator in the Italian Parliament that led Gaetano Mosca to write the first serious attack on Parliament by a leading liberal theorist.[25] Mussolini did not await his second parliamentary address after the March on Rome to express his contempt for the institution, and during its short period of relative freedom under Fascism it did little to show him to be wrong. The prestige of the Republican Parliament, at first reasonably good because of the public's respect for the many persons of high caliber who sat in the Constituent Assembly, has decreased steadily.

The urgent need for parliamentary reform in Italy is obvious to those who have thought of the matter at all, but there is no agreement as to what should be done.[26] The structure, procedure, and functioning of Parliament have all come in for severe criticism.

The size of the Italian Parliament itself seems exaggerated. It takes somewhat over 945 persons to legislate for Italy, while Great Britain gets along with about 700 active parliamentarians, the United States with 535, and Switzerland with 144. Italy's bicameralism, composed as it is of two houses virtually indistinguishable in power or representation, also seems cumbersome and disfunctional. Some reformers would institute unicameralism, others advocate the establishment of the regions and would let the upper house represent them, thus creating a bicameralism analogous to that of federations like West Germany, Switzerland, and the United States.

The two major procedural anomalies in Italian parliamentary practice are the secret vote and committee legislation. Although the secret vote makes it harder for the representatives of vested interests to buy votes, it also makes parliamentarians unaccountable to their parties and to the voters, and it has been the cause of the overthrow of several governments. Committee legislation has the advantage of lightening the load of the legislators, and in the Italian system there is the safeguard that ten deputies can bring the bill to the floor. It does mean, however, legislation in which only a part of the people's representatives participate.

---

[25] *Teorica dei governi e governo parlamentare* (Turin: Loescher, 1887).
[26] See Alberto Predieri, *Aspetti del processo legislativo in Italia. Estratto dagli studi in memoria di Carlo Esposito* (Padova: CEDAM, 1970).

Thus the only original contribution of republican Italy to parliamentary procedure has proved more a failure than a success.

Another serious weakness in Italian legislation is faulty drafting. There is no bill-drafting service like those generally found in Great Britain, the United States, and Switzerland, nor are there the common law courts of the first two countries, which in case of ambiguity in the text can offer binding interpretations.

The Italian Parliament has not succeeded in almost a quarter-century of activity to institute the basic reforms that appear necessary to modernize the structure of government and to accomplish the purposes set forth in the constitution. The fault for this failure, however, lies less with Parliament than with the Italian political system in general and the establishment it supports. The Italian Parliament is actually an efficient machine for producing statutes. In the fourth legislature Parliament took an average of 118 days to pass a government bill voted by the whole houses and an average of 164 days to accomplish the same thing in the case of private member bills. As Predieri points out, this record is not bad for a country in which one to two thousand days are likely to pass before one can get a final judgment from the courts on an automobile accident.[27]

On the other hand, the Italian Parliament finds time to consider an ever-increasing number of *leggine,* until by 1970 it was estimated that about 1500 are brought before Parliament each year. *Leggine* (little laws) are usually presented as private member bills, but the government is not above presenting them from time to time. They normally concern some minor modification in the structure or procedure of some bureau of the public administration. This is the type of rule modification or interpretation that in other countries is handled within the administration.

There seem to be two reasons for this state of affairs. In the first place, if Parliament would get down to the performance of its major function, that of modernizing and renovating the state, it would have no time for *leggine,* but it is prevented from performing this task by a permanent government majority, the general policy of which is to temporize with events and thus preserve the present antiquated and dysfunctional structures and procedures of the state. This situation, unknown to Great Britain, resembles that established during the Republican hegemony in the United States from the Civil War to the New Deal. During this period the Republican party — the party of American business — — maintained for the most part a policy of resisting change, of doing as little as possible to alter the method of government from one so emi-

[27] *Ibid.,* p. 51, footnote 169.

nently suited to the needs of the establishment.[28] Thus the Italian Parliament, thwarted in its efforts to do what it should do and what its members presumably want to do, seeks an outlet for its frustration in the fabrication of *leggine*.

In the second place, however wasteful and inappropriate it may be for Parliament to spend its time on *leggine*, until such time as it is able to achieve a radical reform in the administration, the administrative process is so cumbersome that often the easiest, quickest, and safest way to effect what are substantially minor administrative rulings is through legislation. And in acquiescing to this imposition on its time the Parliament of republican Italy is merely continuing the practice of the Fascist Parliament, which was also called on to fill the breach caused by the conditions of semichaos and semicoma that pertained in the administration then as now.[29]

The basic weakness in the parliamentary system, however, stems from the fact that Parliament was not constructed for the modern state, for the mass of legislation that modern society must have. Under these circumstances Parliament has ceased being a *dramatis persona* in the power structure to become merely a *locus agendi* for the ritual of power. It is no longer Parliament that counts, but rather the parties in Parliament assembled. Let us hope, however, that the weaknesses in the present functioning of the Italian Parliament will not lead the Italian people to forget that Parliament is after all *in posse* a great democratic institution and that it has been well said that "The worst chamber is better than the best antechamber."[30]

[28] For an exposition of this point of view see E. E. Schattschneider, "United States: The Functional Approach to Party Government," in Sigmund Neumann, ed., *Approaches to Comparative Politics* (Chicago: University of Chicago Press, 1956), pp. 194–215.

[29] See Alberto Predieri, *Aspetti del processo legislativo, op. cit.* For a journalistic account, reaching many of the same conclusions, see Camilla Cederna, "Le malattie del parlamento," *L'espresso,* June 13, 1965.

[30] See Leopoldo Piccardi, Norberto Bobbio, and Ferruccio Parri, *La sinistra davanti alla crisi del parlamento* (Milano: Giuffrè, 1967), and more generally, John Clarke Adams, *The Quest for Democratic Law* (New York: Thomas Y. Crowell, 1970), Chapter 6.

5

The President
of the Republic

The members of the Constituent Assembly of 1946 had *carte blanche* for writing the Constitution on all points but one: the so-called institutional question as to whether the new Italy was to be a republic or a monarchy. This question was voted on by the electorate at the time they elected the Constituent Assembly, and the voters' choice was a republic.

The choice was not so obvious as it may seem to Americans (or to Asians or Africans, for that matter); the monarchist cause could be supported with sound reasoning. Of the viable democracies of Europe in 1946 only Switzerland was a republic; Great Britain, Holland, Belgium, Norway, Sweden, and Denmark were and are monarchies, yet their governments were far more attractive to many Italians than the republican governments of Salazar, Franco, Pétain, Hitler, and Stalin. A modern monarchy, however, must be a unifying force, above politics. The House of Savoy, Italy's reigning family, was a divisive force. Vittorio Emanuele III had twice failed his people, first in permitting the March on Rome and inviting Mussolini to form a Fascist-dominated government, and later in fleeing from Rome in 1943, deserting the army and the government officials, leaving no orders behind, delegating no authority, creating a power vacuum that only the Germans were ready to fill. His son Umberto II, who had been king for only a month before the vote, was not sufficiently disassociated from his father in the public mind to make him appreciably more palatable. After his defeat in the election, which was held on June 2, 1946, he abdicated and went into exile at Caiscais, in Portugal. His respected queen, Marie José, daughter of Belgium's great king Albert, retired to Switzerland. Thus June 2 is a national holiday in Italy, commemorating the founding of the republic, and Italy had a president.

In presidential republics, such as the United States and most of the Latin American republics, the two offices of chief of state and chief executive are combined. Anyone with even a slight understanding of the tremendous workload of the American President realizes the advantages of dividing this work between two men, instead of uniting the executive and ceremonial functions in the same position.

Most of the parliamentary republics are actually either secondhand or "reconditioned" monarchies or are copied after them. In the wake of a national calamity such as losing a war, a monarch was deposed and an elected chief of state was substituted, to whom were given much the same powers that the constitutional monarch had possessed. Thus after 1870 Thiers and then MacMahon replaced Napoleon III, after 1918 Ebert replaced Wilhelm II, and after 1943 De Nicola and then Einaudi replaced Vittorio Emanuele III.

The similarity between the constitutional monarch and the chief of state in a parliamentary republic is less real than apparent. The constitutional monarch is not responsible for his public acts and has only formal power. His functions are symbolic and have to do with psychological functions such as those Merriam calls the *credenda* (myths) and *miranda* (pomp and circumstance) of power. The influence he has on politics is not of a juridical nature. As a perhaps impartial and experienced observer he may counsel behind the scenes and to the public he is a symbol of legitimacy, continuity, conservatism, and stability. His is an office that calls for the continual use of such essentially feminine and negative traits as patience, discretion, charm, and impeccable manners, and it is not surprising that three of the most successful constitutional monarchs of this century (Wilhelmina, Juliana, and Elizabeth II) have been women.

When the Third French Republic was established during the period 1870–75 it was the intention of the predominantly monarchist Constituent Assembly to create the position of king and to put an elected president in the office until such time as the many supporters of the Bourbon and the Orléans pretenders and the relatively few Bonapartists could agree on a candidate. Thus the legend was born to the effect that constitutional monarchs and presidents of parliamentary republics are not merely brothers but identical twins.

The Italian Constituent Assembly of 1946 was not plotting a future return of the House of Savoy when it made of the new president little more than an elected constitutional monarch. The ambiguities in the Constitution with respect to the office of the President of Italy are explained by the fact that the Constituent Assembly failed to realize that the French solution of 1870 did not satisfy the needs of Italy in 1948 or its own wishes for Italy's future.

The thought that the Constituent Assembly did not give this problem has been amply provided quantitatively and qualitatively by some of Italy's major jurists, and their theories have been supplemented by the precedents that Italy's Presidents have established.

The ambiguities that surround the office of President and the powers attributed to the President have to do in great part with the nature of his powers and the responsibility, or lack of it, for his own acts.

The Constitution grants the President a wide range of powers, including: (a) the power to nominate certain members of high state organs [e.g., the President of the Council of Ministers (Art. 92), five senators (Art. 59), and five members of the Constitutional Court (Art. 135)]; (b) the power to veto legislation (or more accurately, to remand laws enacted by Parliament for reconsideration) (Art. 74); (c) the power to authorize the submission to Parliament of government bills, (Art. 87); and (d) the power to call special sessions of Parliament (Art. 62), to dissolve Parliament (Art. 88), to dissolve the regional parliaments (Art. 126), and to call elections (Art. 87) and referenda (Arts. 75, 132, and 138).

The Constitution also provides that the President be the presiding officer of the High Judicial Council and the Supreme Council of Defense (Art. 87), and that he perform such typical functions of a chief of state as the ratification of treaties (Art. 87), the promulgation of the statutes (Arts. 87 and 73), executive orders (*decreti aventi valore di legge*), and regulations (Art. 87), the granting of amnesties, pardons, and reprieves (Arts. 79 and 87), the declaration of war (Art. 87), the bestowal of honors (Art. 87), and the appointing of ministers other than the President of the Council (Art. 92). Certain other powers primarily of a formal nature devolve on the President, although they are not mentioned in the Constitution. These include the dissolution of municipal assemblies and the decision of matters in administrative law through the procedure of a so-called special appeal (*ricorso straordinario*).

The Constitution further provides that every presidential act signed by the President must be countersigned by the minister (or ministers) who proposed it and who assumes responsibility for it (Art. 89) and that the President is not responsible for his acts except for high treason and other acts subverting the Constitution (*attentato alla costituzione*) (Art. 90).

The nature of the President's power is primarily of theoretical and academic interest. The office of chief of state is traditionally considered a part of the executive branch of government. In the case of constitutional monarchies the powers attributed (in form but not in substance) to the chief of state are for the most part executive. The powers of the

Italian President, and particularly the real powers, such as the power to remand legislation and to nominate *motu proprio* certain high state officers, are not actually executive powers. This situation is not surprising nor even particularly interesting to American scholars who have been brought up on the theory of checks and balances, but it is perplexing to scholars brought up in the Franco-Italian tradition of Rousseau and has led to some excellent monographs on the nature of the presidency. Some scholars persist in considering these powers essentially executive,[1] while others speak of a fourth presidential power.[2]

The theory of the separation of powers historically is little more than a device for the avoidance of tyranny. The proposition that is the logical basis of the device, that if power is not concentrated in the hands of a single person or group, tyranny will be avoided, is tautological. The particular division among legislative, executive, and judicial powers has no merit other than a supposed expediency. The members of the Italian Constituent Assembly were trying to construct a state that would not be susceptible to tyrannous usurpation. The particular powers and responsibilities they assigned to the office of President were assigned with this end in mind. The President can contribute to the prevention of the return of tyranny in Italy by exercising the powers assigned to him in the Constitution, and little harm has been done if the vague and arbitrary borderlines dividing these three traditional powers have been violated.

Of considerable more consequence is the question of the President's responsibility or lack thereof. Here again, however, the Anglo-American pragmatic approach helps to clarify a situation that is juridically ambiguous, for it is a fact that the Italian President does act on his own motion on matters of prime importance.

One of the occasions on which he so acts is in the nomination of the five life senators and of the five judges of the Constitutional Court. While it is true that these nominations must be countersigned by a member of the cabinet, the dominant theory now seems to be that the countersignature merely affirms the legality of the nomination and

[1] E.g., Salvatore Carbonaro, "La incidenza delle attribuzioni presidenziali in relazione alle funzioni legislativa e giurisdizionale," in *Studi giuridici in memoria di Piero Calamandrei* (Padua: CEDAM, 1958), Vol. IV, pp. 159–216 at p. 170.

[2] E.g., Giuseppe Guarino, "Il presidente della repubblica italiana," *Rivista trimestrale di diritto pubblico,* I (1951), pp. 903–992 at p. 944. On the subject of the president's powers see also Paolo Barile, "I poteri del presidente della repubblica," *Rivista trimestrale di diritto pubblico,* VIII (1958), pp. 295–357, and Mario Grisolia, "In tema di competenza amministrativa del presidente della repubblica," *Rivista trimestrale di diritto pubblico,* X (1960), pp. 70–141.

cannot be refused because of disagreement over the merits of the nominee or the propriety of his nomination. The approval of the minister, then, is quite a different thing in practice (although this difference is not clearly spelled out in the Constitution) from the advice and consent of the Senate, which the American President must have before many of his nominees can be appointed to office.

The nomination of five senators (about 2 per cent of the total) is of so little political significance that the President's right to exercise this power has not been seriously contested. The Christian Democratic Government, however, did claim the right to select the five (out of fifteen) Constitutional Court judges to be nominated by the President. President Gronchi held firm, however, and had substantial backing from Parliament and the jurists. It seems beyond reasonable doubt that the Constituent Assembly in determining that the Parliament, the President of Italy, and the regular judges should each appoint one-third of the judges of the Constitutional Court intended that the President and not the cabinet should make the choice. Had its intention been otherwise, the power would have been granted to the cabinet and not to the President.

The suspensive veto over legislation is another action that the President must take on his own responsibility. So far this action has been exercised sparingly. During his seven-year term President Einaudi promulgated some 3000 laws and only remanded four to Parliament for reconsideration.[3] In none of these cases was the bill reconsidered, and so even without the requirement of a two-thirds vote to overcome a presidential veto that exists in the United States, Italy's first President had a record of having been sustained in all of his vetoes.

This is the more remarkable in that there is divided opinion over the extent of the President's veto power. Many jurists believe that this power may be exercised only in case the President, as upholder of the Constitution, refuses to act on grounds that the law is unconstitutional.[4] President Einaudi did not accept this restrictive interpretation of his power to request a reconsideration of legislation. The messages that accompanied the first three bills he remanded gave their alleged unconstitutionality as the reason for his action, but the fourth bill, which was merely a time extension for a long-standing practice that permitted certain government personnel, notably in the finance ministries, to charge the public for certain services and to keep the money themselves,

[3] Luigi Einaudi, *Lo scrittoio del presidente* (Turin: Giulio Einaudi, 1956), pp. 208–222.

[4] E.g., Alberto Predieri, "Appunti sul potere del presidente della repubblica di autorizzare la presentazione dei disegni di legge governativi," *Studi senesi* LXX (1958), pp. 279–327 at pp. 295–297.

was remanded on the grounds that the extension of this practice was against public policy.[5] Giovanni Gronchi, Italy's second President, appeared to have similar views.[6]

Einaudi's position has had strong support. A reading of the minutes of the meetings of the Committee of Seventy-Five that drafted the Constitution (of which Einaudi was himself a member) shows that it was the intention of the framers of the Constitution to grant the President this power.[7]

Taking into consideration Einaudi's action and Parliament's acquiescence to it as well as the approval of most of the jurisprudence, one can say that the prevailing doctrine now is that the President's powers go beyond a check on the mere constitutionality of legislation to include a check on the compatibility of the proposed legislation with public policy as it may be inferred from the Constitution. A distinction here is made between an *indirizzo generale o costituzionale* (general or constitutional policy) as opposed to an *indirizzo politico contingente o di maggioranza* (contingent or partisan policy). The theory is that the President of the Republic can and should intervene in matters concerning public policy and that he should not interfere in partisan policy.[8]

Unlike the president of France in both the Fourth and Fifth Republics, the President of Italy does not take part in the meetings of the Council of Ministers. He must, however, authorize the presentation to Parliament of all government bills. In theory his power appears to be similar to the power to remand, and it is so considered in most of the jurisprudence. We know less, however, about the actual practice, and particularly about the number of times the President has denied or threatened to deny his authorization. We do know that the power has been used by both Einaudi and Gronchi.[9]

[5] Einaudi, *loc. cit.*

[6] Enrico Mattei, interview with Gronchi in *La nazione* (Florence) and *Il resto del carlino* (Bologna), August 18, 1957.

[7] Meuccio Ruini, "La controfirma ministeriale degli atti del Capo dello Stato," *Foro padano* (1952), Sec. IV, 28. Ruini was chairman of the Committee of Seventy-Five.

[8] See Paolo Barile, *op. cit.*, p. 308; also Einaudi, *op. cit.*, p. xiv: "The political policy (*la politica del paese*) is the concern of the Government that has the confidence of Parliament and is not the concern of the President of the Republic."

[9] The following comment was attached to one of Einaudi's authorizations. The bill in question was for the control (*disciplina*) of emigrants' cooperatives.

"If the bill were intended to facilitate the establishment of serious cooperatives for emigrants I should say that it would result merely in increasing the bureaucracy and the manufacture of red tape. If it is difficult to create

A refusal by the President to authorize the presentation of a government bill to Parliament can be side-stepped by the Council of Ministers by having the bill presented as a private member bill (*proposta di legge,* in the language of the Chamber). If it is passed, however, the President can remand it and if it is passed again, he can still refuse to promulgate it if he feels that in promulgating it he would be breaking his oath to uphold the Constitution. A future President may find himself in a difficult situation on these grounds. He could run the risk of impeachment for breaking his oath either for promulgating or for not promulgating a law depending on whether or not the impeaching authority held the law to be a potent and serious threat to the Constitution.

Perhaps the most important power conferred on the President is the selection of the President of the Council of Ministers. This power is always formally in the hands of the chief of state in a liberal democracy employing the parliamentary system. In states with few and strong parties, however, the chief of state normally has no effective choice.

In Italy not only is there a wide choice among potential Presidents of the Council, but the choice must be made frequently, and the real decision is the President's. It should further be noted that under the new Constitution he actually appoints the new President of the Council, who goes before Parliament for his vote of confidence already in office.

Impeachment proceedings against the President may be instituted for high treason or subversion of the Constitution (Constitution, Art. 90). The adjudicating body is composed of the fifteen judges of the Constitutional Court and sixteen additional persons drawn by lot from a longer list (*albo*) elected by Parliament every twelve years (Constitution, Art. 135, and Constitutional Law of March 11, 1953, No. 1, Art. 10). These persons must have the requisites for eligibility to the Senate (Arts. 134, 135).

The Italian President, like the constitutional monarchs and the President of the United States, may address Parliament, but he does so

---

and sustain serious cooperatives among men who already know each other and the work they are doing in common, it would seem foolhardy to attempt to create cooperatives in Italy that would operate in Patagonia or other distant lands. Only saints or swindlers would dare try. Saints will find the way to do their job probably without forming cooperatives and certainly without seeking state aid. . . .

"Since the bill fortunately only succeeds in complicating the forming of cooperatives for emigrants, its only result will be to put out of business those swindlers who can't find any other method to swindle their fellow men. Therefore, within these limits and on the condition that it does not create too many new government positions for swindler-watchers, the bill may be approved." Einaudi, *op. cit.,* pp. 564–565.

with considerably less prestige. The speech from the throne delivered by the British Queen at the opening of Parliament is an outline of the policy that the Government, fresh from a victory at the polls, proposes to enact. Its importance lies in the fact that the Government is in a position to enact it. The fact that it is uttered by the Queen adds solemnity and legitimacy to the occasion, but her own role is that of an august puppet. The American President informs the Congress on the state of the union either by message (a tradition started by Jefferson) or by an address (a method preferred by Wilson and F. D. Roosevelt and becoming a tradition). This message usually states the President's general policy and his "must" legislation; he speaks with the authority of a popularly elected chief executive but not necessarily for a majority in Parliament, as does the Queen.

The Italian President speaks only for himself. He is not the spokesman for the Government; indeed he must avoid partisan politics. He comes before Parliament clothed only in his own prestige. Einaudi and Gronchi, fortunately, did not lack prestige or ability. Both chose to appear personally before Parliament to read their messages.[10] Einaudi's sole message, however, was a thousand-word address he made on assumption of office.[11] In his capacity as a distinguished economist, on the other hand, he sent a number of unpublished and unofficial messages to the Council of Ministers and to others, in which he expressed and preached his views.[12]

President Gronchi, a professional politician, and not a scholar at heart as was Einaudi, did more public speaking than his predecessor. Gronchi made his inaugural address to Parliament on May 11, 1955, and a second address on December 27, 1957, on the tenth anniversary of the Constitution. Both messages were attacked by the conservatives and reactionaries as partisan intervention in party politics, but both could be defended as messages merely urging the application and the implementation of the principles expressed in the Constitution. Besides making these two formal (and therefore countersigned) messages to Parliament, Gronchi spoke frequently in public along the same lines. To the consternation of the right and of most of his own party, this activity led him to become by January, 1960, according to the Italian equivalent of a Gallup poll, the most popular Christian Democrat in Italy. In certain of these speeches it would appear that Gronchi crossed the boundary delimiting the President's power to safeguard the Constitution and to stimulate its application and implementation and trespassed on the exclusive privileges of the government, as for instance

[10] Aldo Bozzi, "Note sul rinvio presidenziale della legge," *Rivista trimestrale di diritto pubblico,* VIII (1958), pp. 739–773 at p. 741.

[11] Einaudi, *op. cit.,* pp. 4–6.

[12] See Einaudi, *Lo scrittoio del presidente, passim.*

when he attacked the "dictatorship of the parties" that "threatened the freedom of Parliament" and when he expressed doubts as to the ability of private enterprise to do much to help the economic modernization of southern Italy.[13]

The prestige of the office of President of Italy has been enhanced by the caliber of Italy's first Presidents. Enrico De Nicola (1877–1959), a Neapolitan, was elected provisional President by the Constituent Assembly on June 28, 1946. His life-long reputation for austere and scrupulous probity gained him the respect of both statesmen and the general public. On stepping down from the presidency in 1948, he became by law a senator for life. In 1956 he became the first President of the Constitutional Court, a position from which he resigned in 1957. De Nicola had been a minister before Fascism and had served as President of the Chamber of Deputies from June 26, 1920, to January 21, 1924. In 1929 he was appointed senator by the king, but he refused to take any part in the Senate during the Fascist period.

Luigi Einaudi (1874–1961) was elected the first President of Italy May 11, 1948, and served his full seven-year term. Einaudi, a Piedmontese liberal and a lifelong anti-Fascist, was Italy's most distinguished economist. He graduated from law school in 1895. Five years later, after having worked on the editorial staff of *La stampa* (The Press) of Turin, he started a twenty-six-year stint with Italy's other great paper, *Il corriere della sera* (The Evening Courier, actually a morning paper) of Milan. In the meantime he became professor of economics at the state University of Turin and the private Università Bocconi of Milan. In 1943, after the fall of Fascism, he returned to *Il corriere della sera*. Einaudi was appointed senator by the king in 1919, but after the rise of Mussolini he retired from politics. In the post-Fascist period Einaudi served as governor of the Bank of Italy (1945–48) and as Vice President of the Council of Ministers and Minister of the Budget (1947–48).

Giovanni Gronchi (1887–   ), a Tuscan, became Italy's second President in 1955. He was a founder, with the Sicilian priest Don Luigi Sturzo, of the Catholic *Partito popolare* in 1919 and served in the first Mussolini government for ten months (October, 1922–August, 1923). When Sturzo resigned as head of the party (July 10, 1923) Gronchi took over with two others. In 1926 he was expelled from Parliament along with the other 119 opposition deputies. After eighteen years in business in Milan and later in the resistance movement, Gronchi returned to politics in 1944 as a member of the provisional government and in 1946 of the Constituent Assembly. Successively he became president of the Christian Democratic parliamentary group

[13] Barile, *op. cit.*, pp. 339–343.

(1946–48), and President of the Chamber of Deputies (1948–1955).

Antonio Segni (1891–   ), a Christian Democrat from Sardinia was elected Italy's third President in May, 1962. Segni, a professor o law, a rich landowner, twice President of the Council of Ministers, an many times Foreign Minister, was elected by a center-right coalition Segni is best known for his sponsorship of Italy's land reform program that distributed land to the peasants.

In August, 1964, Segni had a stroke and was thereafter unable to perform the duties of his office. As provided in the Constitution, the president of the Senate, Cesare Merzagora, became acting president. Since it was expected that the election of a new President would be difficult, Segni did not resign until December 7, after the local elections, held in November, were over. The center-left government coalition could not agree on a candidate, and the major party, the Christian Democracy, could only agree that the new President must be Catholic. This party selected an official candidate, Giovanni Leone, but could not get out the party vote for him, although the Vatican did manage to persuade the two left-wing Catholic candidates, Fanfani and Giulio Pastore, to retire. Finally the Christian Democracy had to give in and endorse the candidacy of the founder and leader of the Social Democrats, Giuseppe Saragat, who became the candidate of all parties except those of the far right and the left-wing Socialists. Saragat was elected on the twenty-first ballot by the virtually unanimous suffrage of Communists, Socialists, and Republicans and a considerable number of Catholics.

Giuseppe Saragat (1898–   ) is a Piedmontese and Italy's first Socialist President. He took his degree in economics, and his first employment was as an analyst for the *Banca commerciale italiana.* He joined the Socialist Party in 1922 and went into exile four years later, living first in Vienna and then in Paris. In 1945 he became republican Italy's first ambassador to France. In 1947 he broke with the Socialist Party over its pro-Communist policy and formed the Social Democratic Party. At the time of his election (December 27, 1964) he was Minister of Foreign Affairs in the second Moro government. Saragat's reputation as an impartial President above politics has been perhaps unfairly marred by the scission in the Italian Socialist Party and the resuscitation of his old party, the Democratic Socialist Party. Although there is no proof that he did so, it was inevitable that he be suspected of manoeuvering this scission and inspiring the political program his former colleagues subsequently adopted. His prestige has been further handicapped by his tendency to be garrulous by telegraph not only on nonpolitical matters like congratulations to winning athletes and condolences to losers but also on matters that seem to touch on political partisanship, such as the beginning of a telegram in answer to one from striking students in which they asserted that their professors gave them a daily lesson in moral depravity similar to that given by Italy's political leaders. Saragat's reply began, "Dear students: Yours is a civil voice raised in a moment of national sadness."[14] His performance, however, during his seven-year term of office has been sufficiently satisfactory to make him the first President who was seriously considered a candidate for reelection. At the approach of the election held in December, 1971, Saragat remained a major candidate of those forces that wish to keep a Christian Democrat out of the Quirinale, the presidential palace.

Italy's sixth President, Giovanni Leone (1908–   ), was elected on December 23, 1971. Leone is a Neapolitan, a professor of criminal procedure at the University of Rome (the third of Italy's Presidents to be a law school professor), and a career Christian Democrat politician. Leone has served in both houses of Parliament, as President of the Chamber of Deputies, and on two occasions, when his party has been unable to put together a coalition with majority backing, he has headed interim minority all–Christian Democrat caretaker governments. Leone's political career has been based on his ability to get along with everyone. His talent for conciliation, however, may be seriously tested during his presidency. Unlike other presidential elections this one was strictly partisan. At the beginning of the balloting, the official candidate of the Christian Democracy was Amintore Fanfani. When, after a few ballots, it became evident that Fanfani could not muster unanimous support from his own party, and could not overcome this handicap by gaining support from other groups, the Christian Democracy ordered its delegates to abstain from voting until the party could agree on another candidate. Leone thus became the compromise candidate of his party, but not of all parties, and his election represented the victory of the right and part of the center against the Socialist candidate, Pietro Nenni. Leone's major task for the next seven years is likely to be the difficult one of eliciting cooperation among the very forces his election tended to polarize.

[14] See Vittorio Gorresio, "Come si fa un presidente: la corsa al Quirinale," Part III, Ch. 7, *La stampa,* May 30, 1971, p. 3.

6

The Council of Ministers

In Italy the word "government" (*governo*) is used to describe the executive power (Constitution, Art. 92). It is thus connected with the American use of the word "governor."

The Italian government is composed of the Council of Ministers (*Consiglio dei ministri*), which consists of the ministers and a President of the Council.

The President of the Council is much the equivalent of the British Prime Minister or of the French *premier,* although his power and prestige fall about halfway between those of his British and French *confrères.* The multiparty system in Italy and the instability of Italian governments make the President of the Council a far less formidable political figure than the Prime Minister. On the other hand, his position as presiding officer of the Council of Ministers and as the person chiefly responsible for the Government's program gives him far greater authority than that of the French *premier,* who is little more than executive secretary to the President of the Republic, which latter officer presides over the Council of Ministers and formulates government policy.

The number of ministers in the Italian Government varies. There is normally one for each of the nineteen ministries, and in recent years there have frequently been several additional "ministers without portfolio" in charge of such activities as the reform of the bureaucracy, the economic development of southern Italy (*Cassa per il mezzogiorno*), and the relations between the Government and Parliament. Some Governments also have one or more vice presidents, whose position is similar to that of a minister without portfolio. The third Rumor and first Colombo governments, for example, had twenty-seven members, including a president, a vice president, nineteen ministers with portfolio, and six without portfolio. In the third Rumor government these latter were charged respectively with administrative reform, scientific research, relations with parliament, establishment of the regions, U.N. relations, and aid to depressed areas. Each government contained twenty-one deputies and six senators.

The ministries are:

Foreign affairs	*Affari esteri*
Interior	*Interni*
Justice	*Grazia e giustizia*
Budget	*Bilancio*
Finance	*Finanze*
Treasury	*Tesoro*
Defense	*Difesa*
Education	*Pubblica istruzione*
Public Works	*Lavori pubblici*
Agriculture	*Agricoltura e foreste*
Transportation	*Trasporti*
Postal Service	*Poste e telecomunicazioni*
Industry and Commerce	*Industria e commercio*
Labor and Social Security	*Lavoro e previdenza sociale*
Foreign Commerce	*Commercio con l'estero*
Merchant Marine	*Marina mercantile*
State-Controlled Enterprises	*Partecipazioni statali*
Health	*Sanità*
Entertainment and Tourism	*Spettacolo e turismo*

The President of the Republic after consultation with the political leaders either offers the position of President of the Council to a prominent political figure or, if he believes conditions are not ripe for the formation of a new government, he may request a political leader of his choice to make further political soundings. The person to whom the position of President of the Council is offered may refuse it but normally he accepts on the contingency that he will be able to form a government. (The selection by the President of the Republic is called an *incarico* and the contingent acceptance is called acceptance *con riserva*.) If after further consultations the new potential President of the Council fails to gain the necessary support, he declines the offer; if he succeeds, he is then officially nominated.[1] He then chooses his ministers, who are in turn appointed by the President of the Republic (Art. 96). The Government must then go before both houses of Parlia-

[1] This is the procedure that has been followed since 1958. See Costantino Mortati (*Istituzioni di diritto pubblico,* 8th ed. (Padova: CEDAM, 1969), pp. 532–536.

ment for votes of confidence. If at any time it fails to maintain the confidence of either house it must resign.

The President of the Council of Ministers also appoints over fifty undersecretaries (*sottosegretari*) who are not members of the Council of Ministers.

Each minister appoints a chief of cabinet and a private secretary of his own choosing while the undersecretaries, like the ministers, are

Table 2*
Italian Governments — 1948–1971

	President of Council	Parties represented	Date of formation	Duration in days
1	Alcide de Gasperi V	DC, PSLI, PRI, PLI	May 23, 1948	601
2	Alcide de Gasperi VI	DC, PSLI, PRI	Jan. 27, 1950	537
3	Alcide de Gasperi VII	DC, PRI	July 26, 1951	712
4	Alcide de Gasperi VIII	DC	July 16, 1953	17
5	Giuseppe Pella	DC & "technicians"	Aug. 17, 1953	142
6	Amintore Fanfani I	DC	Jan. 17, 1954	14**
7	Mario Scelba	DC, PSDI, PLI	Feb. 10, 1954	497
8	Antonio Segni I	DC, PSDI, PLI	July 7, 1955	669
9	Adone Zoli	DC	May 16, 1957	399
10	Amintore Fanfani II	DC, PSDI	July 1, 1958	190
11	Antonio Segni II	DC	Feb. 19, 1959	400§
12	Fernando Tambroni	DC	Mar. 26, 1960	122
13	Amintore Fanfani III	DC	July 26, 1960	574
14	Amintore Fanfanti IV	DC, PRI, PSDI	Feb. 21, 1962	486
15	Giovanni Leone I	DC	June 22, 1963	165
16	Aldo Moro I	DC, PRI, PSDI, PSI	Dec. 4, 1963	231
17	Aldo Moro II	DC, PRI, PSDI, PSI	July 22, 1964	581
18	Aldo Moro III	DC, PRI, PSDI, PSI	Feb. 23, 1966	852
19	Giovanni Leone II	DC	June 24, 1968	172
20	Mariano Rumor I	DC, PRI, PSI	Dec. 13, 1968	239
21	Mariano Rumor II	DC	Aug. 5, 1969	226
22	Mariano Rumor III	DC, PRI, PSI, PSU	Mar. 29, 1970	130
23	Emilio Colombo	DC, PRI §§, PSI, PSU	Aug. 6, 1970	

* Through the second Fanfani Government the dates of formation and the length of duration of the Governments are taken from Ferruccio Pergolesi, *Diritto costituzionale*, 14th ed. (Padova: CEDAM, 1960), p. 837. Subsequent data have been taken from newspapers.

** This Government failed to receive a vote of confidence from Parliament.

§ During the period between Governments the former Government acts as an interim Government. In the changeover from the second Segni to the Tambroni Government the resignation of the former Government was accepted the evening before the day the new Government was sworn in: thus Italy had no Government for the night of March 25, 1960.

§§ The PRI left the Colombo government in the spring of 1971. The Government then sought and obtained new votes of confidence from both houses of Parliament and continued in office.

normally members of Parliament. The chiefs of cabinet are normally career civil servants in the top grades.

Italian Governments are of brief duration. In the twenty-three-year period following the 1948 election there were twenty-three Governments. On the other hand, the instability of the Governments has been somewhat offset by the fact that several Presidents of the Council and most ministers have served more than once. In fact, only eleven men have served as President of the Council in the quarter-century of 1946–71 and each has been a Demo-Christian. Alcide De Gasperi headed four Governments (eight of those between 1945 and 1948 are included), Amintore Fanfani four, Mariano Rumor and Aldo Moro three each, Antonio Segni and Giovanni Leone two each, and Giuseppe Pella, Mario Scelba, Adone Zoli, Fernando Tambroni, and Emilio Colombo, one each.

The classical function of the Government was to act as the chief executive organ of the state, dependent on and under the supervision and control of Parliament. Although appointed in the past by the king and at present by the President of the Republic, the Italian Government, like that in all liberal parliamentary democracies, must have the confidence of Parliament, and serves at the pleasure of Parliament. As in many but not all parliamentary democracies (Norway, France, and the Netherlands are exceptions), the ministers are normally members of the legislature.

The direct responsibility for the short duration of Italian Governments, however, cannot be placed on Parliament. No Government of republican Italy has fallen as a result of a parliamentary vote of no confidence. Only one, the first Fanfani Government (in 1954), fell because it failed to receive an initial vote of confidence from Parliament. The other twenty-one Governments have all fallen as a result of extra-parliamentary crises, and the presidents of the Council have tendered their resignations to the President of the Republic without going before Parliament in an attempt to explain or resolve the crisis.

In classical theory, therefore, it is Parliament that legislates, and in so doing sets the policy that it is the primary function of the Government to carry out. If at any time the Parliament is dissatisfied with the way the Government executes this policy it may dismiss the Government.

In practice the people's representatives united in Parliament are finding themselves less and less competent to formulate policy and to legislate. As society's demands for state intervention in the fields of economics and welfare increase, as the techniques of pressure-group influence are perfected, the individual legislator is required to resolve problems of an increasingly complicated technical nature and must at the same time stand fast against the persuasion of powerful pressure groups, a persuasion which may be ethically and even legally of a highly questionable character. The point has now been reached where he cannot acquit himself of his duties and he has been forced by the nature of things to delegate much of his power to the Government, and as a consequence the executive and administrative aspects of the Government's activities are almost of secondary importance. Thus the legislative power that was once in the king, and that passed to Parliament in the nineteenth century, has now moved out of Parliament into the hands of the Government and the parties. It is the reality that has changed, however; the traditional forms have altered little. Thus it is the President, in lieu of the king, who still promulgates the law, and it is Parliament that formally enacts it; but more likely than not it is the Government that has willed the law and that propels it through the mass of ritual that gives it its formal sanction. Parliament and the President are still there. Both are more than mere puppets that bow to the bidding of the new master.[2]

The Government has free rein in the field of policy formation so long as it maintains the confidence of Parliament and its policy remains within the general policy directives of the Constitution. The approval of a motion of no confidence or the failure to approve a motion of confidence forces the resignation of the Government. Failure to stay within the general policy directives of the Constitution may not only occasion a motion of no confidence, but it may also result in the intervention of the President of the Republic in the exercise of his duty to carry out the Constitution. The legislative power of the Government is equally extensive. It is exercised primarily in three ways:

1. through the presentation of government bills to Parliament
2. through powers of delegated legislation
3. through emergency powers

The early stages of gestation of a bill, whether it be a government bill or a private member bill, are difficult to trace. In Italy the government bill often first comes to light when the interested minister presents it formally to the Council of Ministers. If after a preliminary examination the Council favors the bill, it is studied carefully, article by article. If it is approved, it is sent to the President for his authorization for its presentation to Parliament, where it is treated in the manner described in the preceding chapter.

The Italian Constitution permits two types of executive legislation, the *decreto legislativo* and the *decreto legge*.

[2] See L. Balladore Pallieri, "Appunti sulla divisione dei poteri nella vigente costituzione," *Rivista trimestrale di diritto pubblico,* II (1952), pp. 811–830.

The *decreto legislativo* is an administrative act that has the force of law as a result of a previous legislative act enabling the government to legislate. The constitutionality of this act can then be challenged before the Constitutional Court, which is powerless to annul administrative regulations. The statute that authorizes the issuance of *decreti legislativi* must set a time limit on the delegation, must state the general purpose of the delegated legislation, and must delimit the subject matter to be covered (Constitution, Art. 76). In Italy delegated legislation is resorted to principally for handling vast technical subjects like the revision of the law codes or decentralization of the administration.

The Italians and the Europeans in general use the term "delegated legislative power" in a quite restricted sense. If the act of the administration is called a regulation, there is no delegation of legislative power. As the line between laws and regulations is a tenuous one, the actual powers of the Government to establish general and prospective norms through the regulatory power can be and are being constantly increased far beyond the use of the power to delegate "legislative" power under Article 76.[3]

The emergency legislative power of the government is exercised through decree laws (*decreti legge*). Parliament must be informed of them the day they are issued. If Parliament is not in session it must be convened within five days, and the decrees are annulled *ex tunc* if within sixty days they are not approved by Parliament (Constitution, Art. 77). In this way the Italian Constitution preserves the classical executive prerogative as an emergency expedient while at the same time it attempts to protect civil liberties by the requirement of speedy notification of Parliament and parliamentary approval. There have fortunately been no crises so far in republican Italy such as to cause the government to issue decree laws.

The Council of Ministers is the supreme policy-determining organ of the Italian state. The President of the Republic, as head of state, is not responsible for policy (*indirizzo politico*), and should not advocate actions of a partisan nature. On the other hand, the President of the Council of Ministers, as chief of the government, along with the ministers who form the cabinet and whom he has chosen as his advisers and assistants, bears the major responsibility for the formulation and execution of policy.[4]

[3] See Enzo Cheli, "Ampliamento dei poteri normativi dell'esecutivo nei principali ordinamenti occidentali," *Rivista trimestrale di diritto pubblico,* IX (1959), pp. 463–528 at 517–518.

[4] Professor Mortati points out (*Istituzioni,* pp. 528–530) that contemporary experience shows that policy formation is increasingly shared with or delegated to special bodies with greater technical competence than that pos-

Under these conditions it is obvious that republican Italy suffers from the fact that in all her history she has had only one Government that has endured for two years. If the Government is to rule and not merely execute and administer, it must form a long-term policy; it must be in a position to enact a coherent and coordinated legislative program. It needs unity of direction and a feeling of its own stability and prestige. Charles Benoist once said of French deputies, *"Improvisés, ils improvisent."* The same unfortunately is true of Italian Governments, which too often have been makeshift coalitions that have temporized with many of Italy's major problems, such as the reform of the bureaucracy, the inadequacy of the schools, and above all the implementation of the Constitution.

---

sessed by the Council itself. In Italy these bodies are often interministerial committees headed by the President of the Council (e.g., the Economic Planning Commission [CIPE]) or a minister (e.g., the *Cassa per il mezzogiorno*). In the case of the Supreme Defense Council the President of the Republic is the presiding officer. A significant aspect of these committees is the presence on them of persons not members of the cabinet, who may be members of Parliament, of the Civil Service, or experts chosen for their special competence.

7

The Constitutional Court

The Constitutional Court[1] is, with the President of the Republic, the Government, Parliament, and the Court of Cassation, one of Italy's major organs of the state. It is composed of fifteen judges who serve for nine-year terms,[2] five of whom are chosen by the judges of the Court of Cassation, the *Consiglio di stato,* and the *Corte dei conti,* five by Parliament in joint session and by a three-fifths vote, and five by the President of the Republic.

This court performs four functions. It judges (1) the constitutionality of state and regional laws and acts having the force of law, (2) conflicts of competence between top constitutional organs of the national government or between state and region or between regions, (3) impeachments, and (4) the admissibility of referenda.

The most important function of the Court is that of passing upon the constitutionality of laws. It is this function, necessitated by a radical change in the relationships among the top constitutional organs, that makes the Constitutional Court the major institutional innovation in the Italian Constitution. Under the *Statuto* of Carlo Alberto, Italy developed a parliamentary democracy with a sovereign parliament based on the French model; under Mussolini the *Statuto* was perverted to the purposes of a demagogical tyranny with a theoretically omnipotent *duce.* In the Italian republic there is no single preeminently sovereign

[1] Informative articles in English on the Constitutional Court include Taylor Cole, "Three Constitutional Courts," *American Political Science Review,* LIII (1959), pp. 963–984; Giuseppino Treves, "Judicial Review of Legislation in Italy," *Journal of Public Law,* VII (1958), 345–361; John Clarke Adams and Paolo Barile, "The Italian Constitutional Court in its First Two Years of Activity," *Buffalo Law Review,* VII (1958), pp. 250–265; and Giovanni Cassandro, "The Constitutional Court of Italy," 8 *American Journal of Comparative Law* (1959), pp. 1–14.

[2] The Constitutional Court judges originally served twelve-year terms but the term was changed to nine years in Constitutional Law No. 2 of 1967.

body. Power is shared among a number of constitutional organs that mutually approve and control each other's acts and all of which are bound to the observance of a rigid Constitution that delimits their spheres of legitimate activity. The principles of this Constitution are those of liberalism, and thus democracy, which may lead to the tyranny of the majority, is subject to the overriding principles of liberalism expressed in the Constitution. In a system that places liberty above democracy some think it wise to invest a body with the power to nullify the acts of Parliament that run counter to the principles of liberty as expressed in the Constitution. In Italy that power is given to the Constitutional Court.

One normally thinks of a constitutional court as a conservative body in that its major function is to preserve the already established constitutional principles from being overridden by radical innovating legislation. The Italian Constitutional Court, however, at least in its early years, has primarily had an innovating influence in that by annulling Fascist and Fascist-inspired legislation, it is often concerned with altering the established legal order to put it into conformity with the new and, for Italy, radical Constitution.

The court exercises its power to declare laws invalid through two different procedures. In one instance the issue reaches the court from another court by a process not unlike the writ of certification in the United States. This is the procedure adopted when a party to a dispute before an ordinary or an administrative court claims that a law affecting the case is unconstitutional, or when the court itself has doubts about the constitutionality of the law. In the first instance the court must give an interlocutory judgment on the constitutional question. If it holds that the question raised is not pertinent to the issue or patently without merit, the court so states and proceeds directly with the case, and the Constitutional Court is not consulted. If, on the other hand, the court holds that the constitutional question has been validly raised, it suspends the trial and refers the question to the Constitutional Court.

A major advantage of this system is that it relieves the Constitutional Court from having to determine the constitutionality of a law in the abstract without taking into consideration the concrete facts of a real dispute. Judges throughout the Western world dislike reaching decisions on hypothetical cases. In this respect the Italians have only followed the traditional practice of the United States Supreme Court.

Less satisfactory is the interlocutory judgment to the effect that the constitutional question is patently without merit. Obviously it is necessary to give some such authority to the judges; else unscrupulous attorneys would systematically avail themselves of the right to raise a constitutional question, thus sending thousands of cases annually to the Constitutional Court, with the result that the Court would be swamped with work and the decisions in the regular courts would be delayed a year or so longer than they are now.

On the other hand, some Italian judges have shown too great a willingness to assume constitutional jurisdiction themselves. This tendency is particularly noticeable in the higher courts and has led to such anomalies as a decision stating that the constitutional question is patently without merit, which required over 5000 words of explanation. The number of words used would appear to constitute substantial evidence that the inadmissibility of the constitutional question was far from patent.[3]

The other type of case in which the Court judges the constitutionality of a law arises when the state claims that a regional law presents an unconstitutional infringement on its own legislative powers, or when a region makes the same charges against the state or another region. On this occasion the state or the region, as the case may be, initiates the legal action, and the dispute goes to the Constitutional Court in the first instance.

When the Constitutional Court resolves conflicts of competence it is not necessarily examining the validity of a law. Here its competence extends to any type of act.

From the political standpoint conflicts of competence between the state and the regions are not intrinsically different from or more difficult than disputes between the state and the regions over the constitutionality of laws. Conflicts of competence between the top constitutional organs, however, are so fraught with political implications that their settlement by a judicial body seems unrealistic.

In Italy, as one jurist has written, "It is not easy to suppose that such conflicts, involving not only the prestige of the highest offices of the state but also the personal prestige of the incumbents, can be peacefully settled by a judicial process without arousing serious political and psychological repercussions.[4] Furthermore, the Constitutional Court itself

[3] Court of Cassation, Decision of April 28, 1965. See also Piero Calamandrei, "Sulla nozione di manifesta infondatezza," *Rivista di procedura civile,* XI (1956), pp. 154–174.

[4] Vezio Crisafulli, "La corte costituzionale tra magistratura e parlamento," in *Scritti giuridici in memoria di Piero Calamandrei* (Padova: CEDAM, 1958), Vol. IV, pp. 273–295, at 295. See also Ferruccio Pergolesi, "La corte costituzionale giudice e parte nei conflitti di attribuzione", *Rivista trimestrale di diritto e procedura civile* (1959), pp. 1 ff., and Franco Bonifacio, "Corte costituzionale e autorità giudiziaria", in Giuseppe Maranini, ed., *La giustizia costituzionale* (Firenze: Vallecchi, 1966), pp. 41–56.

is one of the major organs of the state. Fortunately the Court has so far (1971) been called on to adjudicate conflicts of competence only between the state and the regions.

When the Constitutional Court acts as a court of impeachment its fifteen regular members are joined by sixteen additional members, chosen by lot from a list of names selected every twelve years by a three-fifths vote of Parliament. These additional members must be eligible for election to the Senate, but they need not have legal training. The law does not specify the length of the list. In 1962 for the first time Parliament in joint session elected a panel of forty-five persons from whom these additional members would be chosen by lot for an impeachment trial. The officers subject to impeachment are the President of the Republic, the President of the Council of Ministers, and the individual ministers. There have been no impeachments to date (1971) in Italy, but in 1965 a Christian Democrat ex-Minister of Finance appeared to have escaped impeachment before the Court by an unconstitutional parliamentary procedure according to which an absolute rather than a simple majority was necessary to indict. The vote was 461 for indictment and 440 against, with forty-nine absent, but since an absolute majority (over 50 per cent of the members of Parliament) was not obtained, the former Minister was not sent to trial.[5]

The Constitutional Court was given a fourth function, one not mentioned in the Constitution, by the Constitutional Law of March 11, 1953, No. 1. This function is to determine the admissibility of proposals for referenda, which according to the Constitution (Art. 75) are permissible only for laws that do not concern taxes, budgets, amnesties, or approvals for the ratification of treaties.

In the early years of the Court's operation the Government regularly intervened as *amicus curiae* in defense of every contested law, no matter how brutally fascist or how patently unconstitutional. Later the

---

[5] See Paolo Barile, "La messa in stato di accusa dei ministri," in Leopoldo Piccardi, Norberto Bobbio, and Ferruccio Parri, *La sinistra davanti alla crisi del parlamento* (Milano: Giuffrè, 1967), pp. 211–219. See Alessandro Galante Garrone, "La costituzione e la classe politica," *La stampa*, July 22, 1965, p. 5; Lino Iannuzzi and Livio Zanetti, "Trabucchi dice tutto," *L'espresso*, July 18, 1965, pp. 2–3; Michele Tito, "I problemi fondamentali," *La stampa*, July 21, 1965, p. 1; and Gaetano Tumiati, "A Verona nessuno ha dubito," *La stampa*, July 21, 1965, p. 5. For an essentially objective account of the parliamentary hearings see Fausto De Luca in *La stampa*, *passim*. There seems to be no reason to believe that the man in question, Giuseppe Trabucchi, gained personally from his actions. The accusations were essentially abuse of office in the form of irregular and illegal acts against the interest of the state and for the personal gain of fellow Demo-Christian politicians.

Government ceased to follow this unseemly practice, and now is likely to intervene only in those instances where it can in relatively good conscience defend the law in question. There is also an increase in the occasions in which the parties do not choose to appear before the Court, and not infrequently the Court hears a case *in camera* on the record as received from the trial court.

So far the Constitutional Court, unlike the regular courts of Italy, has been reasonably successful in keeping abreast of its work. In an average year it issues somewhat more than 100 *sentenze* and somewhat more than fifty *ordinanze*. A *sentenza* is a reasoned decision that answers the question submitted to the Court. An *ordinanza* is a usually brief refusal to consider the question. A single *sentenza* dealing with questions brought up from the trial courts often considers two or more of these referrals, which, because of their similarities, may be treated together.

The Constitutional Court has become one of the most prestigious and best functioning of the major organs of the Italian government. It has done more than any other organ and perhaps more than all others combined to make the letter and the spirit of the Constitution a reality in Italy. Without the impetus that it has given there is little likelihood that the considerable advance in the protection and observance of civil liberties of both a substantive (e.g., freedom of speech, assembly, religion) and a procedural (e.g., the rights of defendants before the courts) nature would have occurred.

8

The Administration

The executive, or directive, power of the Italian state lies with the Council of Ministers and its President. The major function of the administration is the implementation of the directives received from the Government. An auxiliary function is to give expert advice to the Government.

The administration in Italy, as in most countries, is organized into a series of ministries that among them perform most of the administrative functions of the state. The division of functions among the various ministries is on the whole reasonable, but the number of ministries is larger than that of most other democracies and probably leads to some additional waste and inefficiency.

The functions of several of the ministries are described elsewhere in this book.[1] We shall give here a brief description of the work carried on by the other ministries.

Ministry of Foreign Affairs

The Ministry of Foreign Affairs performs the duties normally assigned to such a ministry. It is in charge of all ordinary diplomatic intercourse between Italy and the rest of the world. Besides its political and economic divisions (the latter of which appears primarily concerned with Italy's participation in international economic agencies like the World Bank, the Export-Import Bank, and the International Monetary Fund, or with the Common Market agencies), the Ministry of Foreign Affairs has also an Emigration Division and a Cultural Divi-

[1] The Ministry of Justice (Chapter 10), the Ministry of Labor (Chapter 14), the Ministry of State-Controlled Enterprises (Chapter 13), and the Ministries of the Interior and Defense (later in this chapter and in Chapter 14).

sion. The foreign policy of republican Italy has been remarkable primarily for the consistency with which it has supported Washington's foreign policy. During the entire postwar period Italy has been the most faithful European supporter of United States policy.[2]

The Italian Foreign Service is a career service not unlike the American Foreign Service before serious attempts were made to democratize it. Although many individuals in the Italian service are highly competent, the service as a whole tends to represent a limited class and a single point of view.

Ministry of Defense

Italy has a single united Ministry of Defense that administers the army, navy, and air force, and maintains over a half million persons under arms. This total is slightly under that of France and substantially over that of Great Britain.[3] Military service is compulsory for males, but the law permits certain categories of men to be excused. The number excused depends on the ratio between supply of manpower and supposed need.

Except for specialized troops like the *Alpini,* the Alpine regiments, composed of expert mountaineers, where the morale and prestige are high, and to a lesser degree the *Bersaglieri,* who march in double time and are bedecked with dyed chicken feathers, the morale of the army is low. As in most Western democracies, the navy and the air force fare better in this respect.

The method of selecting officers for the armed forces is based on education. Only those men who have received the baccalaureate degree, which permits them to enter a university, may serve as officers. The less-educated and the non-educated serve as enlisted men. Gentlemen's sons who lack the intelligence to get through the stiff Italian secondary schools must also serve as enlisted men, but they are likely to receive special assignments, e.g., as chauffeurs to officers.

The army maintains a military academy in Modena for future career officers; the navy has a similar academy in Livorno; and the air force has one in Nisida (near Naples).

[2] For studies of Italian foreign policy see Lloyd A. Free and Renzo Sereno, *Italy: Dependent Ally or Independent Partner?* (Princeton: The Institute for International Social Research, 1956), and Norman Kogan, *The Politics of Italian Foreign Policy* (New York: Praeger, 1963).

[3] Ercole Bonacina, "In crociera attraverso i ministeri romani: Primo, la difesa," *Il ponte,* XXIV (1968), 1522–31, at 1525.

The Finance Ministries

Three ministries share the responsibility for the financial administration of Italy. Of the three, the Ministry of the Budget and Economic Planning holds the key position. This ministry has no direct contact with the public, but it is in intimate contact with the other eighteen ministries, from each of which it receives budget estimates. The Ministry of the Budget coordinates these estimates among themselves and with the revenue estimate from the Ministry of Finance and prepares a unified national budget. The major technician involved in this work is the *ragioniere generale* (controller general) who works with the chief fiscal officers of the other ministries. The political function is performed by the Minister, who in case of conflict with other ministries must defend the revised unified budget before the Council of Ministers, the supreme authority in this matter.

The unified budget is then sent to Parliament. The Constitution (Art. 81) forbids the Government to introduce new taxes or new expenditures in the budget. Proposals for taxes or expenditures must be presented to Parliament individually.

Parliament is expected to approve the budget, and it is much more likely to do this in Italy than in a presidential democracy like the United States, where there may be open friction between the executive and legislative branches. Parliament, however, may amend the budget so long as new taxes and new expenditures are not envisaged.[4] There appears to be no instance of Parliament having amended a budget, and there are only two occasions when it has failed to approve a budget. In 1893 Parliament refused to approve the budget of the Ministry of Justice. (At that time the budgets of the various ministries were presented as separate bills.) The result was the resignation and replacement of the minister without a government crisis. In 1964 the Chamber of Deputies disapproved of a single item in the budget that dealt with state aid to Roman Catholic schools — and the Moro government fell.

Once the budget is passed either the Government or Parliament may initiate further financial legislation provided only that the law indicate the sources of revenue from which the new expenditures will be met. It is not quite clear whether or not in case of an unanticipated surplus (or of a deficit smaller than that predicted in the budget) Parliament

[4] Luigi Einaudi and Francesco Répaci, *Il sistema tributario italiano,* 5th ed. (Turin: Giulio Einaudi, 1954), pp. 21–22. Mortati, *op. cit.,* p. 649, supports this view. Guido Zanobini, *Corso di diritto amministrativo,* Vol. IV, 5th ed. (Milan: Giuffrè, 1958), pp. 440–441, believes Parliament has no amending power.

can authorize additional expenditures without providing new revenues.[5]

The Ministry of Finance is entrusted with collecting the money due the state. The tax structure is complex and unsatisfactory. There are many burdensome taxes, and there is much tax evasion. A thorough reform, necessitated by Italy's commitment to the Common Market, is being debated in Parliament as this book goes to press.

The *guardia di finanza* is a branch of the armed forces attached to the Ministry of Finance and specially charged to aid in the suppression of fiscal evasions and the capture of evaders. Their work is primarily against smugglers and violators of customs regulations. The placement of these soldiers under the Finance Ministry brings to mind the United States practice of placing the Coast Guard under the Department of the Treasury in peacetime.

The Ministry of the Treasury is in charge of the state's money and its disbursement. It also manages the public debt and is in charge of the *Ragioneria generale dello stato* (the General Accounting Office), the *Provveditorato generale dello stato* (General Purchasing Office), and the Mint.

Ministry of Education (Pubblica istruzione)

The control of education in Italy is highly centralized. All public school and state university personnel are civil servants. Every university chair is created by law, and the content of every course in primary and secondary schools is determined by bureaucrats in Rome.

There are five years of elementary school in Italy and up to nine years of secondary school. The university, which corresponds roughly to the third and fourth undergraduate years and graduate school in the United States, is a place of specialization and not of general culture.

Although the Constitution apparently opposes state aid for private or parochial schools, the Christian Democracy has insisted on subsidizing the many Catholic schools. At the university level all institutions of standing are governmental except the *Università cattolica del Sacro cuore* at Milan, which is a church institution. Widespread student dissatisfaction with secondary and university education has led the Government to propose radical reforms. Opponents of these reforms, however, have enough strength in Parliament to have thus far prevented passage of the school reform bills. The secondary school bill was defeated in Parliament in the spring of 1971, and the university bill is still being debated as this book goes to press.

[5] See Einaudi, *Lo scrittoio del presidente,* pp. 201–207.

The Ministry is also in charge of Italy's public libraries, its art galleries, and its scenery (*bellezze naturali*).

Ministry of Public Works

The Ministry of Public Works is the construction ministry. It is a political plum that the dominant party has rarely let out of its hands. It has a lot of money to spend, and there is a fairly widespread belief that some of it goes toward mending political fences and paying political debts.

The Ministry does the construction work for the state railways; it does port construction work, including dredging, hydroelectric construction, and the erection of public buildings. It directs the *Azienda nazionale autonoma delle strade statali* (ANAS), which builds and maintains the state roads.

Ministry of Agriculture and Forests

The Ministry of Agriculture and Forests, as in the United States, is more of an educational and assistance agency than a law-enforcing agency. It is concerned with teaching people to improve the use of the farm and forest land. Italian agrarian law is a complex and interesting subject. It is more favorable to the state and society and less favorable to the individual than is the Anglo-American common law. Thus subsoil rights pertain to the state and not to the owner of the soil, and the owner of land abutting on water does not have a riparian right, that is, the right to close the shore to the public, as he may have in the Anglo-American system.

The educational work is done on the spot by agricultural college graduates under the supervision of the *Ispettorati provinciali agricoltura* — IPA (provincial agricultural inspectorates). Local boys are generally used, as they know the local dialect. Where the local priest is interested in the physical and economic well-being of his flock and where he is respected, he often gives this Italian equivalent of the county agent the support of his considerable prestige. Other functions of the Ministry include the supervision of the four national parks and of the numerous agricultural experiment centers.

The major administrative work of the Ministry is performed by one of its seven *direzioni generali,* the *Direzione generale della bonifica.* The word *bonifica* covers all types of land and soil improvement and includes reforestation, controlling streams and altering their courses, malaria control, road building, electrification, and resettlement.

The Ministry also supervises the government-owned corporation that operates the state forests (which are, among other things, a major source of lumber) and provides or supervises the provision of low-interest loans to individual farm owners who wish to improve their land.

Ministry of Industry and Commerce

The Ministry of Industry and Commerce performs consultative, fact-finding, supervisory, and inspection work in the fields of industry and commerce. One major division of the Ministry is concerned with the mining industry and another with small business and artisans. Both of these divisions include an inspection service. Other divisions deal with patents and trademarks, with inspection of private insurance companies, with domestic commerce, with industrial production, and with fuel and hydroelectric and atomic power. The last two sections appear to overlap with the Ministries of Foreign Affairs and of Foreign Commerce in that they are all deeply involved in the economic aspects of international organizations.

Ministry of the Merchant Marine

The functions of the Ministry of the Merchant Marine have been carved out of the functions of various other ministries according to a plan reminiscent of the Fascist corporative system, wherein all aspects of a single economic process were lumped together. Thus it has taken fishing from Agriculture, seamen and port workers from Labor, and ports and shipping from Industry and Commerce. The redundancy of this ministry is obvious.

Among its most interesting functions are those relating to labor. Seamen are licensed by this ministry, and their working conditions are inspected by its representatives rather than by the Ministry of Labor. In order to load or unload ships in Italy, port workers must have a license from the Ministry of the Merchant Marine. These licenses are given to members of the various *"compagnie"* that exist in each port. Membership in the *compagnie* is strictly limited. Whenever there is a vacancy, the remaining members, through their union, suggest the name of the new man whom they want licensed. He is often the son or other relative of the man who is retiring. Such nominations are normally approved by the Ministry. Thus among this category of workers a system persists that is similar to the medieval guild. The result is that, whereas the port workers of the rest of the world are among the farthest left of the labor groups, the Italian port workers are to the right of the rest of the labor movement. The monopoly they have is virtually unbreakable, for although port work is mainly heavy exertion for which a strong back is more helpful than either brains or experience, it cannot be carried out effectively unless some of the men are experienced.

Therefore, if the government should fail to maintain the port workers in their privileged position, they could easily tie up the ports of Italy by a strike.

Ministry of Foreign Commerce

Another possibly superfluous ministry is that of Foreign Commerce. This ministry performs the equivalent of the bulk of the work of the economic sections of the American Department of State with respect to trade agreements and economic reporting. It is also concerned with regulating foreign trade and foreign exchange.

The Ministries of Communications

Under Fascism a single Ministry of Communications was in charge of the two large government enterprises, the railways and the postal and telegraphic services. These are now divided between two ministries. The Ministry of Transportation administers the state railways and their subsidiaries and exercises a close supervision over the minor private railways. The Ministry of Postal and Telegraphic Service (*Poste e telecomunicazioni*) is primarily concerned with the management of the postal and telegraphic services. It also operates an extensive postal savings system, but the investment of these funds is managed by the *Cassa depositi e prestiti* in the Ministry of the Treasury.

Ministry of Health

The Ministry of Health (*Sanità*) was established in 1958. Previous to that date most of its functions had been performed by a Health Commissioner. It is divided into five sections (*direzioni generali*): public health (*igiene pubblica*), socialized medicine (*medicina sociale*), veterinarian service, drugs (*servizio farmaceutico*), and general administration.

The public health division is concerned with the administration of the pure food laws and with epidemiology. The socialized medicine division is mainly concerned with maternity and child welfare and with research on certain diseases like tuberculosis, cancer, malaria, and trachoma. The drug business is faced with many controls in Italy. The number of pharmacies and their hours of business are determined by the Ministry, as are the drugs they must stock, and those they may sell only under prescription. The maximum retail prices are also fixed, and except in the case of a patent drug, these prices are low. The control over the drug manufacturing business, however, does not prevent the companies (e.g., Carlo Erba, Montecatini) from making large profits on patent drugs. The control of the manufacture and use of harmful drugs is also a concern of this ministry, as is the administration of the various public health laws concerning pure foods, malaria abatement, health hazards in employment, water pollution, and funeral arrangements.

Ministry of Tourism and Entertainment

The Ministry of Tourism and Entertainment (*Turismo e Spettacolo*) was created in 1959, when the entertainment division of the Presidency of the Council of Ministers and the *Commissariato per il turismo* were joined together and given ministerial rank.

Americans must applaud the interest the Italian state takes in the entertainment field and the not inconsiderable millions it spends in subsidizing the stage, lyric or otherwise. The almost complete disregard for the arts that is the traditional attitude of American national, state, and city governments cannot but seem mean and vulgar in the face of Italy's generosity. The results of the Italian practice, however, show that when subsidy is coupled with stifling controls, the evil may well outweigh the good. A large Roman bureaucracy with limited esthetic sensibilities has its tentacles in every opera house and every theatrical production, exercising sometimes tyrannically and often inefficiently the power of the purse, through the granting and the withholding of subsidies. The helping hand of the government is a heavy hand that may crush as well as sustain.

The state's activities in behalf of the tourist trade include controls over hotels, *pensioni,* tourist agencies, and related services of prime interest to tourists.

Italy, following the modern prejudice that sport has little to do with sportsmanship and physical relaxation, puts the control of sports rightfully in the Ministry of Tourism and Entertainment, for professional athletes are primarily entertainers. Subsidies for professional athletics are funneled through CONI (*Comitato olimpico nazionale italiano*), which is part of the Ministry.

Presidenza del consiglio dei ministri

The *Presidenza del consiglio* in Italy corresponds to the Executive Office of the President of the United States. Both are convenient pigeonholes for a series of small offices and services that do not rate a ministry to themselves either on account of their small size or on account of the wide interministerial scope of their activities. The *Presidenza del consiglio* contains the press offices, the copyright office, and a legal office that writes or edits government bills. Other essentially autonomous bodies, such as the *Consiglio di stato,* the *Corte dei conti,* the state *discoteca* (phonograph record library), the *Istituto centrale di statistica* (Central Statistical Institute), and the *Comitato nazionale per la produttività* (CNP — National Productivity Committee) are formally included under the *Presidenza del Consiglio.*

Italy with nineteen ministries and an active Presidency of the Council of Ministers has one of the least integrated of administrations to be found in the Western world. (Switzerland, for instance, has only seven ministries and the United States only eleven departments, not counting the Post Office.) Fortunately the various functions of government are fairly rationally divided among the ministries as they now stand; on the other hand, no one but the civil servants could lose by the consolidation of the ministries, and both the state and the public should gain by any successful efforts at streamlining the present administration and eliminating duplication of work. Thus there seems little reason for separate ministries for railways and for postal and telegraphic services or for three financial ministries (budget, finance, and treasury) or for separate ministries (1) of industry and commerce; (2) of foreign commerce, and (3) of the Merchant Marine.

The policy-forming function

As was noted in Chapter 6, the Council of Ministers shares its policy-forming functions with certain other bodies. The major bodies that share this power are the Supreme Council of Defense and the Economic Planning Commission. Others include the Interministerial Committee on Prices (*Comitato interministeriale dei prezzi* — CIP), the Committee for the *Cassa del mezzogiorno,* and the Banking Committee (*Comitato pel credito*).[6]

The Supreme Council of Defense (*Consiglio suprema di difesa*) is not an advisory body and is virtually independent of the Ministry of Defense. Its president is the President of Italy, and he calls the meetings and sets the agenda. Its members are the President of the Council of Ministers, the Ministers of Foreign Affairs, Defense, Industry, and the Treasury, and the Chief of Staff. The Council has been meeting on an average of once or twice a year. It is a policy-forming body rather than an advisory body. It is expected to give directives rather than opinions. The Economic Planning Commission (*Comitato interministeriale per la programmazione economica* — CIPE) is attached to the Ministry of the Budget and is responsible for economic planning. The regular members of the Commission are the President of the

---

[6] Mortati, *op. cit.,* pp. 528–529.

Council of Ministers and the Ministers of the Budget, Foreign Affairs, Treasury, Finance, Industry, Agriculture, Foreign Commerce, Public Works, Labor, Transportation, Merchant Marine, Tourism and Entertainment, State-controlled Enterprises, and the *Cassa del mezzogiorno*. The governor of the Bank of Italy and the president of the Central Statistical Institute may also be invited to attend. This Commission avails itself of the services of a research institute for economic planning (*Istituto di studi per la programmazione economica*), which prepares reports for the CIPE and the Ministry.[7]

The advisory function

The function of the ministries, however, is not exclusively administrative. They are also called upon to give advice to the Government; and special bodies, composed of top career civil servants and in some cases supplemented by non-government personnel elected by the category of persons possessed of the expert knowledge sought, are set up in many of the ministries for the express purpose of giving advice. As these bodies are technical rather than political, however, the Government is often required by law to consult them, but it is rarely required to obtain their consent. Decisions are normally political matters that it is appropriate to leave to the Government.

The major advisory body is the *Consiglio di stato* (Council of State). Like the French *Conseil d'état,* this is the top organ of the administration and the supreme administrative court.[8] (For the judicial functions of the *Consiglio di stato* see Chapter 10.)

The *Consiglio di stato* is composed of eighty-seven persons (one president, twelve presidents of section, sixty councillors, and fourteen junior members (i.e., seven *primi referendari* and seven *referendari*). The councillors who enter the service as *referendari* are career officers. The other councillors are appointed by the Government, usually from among the higher grades of the civil service. The advantage of this system is that it permits inclusion on the Council of men representing a wide expertise in matters affecting various facets of state administration. The disadvantage is that it permits perhaps undue governmental influence on a body that should be quite independent of the Government.

---

[7] The CIPE was established by Law No. 48 of 1967. It supersedes the CIR (*Comitato interministeriale per la ricostruzione* — Interministerial Commission for Reconstruction), established in 1945. The CIPE, however, has considerably more extended powers.

[8] For a survey of its structure and functions see Giovanni Paleologo, "Il Consiglio di stato: struttura e funzioni," 16 *Rivista trimestrale di diritto pubblico,* 303–353 (1966).

The administrative half of the *Consiglio di stato* is divided into three sections. To each section is attributed the power or the obligation to advise certain ministries. When the advice sought concerns ministries serviced by different sections, a special commission composed of members of the sections involved may be set up. For matters of greater importance the *Consiglio di stato* meets in *adunanza generale,* that is, in a plenary session, with all the Councillors of both the administrative and judicial sections present.

The *Consiglio di stato* also meets in *adunanza generale* to give its opinion on general administrative regulations before their promulgation. The opinion of a section suffices in the case of many decrees of a less general nature. In at least one case the Government must actually obtain the consent of the *Consiglio* before acting, when it denies a petition for the reacquisition of Italian citizenship (Law 555 of 1912, Art. 9). The Government is also required by law to consult the *Consiglio di stato* on all government bills before presentation to Parliament (Law 1054 of 1924, Art. 14), but this provision is an anachronistic residue of the feudal practice in the days before Parliament when the *Consiglio di stato* was comprised of the chief nobles of the realm. Although still on the statute books, this provision is now disregarded in practice.[9]

The National Economic Council (*Consiglio nazionale dell'economia e del lavoro*), provided for by Article 99 of the Constitution, was established by the law of January 5, 1957, No. 33, after a delay of more than nine years, and the Council met for the first time in the following month.

The Council is composed of eighty members. Fifty-nine represent the various vocational categories; twenty are experts in economic and social affairs and supposedly represent the general (or the consumer's) interest; the other member is the president, and he does not officially represent any group.

The members are appointed for five-year terms by the President of the Republic and are immediately eligible for reappointment (Law No. 619 of 1967. Previously councillors were appointed for three-year terms.) The nominations for the fifty-nine representatives of the vocational categories are made by the various vocational associations according to their membership. Twenty-three represent labor, nineteen represent private business, ten, the self-employed; four, state enterprises, and three, cooperatives. Twelve experts are nominated by various government research bodies, and the nominations are approved by the President of the Council of Ministers after consultation with the Council of Ministers. The eight other experts have been nominated by

[9] Mortati, *op. cit.,* p. 549.

the President of the Republic on the suggestion of the Government.[10] It is not clear, however, that the law prevents the President from making his selections *motu proprio*.[11]

The Council may do three things: it can initiate legislation when two-thirds of its membership is so moved; it gives its opinion when requested to do so by either house of Parliament, the Council of Ministers, or by the regions; and it makes studies on the request of a house of Parliament, of the Council of Ministers, or on its own motion. In practice its main purpose seems to be to advise the government on prospective legislation.

The National Economic Council as it is organized today bears little resemblance to the grandiose body proposed by some of the Christian Democrat members of the Constituent Assembly. Costantino Mortati envisaged an entire hierarchy of organs, based on functional representation and endowed with extensive powers.[12] He was apparently inspired by the typical Roman Catholic corporate theory that developed in nineteenth-century France.[13] Even the watered down council envisaged by the Constitution has been further weakened by the enabling legislation, which gives overrepresentation on the Council to some sectors of the economy and underrepresentation to others. Thus the CNEL has five representatives of the independent farmers (*coltivatori diretti*), a group controlled by right-wing Catholics, and only seven representatives of industrial labor. There are roughly 1,500,000 independent farmers in Italy and roughly 4,700,000 industrial workers.[14]

It is possible, however, that if the National Economic Council acts wisely and if its membership succeeds in representing the public as well as the state, this body may turn into something like a permanent Royal Commission on economic affairs, an advisory body, to be sure, but one whose prestige is such that its counsel is taken seriously into consideration.

There are at least eight other advisory councils attached to other ministries. These councils are likely to be elective if the interests they represent are organized in such a way as to make elections feasible and

[10] Vezio Crisafulli, "Aspetti problematici del sistema parlamentare vigente in Italia," *Jus,* IX (1958), p. 26 (*estratto*).

[11] Mortati, *op. cit.,* p. 552.

[12] Alberto Bertolino, "L'attività economica, funzioni e forme organizzative del lavoro. Il Consiglio nazionale dell'Economia e del Lavoro," in Piero Calamandrei and Alessandro Levi, *Commentario sulla costituzione italiana* (Florence: Barbèra, 1950), I, pp. 407–440, at 440.

[13] John Clarke Adams, "The Origins of the Theory of the Corporate System," *Journal of the History of Ideas,* III (1942), pp. 182–189.

[14] *Annuario statistico italiano* 1969 (Rome: Istituto centrale di statistica, 1969), p. 313.

appropriate; otherwise they are appointive. If we can take as an indication of Italian thinking on this matter the law on the National Economic Council (which set up an election system that is to go into effect when the bodies that will do the electing have been created), the trend would appear to favor elective over appointive councils.

The Council of Agriculture and Forests is the most complex of these councils. It has over 100 members and is divided into five sections, one each for experimentation and phytopathology, for trees and grasses, for land improvement, for animals and hunting, and for forests.

The members of the Council of the Armed Forces, as befits the authoritarian nature of military organization, are appointed, not elected. This body meets as a whole or in sections (army, navy, air force) in accordance with its agenda. The members are the top persons in the military hierarchy and in the Ministry of Defense.

The major advisory organ of the Ministry of Health is the National Health Council, composed of a minority of *ex officio* members and a majority of members appointed by the President of the Republic for three-year terms. The President has a free choice in appointing most of the appointed members from among various categories of persons, most of whom are physicians or veterinarians, but a few members are actually chosen by other government agencies.

The Ministry of Education has three advisory councils. The Council on Education, composed of sixty-eight members, has three sections, one each for elementary, secondary, and higher education. The majority of the members are selected by the class of teachers concerned. The Library Council is a small body of fifteen members of whom ten are elected, three by the librarians and seven by the presidents of academic and scientific institutions. The Antiquities and Fine Arts Council is composed of twenty-six members and is divided into five sections dealing with (1) archaeology, paleontology, and ethnology, (2) medieval and modern art, (3) monumental architecture, urban planning and natural beauty, (4) contemporary figurative arts, and (5) music and drama.

The High Public Administration Council (*Consiglio Superiore della Pubblica Amministrazione*) is attached to the *Presidenza del consiglio* and is an advisory body on general questions of administrative coordination. This body is similar to the advisory councils described immediately above except that its competence extends over the entire administration. It is for this reason that it is placed in the *Presidenza del consiglio*.

The National Research Council (*Consiglio nazionale delle ricerche*) is a large body with over 100 sections. It acts in part as an advisory body to the government and in part as the supervisor of many different scientific research centers. The Council is divided into seven major committees, one each for mathematics, physics, chemistry, biology, engineering, agriculture, and geography. It is placed under the *Presidenza del Consiglio.*

The control function

The *Corte dei conti* (Court of Accounts)[15] exercises a preventive control over the legality of the government's acts, performs a post-audit on the budget, and supervises the financial activities of enterprises to which the state contributes capital. It reports its findings directly to Parliament.

The *Corte dei conti* is composed of over 500 officials, including a president, fourteen presidents of section, seventy councillors, and more than 430 junior members (*primi referendari* and *referendari*). The latter, as in the case of the *Consiglio di stato,* are career civil servants, recruited by competitive examination. The Court is divided into five regular and various special sections. The first regular section (and temporarily one of the special sections) performs administrative work. (The other sections function as special administrative courts. See *infra,* Chapter 10.)

The *Corte dei conti* must register all decrees of the President of the Republic (i.e., all important executive orders). If it considers an act illegal it remands it to the government. The government in turn either drops it, alters it, or returns it to the *Corte* for registration "with reservations." In the latter case the *Corte* must comply with the request but must also notify Parliament fortnightly of all such registrations. In practice this safeguard against the government is inoperative, as Parliament is in the habit of paying no attention to these communications. The *Corte dei conti* must approve all acts of the government involving more than minimal expenditures. Other categories of acts requiring approval by this body include the appointments, promotions, and dismissals of public servants and the final settlement of pensions.

Professional associations
(Ordini o collegi professionali)

The Italian equivalents of the American Bar Association and the American Medical Association are public bodies, organized on a provincial basis. Membership is obligatory for all who wish to practice. The provincial bodies levy dues (*tasse*) on members, admit new members, have powers of discipline over members, and make available their good offices in disputes over fees between members and their clients.

[15] See O. Sepe and F. P. Pandolfo, *La struttura e le attribuzioni della Corte dei conti* (Milano: Giuffrè, 1967).

Government control over the medical orders (physicians, pharmacists, veterinarians) lies with the Minister of Health and over the legal orders (lawyers and notaries) with the Minister of Justice.

Personnel

The personnel that operates the Italian administration consisted in 1964 of about 1,300,000 persons. Almost one-third of them were teachers, about a fourth were military personnel, somewhat less than a fourth were employed in government-operated business enterprises (postal services, railways, telephone and telegraph services, tobacco and salt monopolies, state roads, state forests), and the rest, about 200,000 persons, comprised the civil service in the more restricted sense. The salaries, wages, and pensions paid to all these people amounted to about 40 per cent of the national budget.[16]

The Italian civil service does not enjoy the respect, affection, or confidence of the Italian public. It is accused of being overpaid and underpaid, overstaffed and understaffed, overcautious and overzealous, ineffective and corrupt. Paradoxically, it is perhaps all these things.

In spite of the continued and successful pressure the civil servants exert on the government and the frequent pay increases they receive, their pay is not sufficient to attract the best brains, which normally find more lucrative employment in the service of private enterprise. Yet it is doubtful if the average civil servant is worth more than he is getting, if one takes into consideration his modest ability and his short work week. The official week is normally composed of six six-hour tours of duty from 8:00 A.M. to 2:00 P.M., a total of thirty-six hours. Since a six-hour uninterrupted stretch of office work is beyond normal human endurance, it is safe to assume that the average civil servant works for the government no more than thirty hours a week.

An overall figure of 200,000 civil servants does not appear excessive, but the deployment of this personnel is not rational, with the result that certain offices are overstaffed and others overworked. The extreme centralization of the government that requires approval from Rome for minor decisions of purely local significance results in an inefficient use of the civil servants' energies. The extreme physical decentralization of the ministries in Rome, exemplified by the general practice of having various departments of a single ministry scattered over the city, causes further delay and waste. The inability to recruit

[16] For a straightforward and informative elementary study of the Italian civil service, including an analysis of the reforms proposed and in part enacted since 1945 see Alberto Spreafico, *L'amministrazione ed il cittadino* (Milano: Edizione di Comunità, 1965).

competent and trained personnel to fill vacancies in the upper echelons puts an increasing work load on the remaining top civil servants, at least one of whom is involved in all but the most routine decisions.

The laws and regulations under which the civil service operates are unnecessarily complex, and Parliament continues to modify them by hundreds of special laws excepting some group from this or that provision of a general law or altering the normal procedure to be followed in certain categories of cases. As a result the cautious civil servant is afraid to act for fear of running counter to some codicil to a general provision which may have escaped his attention. The enterprising civil servant who feels obligated to get things done risks his career by cutting corners either consciously or unconsciously. He is at the mercy of his overzealous colleagues who may report his "illegal" methods and the result may be a prison sentence, as in the cases of Prof. Marotta of the *Istituto di sanità* (Public Health Institute) and Prof. Ippolito of the CNEN (*Centro nazionale per l'energia nucleare*). Each was charged with misappropriation of funds. In these cases the courts could only judge whether the men in question had violated the letter of the law, whereas the real questions, which lay outside the courts' competence, were whether these agencies could be operated strictly according to the law and at the same time produce the expected results, and whether a minister would not be open to public criticism if he strait-jacketed an agency of this kind by putting it in the hands of a cautious, bureaucratically inclined administrator who would rather stay safely within the law than serve the public. It appears, for instance, that one of the major achievements of the *Instituto di sanità*, the experiments with antipolio vaccines, was made possible by large unauthorized expenditures. The laws under which the administration works are often antiquated, illogical, uncoordinated, and self-defeating. Trials like those of Marotta and Ippolito have a demoralizing effect on the more active and public-spirited civil servants.

One who would describe the ineffectiveness of the Italian administration risks being accused of hyperbole. In many instances it has been incapable of spending its appropriations. Italy suffered three "natural" disasters during the sixties: the crack of the Vajont dam, the flood of Florence, and the earthquake at Trapani. In each case Parliament generously voted relief funds, but by the end of 1971 the administration had failed to disburse them. Social security payments are unreasonably high in relation to the benefits received. A few years ago there was still a backlog of about 300,000 war pension cases. Some cases dealing with water rights have been before the courts for over 100 years, and a recent budget still contained an item of 350,000 lire for the liquidation of damages caused by the Neapolitan troops in

1859.[17] Direct taxes, particularly income taxes, are collected only in part.

Italians are convinced that theirs is a particularly corrupt administration. This belief is fed by the scandals that are frequently featured in the press. The actual corruption, however, may have a less grave influence on Italian public life than the assumption on the part of the public that corruption is endemic and probably irradicable.

The basic problem with public administration in Italy, however, remains the mentality that permeates the civil service. The civil service is drawn for the most part from Mediterranean Italy; 62.7 per cent of the personnel in the administrative class (*carriera direttiva*) come from the south, although this region represents only 36.8 per cent of the population, while the south supplies 75.9 per cent of the prefects and 77 per cent of the judges.[18] A prominent element in the culture of Mediterranean Italy is the mutual distrust that exists between the government and the governed. The former wish to assert their authority, the latter to subvert it. Further, the southern Italian functionary is generally of a conservative disposition. His civil service position symbolizes his success. His loyalty is to the traditional forces operating in the south and controlling it. The industrial democracy of the north is foreign to him, as are the principles of the republican constitution. They appear to undermine his authority and his prestige, although in fact they need do neither, and thus he looks askance at them and builds ingenious legal barricades against their invasion of his satrapy of futile power.[19]

The founders of republican Italy were aware that a major task before them was the reform of the bureaucracy. Many studies have been made of the problem, and some positive results have been achieved. Measures have been taken to reduce the amount of documentation necessary for certain acts and to simplify the tax structure. Mechanization has accelerated certain processes. Some steps have been taken to improve the public relations of the administration. Responsible elements in the administration itself have cooperated in planning and carrying out these improvements.

In 1954[20] Parliament authorized the government to issue new civil service regulations by decree; two years later a decree of 386 articles

[17] *Ibid.*, p. 82.

[18] *Ibid.*, p. 151.

[19] The following comparison exemplifies the lack of interest in public relations typical of the Italian bureaucratic tradition. In the United States the consumer who pays his electric bill promptly is rewarded with a discount. In Italy the consumer who does not pay his bill within a few days of when the public service wants it to be paid, is fined and his electricity is cut off, both without notice.

[20] Law of December 20, 1954, No. 1181.

was issued.[21] It divides the personnel into four categories: (a) *carriere direttive,* (b) *carriere di concetto,* (c) *carriere esecutive,* (d) *carriere di personale ausiliario.* The first three categories correspond roughly to the administrative class, the executive class, and the clerical class in Great Britain. The fourth category is that of the ushers.

Admission to the Service is normally by competitive examination. Applicants must be between eighteen and thirty-two. If the scores on the examination are equal, preference is given to seventeen types of persons who are either war veterans or close relatives of war veterans. The *carriere direttive* are open to university graduates and to personnel in the *carriere di concetto,* and the *carriere di concetto* are open to graduates of an upper secondary school and to personnel in the *carriere esecutive.*

The *carriere esecutive* are open to graduates of the lower secondary schools who are proficient in shorthand, typing, or the use of business machines. The *carriere ausiliarie* are open to persons with an elementary school diploma. Promotion is by merit or seniority, but at the top level (i.e., director general) the Council of Ministers may appoint persons from other ministries or from outside the Service.

There is no Civil Service Commission in Italy, as there is in the United States, no single body that prepares and administers the entrance examinations. Each ministry has a *Consiglio di amministrazione,* composed of its top political officers and its top civil servants, which is in charge of personnel. There is also a disciplinary commission in each ministry, composed of a director general and two inspectors general. By 1971 there was as yet no special school in operation for training top echelon civil servants like the one Marcel Debré was instrumental in founding in France in 1948. Such a school (*Scuola superiore della pubblica amministrazione*), however, is authorized by the new regulations.

To achieve an effective administration the Italian Parliament must rewrite and rationalize its laws, and must see that the ministers assume responsibility for the policy directives under which the civil servants operate. Ugo La Malfa, secretary of the small Republican party, made reform along these lines a prominent plank in the party platform. It is encouraging to note that the party spectacularly increased its vote in Rome after La Malfa took this stand, an increase that would seem to indicate a desire for change on the part of a significant number of the government employees living in Rome.[22]

---

[21] Decree of the President of the Republic of January 10, 1957, No. 3.

[22] See Ugo La Malfa, "Siamo tutti colpevoli," *L'Espresso,* Rome, November 21, 1964, p. 3. This is a copy of an address made by La Malfa at the Circolo Gaetano Salvemini a week earlier.

9

Local Government

The organs of local government in Italy are the region, the province, the commune, and various and numerous special purpose bodies. Italy is divided into twenty regions (of which five have been given special powers), into ninety-three provinces, about 8000 communes, and countless special purpose bodies. Since the regions are an innovation superimposed on the preexisting local government, we shall start this description with the province, passing on to the commune, to the prefect (the instrument of central control), and to the special purpose bodies, and shall finish the chapter with a description of the regions.[1]

The province

The Italian province (*provincia*) is copied from a creation of Napoleon Bonaparte, the French *département*. Since there are roughly the same number of *province* and *départements* and France is about twice as large as Italy, the average *provincia* is about half as big as the average *département*.

The province serves both as a territorial division for hierarchic decentralization and as the traditional unit of local government (Constitution, Arts. 128–129). It takes its name from its principal city (in this it differs from the *département*), and few cities in Italy manage to reach any distinction without serving as provincial capitals.

[1] Students who read Italian who seek more detailed information on local government should consult G. Solmi, *La provincia nell'ordinamento amministrativo vigente* (Padova: CEDAM, 1953); Guido Zanobini, *Corso di diritto amministrativo,* particularly Vol. III, 6th edition (Milano: Giuffrè, 1958); Costantino Mortati, *Istituzioni di diritto pubblico,* 8th ed. (Padova: CEDAM, 1969), Vol. II, pp. 819–932; and Paolo Barile, Federico Mereu, and Marco Ramat, *Corso di diritto,* Vol. I (*Principi di diritto generale. Diritto pubblico*), (Firenze: La nuova Italia, 1970), pp. 383–418.

The government of the province consists of a locally elected *consiglio provinciale* (provincial council) and an executive body, the *giunta provinciale,* elected by the council from among its own members. The council is composed of forty-five members in the four provinces with over 1,400,000 inhabitants (Milano, Roma, Napoli, Torino), of thirty-six members in the other provinces with over 700,000 inhabitants, of thirty members in the provinces with over 300,000 but not over 700,000 population, and of twenty-four members in the remaining provinces. It is elected for a five-year term. There is no provincial government in Aosta or in Molise, as these former provinces are now regions, and there are no direct provincial elections in Sicily.

The *giunta* is composed of nine members in the four largest provinces, of seven members in the two middle categories, and of five members in the twenty-six provinces with 300,000 or fewer inhabitants. One of the members of the *giunta* is designated president of the province.

The functions of the province are few and lie primarily in the fields of finance and public services. The province collects some taxes and administers provincial property. The province's public services include (1) maintaining the provincial roads, (2) caring for abandoned children and the indigent insane, (3) health services, such as free vaccinations, free quinine for malarial workers, and the maintenance of a medical laboratory, and (4) the maintenance of secondary school buildings.[2]

---

[2] An idea of what a progressive provincial government in Italy does can be had by examining the electoral platform of the Christian Democracy for the province of Torino in 1960. Professor Giuseppe Grosso, the president of the province, said that in the previous four years the province was particularly concerned with road building "in order to give breathing space to Torino and Piedmont," and that in that period the Torino-Ivrea-Val d'Aosta *autostrada* (thruway) was completed and the Ceva-Savona highway was opened to the public, and that in the next four years the province must see to it that the Torino-Asti-Alessandria-Piacenza *autostrada* and the Fréjus tunnel were completed. The province obviously did not pay the entire cost of these means of interprovincial and international communication, but it had borne the initial planning costs itself and would contribute to the building costs. Professor Grosso continued that the province had taken over 1826 kilometers of communal roads and had planned to spend twenty-six billion lire putting them in shape, and that the first part of this task would soon be under way with five billion lire from the province and five billion lire from the state. Another major provincial expenditure was for schools. In the previous eight years five new specialized secondary schools were built and two more were under construction. Professor Grosso promised a half dozen new schools if he and his party won the election. Among the province's other major achievements in recent years, according to Grosso, were a billion lire home for abandoned children and a 225 million lire addition

The Sicilian regional law on local government abolishes the provinces as organs of local government (but not as deconcentrated units of the central government). It gives the communes freedom to establish *liberi consorzi,* which differ from the provinces of the rest of Italy in that rather than being divisions of the state or the regions imposed from above they are agglomerations of communes voluntarily formed by the communes themselves.

The deliberative body of the Sicilian *libero consorzio* is elected indirectly by the common councillors and not directly by the general electorate, as are the provincial councils in the rest of Italy. The Sicilian system would appear in theory to be a distinct improvement for two reasons: (1) it tends to create an atmosphere of cooperation between the commune and the *libero consorzio,* two organs of local government whose functions should be coordinated, and (2) it relieves the voter of the onus of participation in an unnecessary election.

In practice, however, the Sicilian provinces have not been abolished. In the first place, they remain the territorial divisions of the state and the seats of the nine prefects in Sicily. In the second place, the Sicilian communes have not seen fit to form themselves into *liberi consorzi* for local purposes, and about the only practical result of the Sicilian law is the indirect election for the provincial council.

The commune

The commune, the smallest unit of local government in Italy, takes the place of both the municipality and the town (or township) in the United States and of the borough and the rural district in Great Britain. Thus every bit of Italian territory lies within the boundaries of a commune, and all communes, whether they be of the size of Milan and Rome or whether they have a population of a few hundred, have the same legal structure. Also, like the French commune (and the Italian province and the French *département*), the Italian commune is both a unit of local government and an administrative unit of the central government.

The urban commune is a city. The rural commune is normally composed of a number of hamlets called *frazioni.* Although the *frazioni* have no independent power, they often constitute separate election districts, and many have their own branch offices and their own budgets.

---

to its tubercular hospital (*La stampa,* October 6, 1960, p. 2). In recognition of his services as president of the province Grosso was elected Mayor of Turin in 1965. This is an indication of the relative importance of provinces and major cities.

In many parts of Italy there used to be a system of local government similar to the Anglo-American one. The Renaissance was born in city-states, and the importance of cities in northern Italy in the Middle Ages is attested to by the *Lega lombarda* and the writings of Marsilio of Padua. As late as the nineteenth century municipalities had individual charters in the *Regno Lombardo-Veneto,* in Tuscany, and in the Papal States, and, depending on its size and its local traditions, each municipality (or each class of municipality, as the case may have been) exercised the specific authority granted it.[3]

The basic organs of the commune are the common council (*consiglio comunale*), the *giunta comunale,* and the *sindaco.*

The common council is the deliberative body. (The Anglo-Americans, but not the Italians, would say the legislative body.) Depending on the population, the commune is composed of between eighty and fifteen popularly elected councillors,[4] who serve for five years. The election system of the limited vote,[5] used in communes with a population of 5,000 or less, virtually assures a stable majority in the council, and the elections therefore take place with some regularity. Since the elections are not automatic but must be decreed by the central government, the term of office is approximately rather than exactly five years.

The system of proportional representation used in the elections in the larger communes, those with over 5,000 inhabitants, leads frequently to an *impasse* that requires the dissolution of the council and the appointment of a prefect called the *commissario prefettizio* (prefectoral commissioner) to take over all the functions of the dissolved council, its *giunta,* and its chief executive, until new elections are held.

When a common council or a provincial council is dissolved, the law requires a new election within three months, or if the decree of dissolution specifically so states, within six months. This law, however, is a

[3] Zanobini, *Corso,* Vol. III, p. 127.

[4] The six communes with over 500,000 population (Rome, Milan, Naples, Turin, Genoa, Palermo) have eighty-member councils. Communes with between 250,001 and 500,000 population have sixty-member councils. Communes with between 100,001 and 250,000 population have fifty-member councils. Communes with between 30,001 and 100,000 population have forty-member councils. Communes with between 10,001 and 30,000 population have thirty-member councils. Communes with between 3,001 and 10,000 population have twenty-member councils. Communes with less than 3,001 population have fifteen-member councils.

Communes that are provincial capitals have forty-member councils even if their population is less than 30,001. There are three such communes: Sondrio (Lombardia), Enna (Sicily), and Nuoro (Sardinia).

[5] See Chapter 11.

dead letter, and the government has permitted communes of the importance of Florence and Naples to go years without locally elected governments.

The *giunta comunale* is the executive committee of the common council. It is elected by the council from among its own members and is composed of from three to thirteen councillors, including the presiding officer, the *sindaco* (mayor). The election is by a majority vote (of the councillors attending, provided a quorum is present) on the first two ballots and thereafter by a plurality. For the election of the *sindaco* two-thirds of the councillors constitute a quorum.

Like the French *maire,* the Italian *sindaco* is a servant of two masters. He is not only the locally chosen chief executive of the commune; he is also the agent of the central government and is responsible for the performance of certain functions of the national government. The most specific of these functions are those concerned with registering births, marriages, deaths, and migrations. Copies of the documents resulting from these functions, as well as good conduct certificates, are obtained from the *sindaco* acting as a state official. The broader and vaguer powers he exercises in this capacity include the maintenance of public order, public safety, and public health, and the issuance of building permits, which is a state function in Italy.

The most important difference between the similar models of local government in France and Italy is that Italian mayors cannot serve simultaneously as deputies to Parliament, while French mayors can and do. The purpose of this prohibition in Italy may have been an attempt to improve communal government by insisting that the duties of a chief municipal executive required the full attention of the man elected to perform them. The result, however, seems to have been a further weakening of communal government by reducing the political influence of the mayors. On the other hand, Bordeaux is thought to gain more than it loses by having as its perennial mayor Jacques Chaban-Delmas during the years he has served as President of the National Assembly and as Prime Minister. Likewise, Lyons was doubtless well served during the almost half century that Edouard Herriot was its mayor and at the same time deputy, cabinet member, or Prime Minister in Paris; and in Marseilles Gaston Deferre, the Socialist leader, follows the same pattern by being perhaps more the Marseillese ambassador to Paris than the chief administrative officer in Marseilles. In contrast to these figures, Italy's mayors are a politically insignificant lot. It is difficult for them to make a reputation for themselves as administrators because they need authorization from Rome for so many of the things they would like to do, and it is equally difficult for them to exert political influence on a national scale because they are deprived of a seat in Parliament and the political base in Rome that goes with it.

The chief technical advisor of the *sindaco,* particularly in the smaller communes, is the *segretario comunale,* the top permanent communal official. He is the person who knows best what the commune has done, must do, and may do.

The functions of the Italian communes are similar to those of smaller local government units in other countries. In comparison with the United States municipalities, the Italian communes exercise more stringent zoning controls, particularly of an esthetic or historic nature. On the other hand, the ordinance-making power of the Italian commune is more limited. There are no local magistrates in Italy, and the maximum penalty for an infringement of a local ordinance is a fine of 4000 lire ($6.50). Fire protection, normally a municipal function in the United States, is handled by the central government in Italy. The public schools are maintained and controlled from Rome.

Until recently the Italian communes had to bear the costs for various governmental services over which they had no authority or control. These included the building and maintenance of the public schools, of the courthouse for the local judge, and of other public buildings. Since the taxing power of the communes (and the provinces) is so limited[6] that they cannot perform their functions without grants-in-aid, it is absurd to expect them to assume financial responsibility for these other services. A law enacted in September, 1960, released the communes and the provinces from many of these financial responsibilities. In 1968 the state was diverting about 10 per cent of its current expenditures to local government units.[7]

As intimated in the previous paragraph, the financial condition of the communes is precarious. Of the thirty-two communes with a population of over 100,000, only half operated on a balanced budget in 1961. Except Prato, in Tuscany, all of these were either in continental Italy or in the contiguous region of Emilia Romagna. The half operating on a deficit included La Spezia in Liguria, Florence in Tuscany, and the fourteen cities with at least 100,000 population to the south of Florence. Three of these sixteen cities, Naples, Reggio Calabria, and Messina, succeeded in disbursing as wages and pensions more than their total intake.[8]

The prefect and the prefecture

The functions of Italian local government, as described above, do not differ in a substantial manner from Anglo-American local govern-

[6] See *Annuario parlamentare, 1963–64,* pp. 4117–4136, for a detailed description of local taxes.

[7] Statistics derived from *Annuario statistico, 1969,* pp. 333–334.

[8] *Annuario statistico, 1963,* p. 380. In the case of Messina the expenditures for this one item were over 130 per cent of the total receipts.

ment. The difference becomes obvious only on examining the powers of control exercised by the central government. These powers are exercised by a tin god known as the *prefetto* (prefect), assisted and advised by certain auxiliary organs such as the *giunta provinciale amministrativa* and the *consiglio di prefettura*.

The prefect is the representative of the state in the province. He is a high official of the Ministry of the Interior. The majority of the prefects are career men who have worked up the ladder of the hierarchy to the prefectures (from three grades of councillors through two grades of vice prefects to two grades of prefects). The hierarchy contains about 1500 persons, of whom fewer than 10 per cent have the rank of prefect. Not all prefects, however, are career men, and the government is free to appoint anyone to the position and to transfer or remove prefects at will with the proviso that career prefects continue to get paid.

In the interests of public order, or generally in emergencies, the prefect still has on paper almost unlimited decree power. Leading Italian jurists, however, have been almost unanimous in considering these articles unconstitutional, and the Constitutional Court has limited their potential.[9]

The prefect's inclusive powers over the deliberations of the provincial and communal governments rest on the legal fiction that local governments are purely administrative bodies and that as such all their acts, even the deliberations of the councils, are reversible by a higher administrative authority, always on grounds of illegality and sometimes on lack of merit.

The law does not require the formal approval of the prefect for most of the acts of the provincial and communal councils and *giunte,* but only that he be notified. He has twenty days from the date of notification to exercise his veto power, which he can use only on the grounds of the illegality of the act. At any subsequent time, however, the government may still annul any act of a commune or province on grounds of illegality.

The prefect's *visto* (approval) is required for local government contracts, and in these cases the prefect may refuse his approval on the lack of merit as well as the illegality of the proposed contracts. If the contracts involve large sums (the exact limit varies with the population of the commune or the province), the approval of the prefect must be obtained before the contract is negotiated. This type of control is called *controllo preventivo,* and the permission is called an *autorizzazione* (authorization). Other types of act that require an *autorizzazione* include acts that accept donations and acts that impose special taxes.

---

[9] See Constitutional Court decision 8 of 1956 (in *Giurisprudenza costituzionale,* Vol. I. [1956] 602–607) and Mortati, *op. cit.,* pp. 643–645.

Besides these so-called negative controls by which the prefect stops local government agencies from acting, the prefect has certain positive controls, *controlli sostitutivi,* that empower him to act in matters concerning which the local government bodies are required to take action but have failed to do so. Normally, however, the *controllo sostitutivo* is exercised by the *giunta provinciale amministrativa* and not by the prefect.

The prefect's ultimate power over local government is his power to dissolve the provincial or common councils and their respective *giunte,* and to relieve the provincial president or the *sindaco* of his position. The decree that dissolves a council appoints a *commissario prefettizio,* who is usually a prefect, to administer the province or commune pending the next elections. The power of dissolution is legally in the hands of the government and not of the prefect, but the latter may be the instigator of the decree of dissolution. Political expediency rather than objective juridical criteria determine the occasions on which the power is used.

Although the prefect is an administrative officer, his functions are in good part political. In other words, although *de iure* he represents the state, *de facto* he represents the government. One of his principal concerns is to help the government make a good showing in his province whenever there is an election; another is to show courtesy to and do favors for friends of the government. According to his special talents a prefect may be particularly suited to duty (1) in the south, (2) in the Catholic north, or (3) in the red belt. In the south the local governments are usually right or center right and near bankruptcy, and therefore particularly dependent on Rome. The local parties are generally headed by cliques of purely local significance. Here the prefect's job is to buy the support Rome needs by doling out or withholding the favors in his power to bestow.

In the strongly Catholic provinces north of the Po the prefect must be a diplomat of considerable skill. Here the local government units are relatively wealthy and therefore less tolerant of the prefect's presence. Most of his dealings are with warring factions in the Christian Democracy, each of which has its friends in Rome and therefore is dangerous for the prefect to antagonize. In this situation it is sometimes the local leaders and not the prefect that have the upper hand. In the red belt the prefect must do what he can to discredit the local government and give aid and comfort to the opposition. He must be careful, however, not to become overzealous, for "the tactics of harassment may backfire . . . left wing councils deliberately court the veto of welfare schemes, . . . they sometimes succeed in appeals against prefectoral decisions to the Council of State, and . . . under close prefectoral surveillance they have avoided the scandals that have occurred in many of the centrist and right wing communes and have produced the most respected local government performances in the country."[10]

A distinguished authority has said that Italy will never be really democratic so long as there persists that type of centralized government of which the prefect is the symbol. "Those who speak of democracy . . . of popular sovereignty, and of self-determination, and forget about the prefect don't know what they are talking about. Elections, . . . parliaments, constitutional assemblies, responsible ministers, are but a solemn farce when the government remains centralized in the Napoleonic fashion. . . . In countries where democracy is more than a vain word people manage their own local affairs without awaiting the suggestions or the permission of the central government. . . . A political class cannot be formed if the person elected to manage the municipal . . . affairs is not fully responsible for his own actions. If some one can give him orders and countermand his acts the elected official has no responsibility and does not learn how to administer. He merely learns to obey, to intrigue, to recommend, and to seek influence."[11]

In spite of Professor Einaudi's strongly worded admonition, there seems little chance of getting rid of the prefect. Mario Scelba, a former Interior Minister, cannot claim the prestige and the intellectual preeminence of Italy's first president, but his opinion on the use of prefects as given in an interview to *La nazione* unfortunately carries more political weight than that which Professor Einaudi can muster. Scelba said that "if the prefect did not exist it would be necessary to create him. His function is essential; he cannot be dispensed with."[12] On the other hand, Costantino Mortati, one of Italy's most distinguished jurists, concludes the section on prefects of his treatise on public law with this comment: "In reality the prefect remains an instrument of the domination . . . of the party in power, an instrument of political corruption and malpractice."[13]

It would appear, therefore, that for the present Italy will have to be satisfied with the modest retrenchment in the power of the prefects as a result of parliamentary activity and the decisions of the Constitutional Court.

[10] Robert C. Fried, *The Italian Prefects* (New Haven: Yale University Press, 1963), pp. 256–257.

[11] Luigi Einaudi, "Via il prefetto," *Gazzetta ticinese,* July 17, 1944, reprinted in Luigi Einaudi, *Il buon governo* (Bari: Laterza, 1954), pp. 52–59, at 53–54.

[12] *La nazione,* September 25, 1960, p. 1.

[13] Mortati, *op. cit.,* p. 764.

The giunte provinciali amministrative

The *giunta provinciale amministrativa* (GPA) is composed of ten members; the prefect (or his substitute), the provincial representative of the Ministry of Finance (*Intendente di finanza*), four other officials of the prefecture, and four persons elected by, but not members of, the provincial legislature (*consiglio provinciale*). It determines the expediency of the *deliberazioni* of local government bodies that have to do with finance. By the exercise of this power an unfriendly GPA can hamstring a communal (or provincial) council by refusing its consent to any nonobligatory expense. The left wing councils particularly complain that this power is used to prevent them from functioning properly.

The consiglio di prefettura

The *consiglio di prefettura* is an advisory body composed of the prefect and two assistants. The prefect may always and must sometimes seek the advice of this council.

The *consiglio di prefettura* appears to be a useless body. Its lack of "any independence whatsoever from the administration . . . gives a virtually illusory value to its opinions," and the only thing other than inertia that has prevented its abolition is that it does little if any real harm.[14]

Minor advisory committees

The prefect is also surrounded with a number of special committees to advise him on technical matters. These include a public health committee, a public welfare committee (*comitato provinciale di assistenza e beneficenza pubblica*), and committees on insane asylums, drug stores, and retail liquor stores. There even appears to be a special advisory committee on the licensing of operators of boilers.[15] These committees are normally composed of *ex officio* and appointed members.

Provincial health officers

Parliament has freed two technicians, the *medico provinciale* and the *veterinario provinciale* (provincial physician and provincial veterinary) almost completely from prefectoral supervision and has made them responsible for public health administration within the province. This practice, which seems normal enough to an American, is novel to Italy,

---

[14] Zanobini, *Corso,* III, p. 106.
[15] *Ibid.,* p. 109.

where experts are supposed to be on tap only and administrative power is normally left in the hands of persons trained in the law.

The questore and the questura

After the prefect the most important state officer in the province is the *questore,* the chief of police. His headquarters are called the *questura.* Most police work other than traffic control in the cities is done by the national police, who are mainly responsible for public order and for crime detection. The *questore* is the prefect's chief assistant in all that concerns public safety and public order.

A number of ministries are deconcentrated to the degree of maintaining provincial offices, whose names are often difficult and perhaps fruitless to translate. Among these are the Ministry of Finance with its *Intendenze di finanze,* the Ministry of Agriculture with its *Ispettorati provinciali* (see *supra,* Chapter 8), the Ministry of Education with its *Provveditorati agli studi,* and the Ministry of Public Works with its civil engineers' offices (*Uffici del genio civile*). Other central administrations have preferred to decentralize to larger units, comprising several provinces and sometimes more than an entire region. Included among them are the Superintendencies of Antiquities and Fine Arts, the state railways, the postal and telephone services, the *Corte dei conti,* and the *Avvocatura dello stato.* For the last two bodies see *infra,* Chapter 10.

Special local government units
(l'amministrazione autarchica non territoriale)

Italian law requires or permits, as the case may be, the establishment of special purpose local government units. Many of these units can be classified in one of the following categories: charitable bodies, *consorzi,* and chambers of commerce.

(*a*) *Charitable bodies.* Each commune is required by law to set up an *Ente communale d'assistenza* (ECA). The funds for these bodies come in part from the commune and in part from private donations. There is a long tradition in Switzerland that wealthy people without heirs leave part or all of their estates to their commune for charitable purposes, and this practice is not infrequent in north Italy.

The ECA is administered by a committee whose members are elected by the common council and approved by the prefect. The number of committeemen depends on the population of the commune. The ECA, like other semi-independent local government units, is under the tutelage of the prefect. He can annul its acts on legal grounds. The control over the merits of the acts of the ECA is exercised by the *Comitato provinciale di assistenza e beneficenza pubblica* (Provincial Social Welfare Committee) of whose eleven members three are elected by the *Consiglio provinciale,* five, including the prefect, are government officials, two are labor representatives, and one is appointed by government officials.

Other state-controlled charitable institutions may be established to operate in different territories (i.e., a *frazione,* or two or more communes), and the state is permitted to unite and divide existing bodies.

(*b*) *Consorzi.* The word *consorzio* (pl. *consorzi*) in the present context refers to a special body set up by two or more communes or provinces to carry out certain of their functions. *Consorzi* may operate public utilities; they often supply agricultural services. The ECA may also form *consorzi.*

Consorzi are under the same tutelage of the prefect as are the provinces and communes. If the *consorzio* operates in more than one province the prefect of the province in which its head office (*sede*) is located is responsible.

The state itself is a member of some *consorzi* that are primarily local in their operation but which affect national interests. An example is the *Consorzio autonomo per le opere del porto di Genova,* a Genoa port authority somewhat comparable to the New York Port Authority, jointly managed by the states of New York and New Jersey. Another *consorzio* with state representation is the *Ente autonomo per l'acquedotto pugliese* (Puglie Aqueduct Authority).

(*c*) *Chambers of Commerce.* The *Camera di commercio, industria, artigianato e agricoltura* (Chamber of Commerce, Industry, Crafts and Agriculture) is often referred to in Italy by the shorter title, Chamber of Commerce. This is a public body representing the business interests within a province. These chambers exercise a limited control over the economic life of the province. They have a taxing power, they gather statistics and prepare official lists of certain types of industrial and commercial experts, and their authorization is necessary for certain activities (e.g., selling silkworms), and they have the power to require certain other actions (e.g., replanting of olive trees).[16] Their major function is the compilation of the local commercial usages that will be applied in local contracts.[17]

[16] Decree of the President of the Republic, No. 987 of 1955, Arts. 63 and 72.

[17] See, for example, Camera di Commercio, industria e agricoltura, *Raccolta degli usi e delle consuetudini commerciali della provincia di Firenze,* Firenze, 1953.

The regions

One of the major innovations of the Constitution is the division of Italy into regions and the granting of a degree of local autonomy to each. The regions generally correspond to geographically distinct territories, each with a local history and culture. The regions had long been recognized *de facto,* but since Italian unity they had exercised no juridical functions.

The nineteenth-century liberals who united Italy had feared regionalism. They saw the need for national unity and were therefore willing to follow the pattern of Napoleon, who in his passion for unity destroyed the French regions (*provinces*). The twentieth-century liberals, having suffered under the centralized government of Mussolini, saw the region as yet another device to thwart some future scoundrel who might seek tyrannical power.

Another factor that encouraged the Constituent Assembly to create the regions and to grant them some autonomy was the fear of losing territory. Italy was fighting diplomatic battles to keep the province of Aosta from going to France, to keep the province of Bolzano from being ceded to Austria, and to draw the most favorable frontier possible on the Yugoslav border. Besides these international troubles to the northwest, north, and northeast, a number of vociferous Sicilians were clamoring for independence with apparently some slight intention of joining the United States of America.

Being unwilling to grant the core of Italy the degree of autonomy that its policy of appeasement made it advisable to offer the periphery, the Constituent Assembly created two classes of regions. Special grants of autonomy were to be bestowed on Val d'Aosta, Trentino-Alto Adige, Friuli-Venezia Giulia, Sicily, and Sardinia, and denied to the other regions. The special autonomy would be granted in special charters for each of these five regions (Constitution, Art. 116).

Val d'Aosta, as a result of French aspirations to the territory, had been made a semiautonomous region in 1946. Semiautonomy for Sicily was considered of such urgency that the provisional government prepared and promulgated a hastily and ill-conceived constitution for that difficult isle. Almost two years later the constitutions of Sardinia, Val d'Aosta, and Trentino-Alto Adige were promulgated. The constitution of Friuli-Venezia Giulia was finally enacted by the constitutional law of January 31, 1963, and the regional government started operating in 1964. The constitutional amendment of December 27, 1963, No. 3, detached the province of Molise from the Abruzzi and established the twentieth region of Italy. Molise with a resident population of 358,052 in 1961 became the second smallest region (Val d'Aosta had 100,959 inhabitants). Pressure from local interests rather than sober administrative policy appears to have motivated the establishment of this region.

In 1953 Parliament enacted a law setting up the institutions of the ordinary regions and determining their powers, but other essential legislation was not enacted until 1970, and the first elections for these regional councils were held in June of that year. By the spring of 1971 the assemblies had in most cases managed to write their constitutions and to submit them to parliament for approval. Most of the regions, however, had formed governments while awaiting approval of their constitutions. The three regions in the "red belt" — Emilia Romagna, Tuscany, and Umbria — had set up coalition governments with the Communists.

The examination of the regional constitutions by parliament takes time and care. It is important that they include no unconstitutional provisions and that they make provision for carrying out all the functions delegated to them. It is not expected that the regions will be in operation before 1972.[18]

The organs of regional government are similar to those of the province and the commune. Each has a single-chamber deliberative body called a *consiglio* (the Sicilian body is called *assemblea*), a *giunta,* and a president. The regional councils, however, have presidents that are distinct from the presidents of the *giunte.* All these officers are supervised by a superprefect called the *commissario* (commissioner), appointed by the central government. The *commissario* is assisted by a committee similar in makeup and powers to the GPA.

The veto power of the *commissario,* however, does not extend beyond the administrative acts of the region. When the region exercises legislative power in a manner that the *commissario* deems illegal or contrary to the national interest or the interest of another region, he must inform Rome. The Government may then exercise a suspensive veto, which in turn may be overridden by another vote in the regional council supporting the act by an absolute majority. If the Government is still opposed it has a choice of actions, depending on whether it claims the regional law is (1) illegal or (2) inexpedient. In the former case it takes the dispute to the Constitutional Court; in the second case it takes it before Parliament for action. If Parliament in effect vetoes the regional law the region can take the act of Parliament before the Constitutional Court, which must decide whether or not Parliament was justified, on the grounds of national interest or the interest of another region, in acting as it did. It is worthy of note that the state's power to

[18] The draft constitution of Piedmont is printed in full in *La stampa,* December 8, 1970, p. 11. For a discussion of the "red belt" constitutions see Paolo Barile, "Gli statuti delle regioni rosse," *La stampa,* January 12, 1971, p. 8.

overrule regional bills that it deems contrary to the national interest lapses when the bill has been approved by the *commissario*.[19]

The Government may dissolve the organs of the regional governments, after it has heard the advice of a special thirty-man parliamentary committee. The decree of dissolution must also name three commissioners from the region who are to take over the regional government. Their major responsibility is to prepare new elections within a three-month period.

The major differences between the autonomy granted the special regions and that granted the ordinary regions lie in the exclusiveness of the legislative power granted the special regions over certain matters (the ordinary regions have only concurrent powers) and in the greater taxing power of the special regions.

After sixteen years or more of regional governments in operation it is not possible to give much of an evaluation of this attempt at decentralization. The five experiments have produced varying results.

The northeastern regions of Trentino-Alto Adige and Friuli-Venezia Giulia appear to operate efficiently and without fanfare. The others have made a less positive impression. Sardinian administration has bogged down. Val d'Aosta has suffered from government scandals and party indiscipline, and the regional government of Sicily has been an embarrassment and a disgrace.

Perhaps the biggest incognito of the regional governments is their financial position. Like other units of local government in Italy, the regions have a limited direct taxing power and are expected to live off percentages of state taxes that are turned over to them. The state has been extremely liberal in the case of the five semiautonomous regions, each of which was still solvent at the time of writing. It is not healthy, however, for governments to live off handouts. If they have no responsibility for or control over their income they can hardly be expected to have a more highly developed financial maturity than the adolescent spending his allowance. The real catch, however, will come as state funds are made available to all regions. The subsidies to the five semiautonomous regions as established in their constitutions vary greatly. It is true that the regions do perform some of the work that previously was done by the state, but the price paid seems more than it is worth. Professor Einaudi estimated that if the Trentino–Alto Adige subsidies were applied on a state-wide basis the regions would be receiving 18 to 19 per cent of the state's annual income, while if the Sicilian subsidies were applied, the regions would be spending 61 to 62 per cent of the

[19] See Livio Paladin, "Il limite in merito delle leggi regionali," *Rivista trimestrale di diritto pubblico,* VII (1957), pp. 624–666.

annual Italian national income.[20] The compromise solution reached in the 1970 law on regional finance assigns funds to the regions on a per capita basis and gives supplementary grants to poor regions. This is the system the Swiss employ in giving special aid to their poor cantons.

The advent of the regions should logically lead to a reassessment of the role of the provinces. Ugo La Malfa, secretary of the Republican party, has strongly advocated the elimination of the province as a unit of local government. This will be difficult to accomplish, however, as the provincial councils are provided for in the Constitution (Arts. 128 and VIII). Useless organs of government are loath to die, and their tenacity in clinging to an ignoble and unproductive life is greatly aided when, as in Italy, they are protected by the massive inertia of a weary but selfish bureaucracy. The future role of the provinces should probably be that of decentralized organs of the region. The continued election of provincial councils — along with communal and regional councils — will be likely in the long run to bore the voter and thereby reduce the seriousness with which he participates in the political process.

The efficiency of the regions could doubtless be increased if their boundaries were altered to change historical divisions into viable socioeconomic units, and the Constitution gives Parliament the power to do this. This is not the place to make highly controversial recommendations, all of which would find strong attackers and defenders. Brescia and Bergamo, however, have conceivably more in common with the Veneto than with Milan, and it is certainly arguable that small and relatively poor regions like Umbria and the Marche could benefit by incorporation into their larger and wealthier neighbors, Tuscany and Emilia Romagna. So far Parliament's single action, that of creating a separate region of Molise, has been in the wrong direction.

[20] Luigi Einaudi, "Che cosa rimarrebbe allo stato?" in Luigi Einaudi, *Prediche inutili, dispensa sesta* (Turin: Giulio Einaudi, 1959), pp. 335–359, at p. 357. See also Einaudi and Répaci, *op. cit.,* pp. 426–428, for a detailed list of the taxing powers of the regions.

10

The Judicial System

The Italian judicial system consists of a series of courts and a body of career judges, resembling that of France. In both states the judges are career civil servants; there is a tendency towards a plural bench, and there is interchangeability between the positions of judge and of prosecuting attorney in a single career service. Finally, both countries have set up in their postwar constitutions a new institution, the High Judicial Council, which is intended to guarantee the independence of the judiciary.

The Courts

Italian courts either form part of the regular court hierarchy, or they are special courts outside this hierarchy, having a specific and limited competence.

The ordinary courts

The Italian judicial system is unified. There are no regional courts in Italy corresponding to the American state court systems. Every Italian court is part of the national network.

The lowest rung in the Italian judicial hierarchy is the *conciliatore*, the Italian equivalent of the French *juge de paix*. The *conciliatore* has only civil jurisdiction, receives no salary other than fees, and is chosen from among the educated men in the community respected for their honesty and impartiality. He hears cases involving up to 50,000 lire ($80), and his decisions can be appealed to the next higher judicial authority, which is the pretor.

The pretor (*pretore*) is the lowest of the career judges. He has jurisdiction over minor civil and criminal matters within his district (*mandamento giudiziario*). There are about a thousand such districts, but there are many more than a thousand pretors, as the more populous districts keep many pretors busy. The pretor is the only Italian judge, other than the *conciliatore,* who judges alone. Although he is at the bottom of the judicial hierarchy, he is not a man without power. His jurisdiction in criminal cases extends to those crimes for which the maximum penalty is three years' imprisonment.

The court above the pretor is the tribunal (*tribunale*), of which there are about 150 in Italy, one in every provincial capital and in some fifty other towns, mostly in Piedmont or southern Italy. These courts have a plural bench, like the French *tribunaux*. Three judges hear a case. The tribunals have more than 450 judges, however, because in the larger towns there is more than one section of the tribunal. These courts have original jurisdiction over civil cases involving too much money for the pretors' competence and criminal cases involving crimes for which the punishment is beyond the competence of the pretors to impose. They also act as appellate courts for the cases previously tried by the pretors.

Civil and criminal appeals may be taken from the tribunals to a court of appeals (*corte d'appello*), of which there are twenty-three. There is a court of appeals located in each regional capital except Aosta and Campobasso. There are extra courts in Brescia (Lombardy), Lecce (Puglie), and Catania, Caltanissetta, and Messina (Sicily), and a special section of the Catanzaro (Calabria) court sits at Reggio di Calabria. Cases before the court of appeals are heard by five judges, and questions of both fact and law are reviewed.

In its normal guise the court of appeals has only appellate jurisdiction. Judges from the court of appeals, however, form a number of courts of specialized jurisdiction, some of which hear cases in the first instance.

The most important of these specialized courts is the court of assizes (*corte d'assise*), which has primary jurisdiction over major felonies. It is composed of two judges and six laymen, who judge the law and the facts together, and not separately as do judge and jury in the Anglo-American system. An appellate section, composed again of two judges and six laymen, hears appeals from the court of assizes. The educational requirement for the laymen, which for the courts of the first instance was eight years of school, rises to eleven for the appellate section.

The *tribunale regionale delle acque pubbliche* (water rights court) has competence over the highly technical problems concerning water rights. It is composed of a regular five-judge section of the court of appeals with the addition of three engineers designated by the Ministry of Public Works. Not every court of appeals has a *tribunale regionale delle acque pubbliche;* thus some of these water courts have a wider territorial jurisdiction than that of the other sections of the same court of appeals.

A special appeals court, the *tribunale superiore delle acque pubbliche,* composed of five regular career judges, four Councillors of State, and three experts from the High Council of the Ministry of Public Works, hears appeals from the regional water rights courts.

The highest court in the regular hierarchy is the Court of Cassation (*Corte di cassazione*). Like its French equivalent this court has only appellate jurisdiction, gives judgment only on points of law, and either sustains or quashes the decision of the lower court. When it quashes a decision and the case is remanded to a lower court for further proceedings, it is sent to a court or a section of a court other than that from which the case was appealed. The Court of Cassation is composed of more than 150 judges. It is divided into three civil sections and four criminal sections, the former with about twenty-five judges each and the latter with about twenty each. Only seven judges, however, hear a single case. Two further sections, called the united sections (*sezioni unite*), one of which is for civil cases and the other for criminal cases, and which are composed of the highest ranking judges of the other seven sections, hear the most important cases. Here the bench is composed of eleven judges. The chief justice (*primo presidente*) assigns the cases to the sections, including the united sections.

The special courts

The Constitution states that there shall be no special courts (Art. 102), although the following articles establish or sanction two types of such courts. These are (a) the administrative courts and (b) the courts martial. There also remain in Italy a vast network of tax courts and, on paper at least, a High Court for Sicily, the continued existence of which appears to be a violation of the spirit and the letter of the Constitution. The Constitutional Court seems to have relieved the High Court of all its powers, and the body has not met in over a decade and has no address.[1] The Constitutional Court has sanctioned the continued operation of the tax courts until Parliament at its discretion determines to abolish them.[2]

[1] See decision No. 38 of 1957 and a 1970 decision reported in *La stampa,* January 24, 1970, p. 9.

[2] Decision of March 13, 1957, No. 41, reported in *Giurisprudenza costituzionale,* II (1957), pp. 511 ff.

(*a*) *The administrative courts.*[3] Like the French, the Italians have a system of administrative justice that is separate from the regular judicial system. The French system, however, is unitary and is independent of the regular courts in that the decision of the highest French administrative court, the *Conseil d'état,* may not be appealed to the Court of Cassation. The Italians, on the other hand, have a dual system composed of two distinct judicial hierarchies, the one culminating in the *Consiglio di stato,* and the other in the *Corte dei conti.* In each case appeals on questions of jurisdiction may be taken to the Court of Cassation and on questions on the constitutionality of law, to the Constitutional Court.

The American student should bear in mind that neither of these systems has much in common with the administrative tribunals of the United States. The American administrative tribunals are essentially regulatory bodies that supervise and control certain facets of American life. The French and Italian systems have as their primary purposes (1) the protection of the individual against arbitrary or negligent acts on the part of the administration, and (2) the supervision and control of public funds. In America the former function is performed by the regular courts, by the Court of Claims, and by private bills, and the supervision of public funds is performed by the Controller General, working where necessary in conjunction with the regular courts.

(1) *The Consiglio di stato.* Like its French counterpart the *Conseil d'état,* the *Consiglio di stato* (Council of State), is the top organ of the administrative branch of the state. In both countries the judicial sections of the Council serve as administrative courts that hear cases in the first instance or on appeal.

The *Consiglio di stato* is composed of eighty-seven members (Law of December 21, 1950, No. 1018). It is divided into six sections, of which three perform its judicial functions. The Councillors alternate periodically between the administrative and the judicial sections. The judicial sections consist of about twelve judges, eight of whom hear a single case. There is no appeal from the decisions of the *Consiglio di stato* except one on jurisdictional grounds to the Court of Cassation. In case a particularly important question arises, or one that has been decided differently by the single sections, the Council may hear it *in adunanza plenaria* (in plenary session). This means the top councillors

[3] Informative articles in English on administrative courts and administrative law include Giovanni Miele *et al.,* "Italian Administrative Law," *International and Comparative Law Quarterly,* 1954, 421–453; and Giuseppino Treves, "Judicial Review in Italian Administration," *University of Chicago Law Review,* XXVI (1959), 419–435.

from each judicial section meet together to hear the case. A separate section of the *Consiglio di stato,* called the *Consiglio di giustizia amministrativa per la regione siciliana,* sits at Palermo.

There are important differences between the French and Italian Councils of State. In Italy the jurisdiction of the *Consiglio di stato* is limited to the annulment of administrative acts; these courts do not award damages to persons whose rights have been adversely affected by acts of the administration. To use the French terminology, they hear the *recours pour excès de pouvoir* and not the *recours contentieux de pleine juridiction,* which latter in Italy are within the competence of the regular courts. The precise distinction made in Italian law is between rights and *interessi legittimi* (legitimate interests). Legitimate interests are defined as individual interests strictly connected with public interests and protected only through the protection of the latter.[4] A citizen, for example, has a right to damages before the regular courts against tortious action on the part of the administration, but he has only a legitimate interest with respect to the validity of an ordinance that adversely affects him.[5]

Another major distinction between Italian and French administrative law is that whereas in France the *Conseil d'état* determines only the legality of administrative acts and the responsibility of the state for damages, in Italy the *Consiglio di stato* has the right to judge the merits of administrative acts. The *Consiglio di stato,* however, exercises this latter power with diffidence and discretion, and the cases in which the power can be used are spelt out in the law.[6] It is mainly used when the administration refuses to act in accordance with a previous decision of the *Consiglio di stato* and the action is of a mandatory rather than a discretionary nature. In these cases the court, besides annulling the administrative act, may act in its own right.

The traditional function of the *Consiglio di stato* was to serve as a consultative body to the monarch, in something like the way the *curia regis* of William I functioned. Originally, therefore, the *Consiglio di stato* merely advised the king on legal matters, and its decisions were not binding. In this case the jurists spoke of *giustizia ritenuta,* accord-

---

[4] Roberto Coltelli ("Note sui limiti della tutela degli interessi privati nel giudizio amministrativo di legittimità," 17 *Rivista trimestrale di diritto pubblico* (1967), pp. 340–383) criticizes the *Consiglio di stato* for its tradition of unnecessarily restrictive interpretations of *interesse legittimo* and the consequent lack of protection afforded the individual.

[5] For a discussion of *interessi legittimi* see Mortati, *op. cit.,* pp. 168–172. For the whole field of administrative justice see Guido Zanobini, *Corso di diritto amministrativo,* Vols. I-VI (Milan: Giuffre, 1958–59), and Enrico Guicciardi, *La giustizia amministrativa* (Padua: CEDAM, 1957).

[6] Royal Decree of June 26, 1924, No. 1054, Art. 27.

ing to which the power of judgment was retained by the monarch.[7]

In Italy today this essentially anachronistic system is still in operation side by side with the more modern system of administrative justice attributed directly to the *Consiglio di stato.* It is therefore possible for the Italian citizen with an *interesse legittimo* to protect, either (1) to start action before the *Consiglio di stato,* or (2) to take a *ricorso straordinario al presidente della repubblica* (extraordinary plea to the President of the Republic). In the latter case the plea goes from the Minister of Justice to the *Consiglio di stato* for its opinion, which opinion the Minister normally accepts. Recourse to this pleading precludes any future appeal directly to the *Consiglio di stato.*[8]

The redundancy of these procedures, both of which lead to the *Consiglio di stato,* is much to the distaste of those theorists who seek symmetry, logic, and simplicity in the legal process. The justification for the retention of the *ricorso straordinario* lies in its rules of procedure. It permits appeal within 180 days instead of only sixty days after notification, as is the case with the regular procedure and it is cheaper in that a lawyer is not necessary.

(2) *The Corte dei conti.* The Court of Accounts is a special administrative court that is somewhat analogous to the French *Cour des comptes.* Like the *Consiglio di stato,* the *Corte dei conti* is both an administrative and a judicial body.

The judicial functions of the *Corte dei conti* deal primarily with fiscal matters. It decides cases concerning the handling of public moneys and concerning the responsibility of public servants in their official capacity for tortious actions against the state. It also hears cases dealing with government pensions, including war pensions, and cases concerning the rights of its own members that arise from their employment contract. As a result of a Constitutional Court decision denying the power to serve as provincial courts of the first instance for fiscal matters to the *Consigli di prefettura,* the *Corte dei conti* has decentralized itself and established regional branches to handle cases arising from local government activities. Appeals from the *Corte dei conti* can be taken to the *sezioni unite* (united sections) of the same court, and on jurisdictional grounds to the Court of Cassation. There is no appeal

[7] For the different administrative law systems, see Henry Puget and Georges Maléville, *La revision des décisions administratives sur le recours des administrés* (Bruxelles: Institut international des sciences administratives, 1935).

[8] See Vittorio Bachelet, "Ricorso straordinario al capo dello stato e garanzia giurisdizionale," *Rivista trimestrale di diritto pubblico,* IX (1959), pp. 788–843, and Guglielmo Roehrssen, "Il ricorso straordinario al capo dello stato, sopravvivenza o abolizione?" *Rassegna dei lavori pubblici,* (1957).

from the *Corte dei conti* to the *Consiglio di stato* as there is in France.

A procedural peculiarity of the *Corte dei conti* is its wide powers of decision. This body has the extraordinary power, not granted the regular courts or the *Consiglio di stato,* to go beyond the original petition or the issues raised by the parties.

Eight of the nine sections of the *Corte dei conti* at Rome are judicial sections, and six of these hear pension cases exclusively. The judicial sections are composed of approximately ten members each. The law requires an uneven number of judges and at least five to hear each case (at least eleven before the *sezioni riunite*).

(*b*) *The courts martial.* The courts martial (*tribunali militari*) have criminal jurisdiction over cases involving military personnel on active duty and even over reserve personnel on unlimited leave, with respect to certain military crimes. Until the law of March 23, 1965, No. 167, was passed, the military courts claimed a vast jurisdiction over reserve personnel and actually convicted two journalists for writing articles critical of and distasteful to the army.[9] There is appeal from the courts martial to the Court of Cassation. Whereas the appeal to the Court of Cassation from the *Consiglio di stato* and from the *Corte dei conti* is limited to questions of jurisdiction, the Constitution gives a general appeal from the courts martial on points of law. According to some authorities this constitutional provision renders superfluous the continued operation of a court of military appeals.[10]

(*c*) *Other special courts.* Numerous other special courts exist in spite of the constitutional admonition that they should be abolished by December 31, 1952. They all deal with fiscal problems and can be classified under six major types.

1. Courts judging disputes over taxes on land improvements (*terreni e fabbricati*).
2. Courts judging disputes over direct taxes and indirect business taxes.
3. Courts judging disputes over assessed value of shares and bonds.
4. Courts judging disputes over stamp taxes and certain other special taxes.
5. Courts judging disputes over tariffs, alcohol and sugar taxes, etc.
6. Courts judging disputes over local taxes.

[9] See Piero Calamandrei, *Dall'Arcadia a Peschiera* (Bari: Laterza, 1954).

[10] See Mortati, *op. cit.,* p. 1208; also decision of the Constitutional Court of July 8, 1957, No. 119, in *Giurisprudenza costituzionale,* II (1957), p. 1082.

These special courts are made up in various manners, but the majority of the judges appear to be civil servants drawn from the administration.

The courts under Nos. 1, 2, and 6 above are in three grades (usually communal, provincial, and national), thus allowing two appeals. Those under Nos. 3, 4, and 5 are in two grades. The reluctant taxpayer who has appealed all the way up the ladder without getting the relief he seeks may then start near the bottom of the ladder in the regular courts (normally the *tribunali*) and work up in three more grades to the Court of Cassation.

In 1953 the Minister of Finance, on the basis of a study made in his ministry, presented a constitutional law (it would be called an Amendment to the Constitution in the United States) to legitimate the continued existence of these courts. The proposal was not acted on, but on the other hand no steps appear to have been taken to abolish them.[11]

The Legal Officers

The judges

With certain exceptions, mostly at the top and bottom of the ladder, Italian judges, like their French brethren, are career civil servants. The exceptions include the *conciliatori,* the lay judges of the Courts of Assizes, and some of the judges on the special courts.

Entrance to the service is by an examination taken after graduation from law school. As a career, that of judge normally appeals to the moderately good student. The good student prefers the bar, where a fortune can be made if he is very good and where he can choose the town in which he wants to live and the type of cases he wants to take.

The career usually starts with a tour of duty as pretor in a rural center. As is likely to be the case in a large hierarchy with few posts at the top, progress up the ladder often depends on other qualities than pure ability. Influence is much sought after, and often appearances count more than realities. A clearly written opinion may bring more credit than a just decision.[12]

[11] See Luigi Einaudi and Francesco Répaci, *Il sistema tributario italiano* (Turin: Edizioni scientifiche Einaudi, 1954), pp. 462–480, and Gaetano Azzariti, "La mancata applicazione della costituzione e l'opera della magistratura," *Scritti giuridici in memoria di Piero Calamandrei* (Padua: CEDAM, 1958), IV, pp. 3–24.

[12] See Piero Calamandrei, *Elogio dei giudici* (Florence: Le Monnier, 2nd ed., 1938, and 3rd enlarged ed., 1955); and Piero Calamandrei, *Processo e democrazia* (Padua: CEDAM, 1954), translated as *Eulogy of Judges* (Princeton: Princeton University Press, 1942), and *Procedure and Democracy* (New York: New York University Press, 1957).

There are more than 6000 career judges in Italy, and only about 100 in England. One reason for this difference is that in Great Britain (as in the United States) it is the general practice to try a case in the first instance before a single judge, whereas all but the lowest of the Italian courts are presided over by a panel of judges. The Franco-Italian predilection for the plural bench seems to be based on the theory that three men are less likely to be prejudiced than one.[13] The Anglo-American reply is that one man is more responsible than three. In the Anglo-American system a single man has the moral responsibility for the decision; he cannot shirk this resposibility by putting the blame on his associates. The sense of responsibility of the Anglo-American judge is further enhanced by the fact that his assent to or dissent from the court's decision, even when he is a member of a plural bench, is part of the official court record, whereas in France and Italy dissenting opinions are not permitted, and there is a fiction of unanimity in each decision.[14]

Another reason for the small number of British career judges is their great prestige. They do not form a civil service entered upon in youth. They are appointed after reaching intellectual maturity from among the most distinguished barristers of the realm. The high office of judge thus becomes the culmination of the career of the best legal minds in England. No wonder that the British are willing to entrust the solution of legal disputes to a single man, with or without the assistance of a jury.

Still another reason for the remarkable difference between the number of judges in England and in Italy is found in the greater celerity of justice in England and the relatively small number of appeals. An Italian observer has considered that an essential element in that celerity is the sense of loyal collaboration that exists between lawyers and judges in England.[15]

Like so much of the world in the seventies, the Italian judges acrimoniously disagree over a fundamental postulate in legal philosophy. Many of the older judges and a few of the younger ones subscribe to the traditional concept of the judicial function, i.e., that of objectively and impassibly applying the general precepts of the law to the specific

[13] See Montesquieu, *De l'esprit des lois,* Livre VI, ch. vii, "Du magistrat unique."

[14] For a strong advocacy of the Anglo-American system and a proposal that it be adopted in Italy, at least for the Constitutional Court, see Costantino Mortati, "Considerazioni sul problema del "dissent" nelle pronuncie della corte costituzionale italiana," in *La giustizia costituzionale. op. cit.,* pp. 155–172. Mortati, a distinguished professor of constitutional law, is now serving as judge of the Constitutional Court.

[15] Calamandrei, *Processo e democrazia, op. cit.,* p. 135.

facts brought before their notice. According to this doctrine a judge has no moral responsibility for his decisions so long as he has followed the law, and the judicial function becomes one that a scientifically oriented society might better entrust to computers. Most of the younger judges and a smattering of the older ones believe that the law must inevitably be interpreted according to some standard of values, that the proper standard of values for interpreting the Italian law is the letter and particularly the spirit of the Constitution, and furthermore, that when laws enacted by a fascist state with a far different social philosophy are still in effect and are being applied today, they should be construed not in the light of their fascist past but rather in accordance with the principles of liberal democracy as found in the Constitution.[16]

Although this basic split extends to all branches of the law, it is in the application of the criminal law that the contrast and the tension are greatest, for it is the fascist criminal law that is most at variance with the principles of the new Constitution.[17] The intolerance shown by many judges for modern social values, particularly the values affirmed by conspicuous elements of the younger generation, and their consequent incomprehension of these values are in part the result of the social and regional class from which an unfortunately large number of the judiciary are recruited. A traditional predilection for the law, strengthened in many cases by the lack of an economically viable alternative to government service, brings into the judiciary a disproportionate number of the sons of the petty bourgeoisie of the small towns in the south of Italy, men of drab cultural horizons, hemmed in by puritanical repressions and hypocrisy, whose background gives them few clues to an understanding of the value system of a modern city. The conventional morality of the middle class of a small southern town is not an acceptable standard by which an industrial society can operate. Some of the young men from this background have the sensitivity, the humanity, and the versatility to adapt themselves to their new surroundings; others who feel incompetent and ostracized in their new

[16] For a general discussion of the problem see Calamandrei, *Processo e democrazia, op. cit.*

[17] For an account of the political schisms in the judges' professional associations see "La Magistratura in Italia," *Il ponte,* XXIV (1968), pp. 715–928 and particularly Luigi Bianchi D'Espinosa, "Il problema politico-giudiziario della Cassazione" (pp. 762–796). See also Roberto Sciacchitano, "Magistrati divisi," *Il ponte,* XXVI (1970), pp. 231–37, and the comment of Marco Ramat that follows, pp. 237–39. For an account of the dispute between the Constitutional Court and the Criminal Divisions of the Court of Cassation on these matters, see Giovanni Conso, *Costituzione e processo penale* (Milano: Giuffrè, 1969).

environment want to compel a modern society to fit itself into an outmoded and uncongenial mold.[18]

The prosecuting attorney

The Italian judge does not spend his life on the bench, however. The same hierarchy includes the judges (*la magistratura*) and the prosecuting attorneys (*il pubblico ministero*). In this way a judge will spend a part of his time as a prosecutor. The prosecuting attorney (*procuratore* or *procuratore generale*) has several duties in Italy that he does not have in the United States. Besides prosecuting criminal actions, he appears in a number of civil actions. He is required by law to intervene in all cases concerning marital and labor disputes; he may intervene as a sort of *amicus curiae* in any other civil case.

There comes naturally to the American observer a sense of concern over this close association between the prosecution and the judges. When they are all one family as they are in Italy there would seem to be a danger of prejudice, a danger that may well be increased by the fact that the defense attorney is an outsider who chose the potentially more lucrative profession of the bar.

Consiglio superiore della magistratura (High Judicial Council)

The *Consiglio superiore della magistratura* was envisaged by the writers of the Constitution as a safeguard against undue political interference with the judiciary and to make the judiciary independent of the executive branch. The necessity of offering some protection to the judiciary from political pressure was obvious at that time because of the way Mussolini, Hitler, and Pétain had shortly before made a mockery of justice.

According to Article 104 of the Constitution, the *Consiglio superiore della magistratura* is presided over by the President of the Republic, and the *Primo presidente* and the *Procuratore generale* (Chief Justice and Chief Prosecutor) of the Court of Cassation are *ex officio* members.

[18] A spectacular case that featured the incompatibility between the culture of a part of the judiciary and the modern world dealt with the indictment of three high school students who published a survey of the sexual habits of their peers. The prosecution, after failing to convince the court that a crime had been committed, appealed the case and petitioned the Court of Cassation for a change of venue on the contention that a fair trial could not be held in iniquitous Milan, where the students had much popular support. The Court of Cassation transferred the case to Genoa, where nothing came of it, because the public prosecutor there decided against reopening the case. See "Il processo contro 'La Zanzara' — testo stenografico del dibattimento," Supplement to *L'Espresso* for April 10, 1966.

Of the twenty-one elected members fourteen are chosen by the judges from among themselves and seven by the houses of Parliament in joint session from among full professors of law and lawyers with fifteen or more years of practice. Elected members remain in office for four years and are not immediately reeligible.

The competence of the Council was to be over recruitment, assignment, transfer, and promotion of judges, and disciplinary procedures against judges "under the law" (Constitution, Arts. 105–107, 110).

The *Consiglio superiore della magistratura* is one of the institutions provided for in the Italian Constitution that was implemented only after a considerable delay, by the law of March 24, 1958, No. 195. Rarely has implementing legislation been so grudging and so filled with apparently unconstitutional provisions. The law originally permitted only the higher judges to vote for the fourteen members of the Council that were to represent the profession. A 1967 amendment (Law 1198 of that year) gives the vote to all the regular career judges but by limiting the eligibility of the junior judges guarantees the election of six judges of the Court of Cassation, four Appellate judges, and four Tribunal judges, and denies eligibility to the pretors. It sets a rule of a three-fifths majority for the election of the seven members chosen by Parliament (a provision not mentioned in the Constitution) and it empowers the Council to decide on matters concerning the judges' status only on request of the Minister of Justice. (The principal purpose of the establishment of the Council was to take out of the hands of the Minister the matters over which it was given competence.) Furthermore, the law provides an appeal against the Council on questions of status to the *Consiglio di stato* and on disciplinary questions to the Court of Cassation. Each of these provisions weakens the *Consiglio superiore della magistratura,* either by making it a less representative body than that the framers of the Constitution had in mind or by curtailing its autonomy, the attribute that was its sole *raison d'être.* Italian jurists question the constitutionality of each of these provisions,[19] but so far (1971) the Constitutional Court has declared the unconstitutionality only of the provision making the Council's deliberations dependent on a request from the Minister of Justice.[20]

The major problem it faces is its relation with the Minister of Justice, who has traditionally been head of the judicial service. In Great Britain and the United States federal government, where judges are appointed for life, removable only by impeachment, and rarely promoted, there is no Ministry of Justice in the European sense. American

[19] Paolo Barile, "Un' opera da compiere," *La magistratura,* XVIII (March, 1964), p. 5.
[20] Decision No. 168 of 1963.

judges are in no way dependent on the Attorney General or the Department of Justice. In Italy, however, the top civil servants of the Ministry of Justice and the political leaders of the dominant party or coalition have not abdicated their position of authority over this major sector of Italian public life.[21] Neither the Constitution nor the enabling legislation has clearly delimited the spheres of authority of the Council and the Ministry, and this vagueness appears to give the advantage to the traditional organ, on whose side the weight of inertia must be counted. The efforts to free the judiciary from government control have led to the same type of ambiguity and redundancy that has resulted from analogous attempts to decentralize local administration. New "democratic" institutions have been set up, but the old "autocratic" institutions have not been sufficiently cut back to permit the new institutions to function effectively.

The Avvocatura dello stato

The *Avvocatura dello stato* is a special body that supplies the state with legal counsel to the number of about 175 lawyers. It is the purpose of this body of career civil servants to defend and protect the interests of the state at law. In the United States this work is carried out by the Solicitor General and his staff. In both countries, besides representing the state in court, this body gives legal opinions to the government. Unlike the *procuratori generali*, who are interchangeable with the regular judges, the *avvocati dello stato* are not part of the judicial career service.

The Legal System

Codified law and common law

Italian law, like French law, is codified; all the laws pertinent to the basic branches of the law are found in a unified code. In Italy there are four such codes: the civil code, the criminal code, the code of civil procedure, and the code of criminal procedure. The difference between the continental and the Anglo-American legal systems, however, does not lie in the fact that the one has codes and the other has not; every one of the fifty American states, as well as the Federal Government, has a criminal code, and every so many years the Federal Government recompiles, from the United States *Statutes at Large,* a huge volume arranged by subject matter, called the *United States Code.*

Although codes exist in the Anglo-Saxon common law countries, the

[21] See Piero Calamandrei, *Processo e democrazia,* Ch. III.

judges are empowered to give interpretations of the codes or any other statutes, which are binding on all future decisions, so long as the interpretation is essential to the settlement of the question at issue in the case before them.[22] (Any other interpretation is an *obiter dictum* and is not binding.) In Italy precedents are not binding, and it is both possible and legal for a lower court to refuse to apply an interpretation of the Court of Cassation. Examples were cited in the press in 1960, when on two occasions the Court of Appeals at Rome refused to accept the ruling of the Court of Cassation.[23]

The civil codes

The civil code and the code of civil procedure were revised at the end of the Fascist period, when Count Dino Grandi was Minister of Justice. Grandi, like all active Fascist leaders in the early period, had been guilty of instigating or approving illegal violence, but perhaps his long career as Ambassador to the Court of St. James had imbued him with a respect for law. At any rate, the best legal minds of Italy were called on to prepare these revisions, including such a prominent anti-Fascist as Piero Calamandrei. These men were able to restrain the pro-Nazi faction that wanted to do away with the Roman tradition of Italian law and create a Fascist law on the Teutonic model. Instead, the basis of the Roman law system was preserved, and the codes are generally considered an improvement over their predecessors, which dated from 1865 (Civil Code and Code of Civil Procedure) and 1882 (Commercial Code).

One of the main breaks with tradition in the civil codes is the increased "orality" of the civil procedure. The old system, like that of France and French Switzerland, consisted primarily of an indefinite series of written documents that passed between counsel for the parties and the judges. The new Italian system tries to bring these persons together to talk things over and thus expedite matters. Even under the new procedure an average civil case is not likely to be settled in less than two years.

The criminal codes

Italy's criminal code and code of criminal procedure are a far greater menace. They are the products of the brilliant but warped mind of

[22] For an analysis of the difference between Franco-Italian civil law and Anglo-American common law, see Lon L. Fuller, *The Anatomy of the Law* (New York: Frederick A. Praeger, 1968), pp. 89–112.

[23] *La stampa,* May 29, 1960, p. 12.

Alfredo Rocco, who was the Fascist Minister of Justice during the middle period of Fascism. These codes, unlike the civil codes, are truly Fascist. There has been continued talk about drastic revision of these codes ever since the overthrow of Fascism, but they are still (1971) in effect, although some of their more patently unconstitutional articles have been repealed by Parliament or declared unconstitutional by the Constitutional Court. This code created many new crimes and increased punishments. It is a mean code, which stands very much on its dignity and exacts its pound of flesh.

Following the teachings of Italy's great penologist, Cesare Beccaria, the pre-Fascist code included no death penalty. The Rocco code reintroduced it, not only for crimes against the state, which were the most serious crimes, but also for any two lesser crimes, the punishment for each of which was normally life imprisonment. This was considered necessary so that no crime would go unpunished! Republican Italy has again abolished the death penalty except by courts martial in time of war, and a 1962 law permits parole of prisoners sentenced for life after twenty-eight years of imprisonment.

A few other observations, chosen almost at random, show the spirit that pervades the Rocco code. The state can appropriate all the property of a condemned man in order to pay his expenses in prison. The previous code only protected the safety of the state: the Rocco code made crimes of all acts which damaged "fundamental political interests with respect to which the state intends to affirm its personality" (Book II, Title I). An example of such an action would be any of the books written by the anti-Fascist exiles in which they told the truth about the government of their country. Another new crime was the failure to report an act against the personality of the state (Art. 364). Still another was the vilification of the Roman Catholic religion. It was also a crime to vilify other tolerated religions, but in these cases the penalties were smaller.

There are many points of divergence between the Italian and the Anglo-American systems of criminal justice. Perhaps the basic difference is in the concept of the purpose of criminal justice. In Italy the purpose is the logical one that the judgment of the courts be as nearly just as possible. In order to arrive at just decisions the judges are not supposed to presume the innocence of the accused but to assume an attitude of impartiality at the beginning of a trial, and they are allowed a greater leeway in questioning the accused and the witnesses than that granted the Anglo-American judge. In doubtful cases the Italian judges, like their learned Scottish brethren, may do what English and American judges cannot do, that is, give a verdict of not proven (*assoluzione per mancanza di prove*). Acquittals may be and frequently are appealed by the prosecuting attorney's office.

In the Anglo-American system of criminal justice the motivating force is the desire to protect the accused against an unmerited conviction. Fair play, rather than justice, is the motto. A presumption of the innocence of the accused is the postulate from which the trial devolves. The judge is more limited in his direct intervention in the case and acts much as a referee in a sporting event, overseeing the contest between the opposing parties and pronouncing the winner. One of the parties, the state, is always considered the stronger, and is thus given a handicap: it can win only if it proves the guilt of the accused "beyond reasonable doubt." If it fails to do this, the accused is found not guilty, and because of the principle of double jeopardy he may normally never be tried again on the same charge. In the American procedure, furthermore, the accused cannot be forced to be a witness against himself, and has a right to the assistance of legal counsel at all times, and to cross-examine adverse witnesses. In Italy, however, the rules of evidence, particularly of hearsay evidence, are not so strictly construed, and there is no effective equivalent of the writ of *habeas corpus*.

Although the accused in Italy is not considered guilty before the verdict in the trial, his defense is prejudiced by several factors. For one thing, in place of the indictment (or, in some states, information) proceedings common to Anglo-American practice, the suspect in Italy is examined by a judge. If the crime of which he is accused is minor, the *pretore* who will later judge him determines whether he will be brought to trial. In the case of more serious crimes this function is performed by a single judge of the court that will try him, who while functioning in this capacity is called the *giudice istruttore*.

A significant partial reform was enacted in 1969 (Law 932 of that year). This law is intended to protect the rights of the accused before trial. It gives a person the right to remain silent during an interrogation and requires that the police warn him that what he says may be used against him. The police must further inform him of his right to the assistance of an attorney of his own choosing, and they must at his request inform his family that he is being held. A 1970 law (No. 192) has also significantly reduced the time persons can be held in jail pending trial. In certain instances the police have meticulously followed these new procedures, but in some of the cases that have been most played up in the press — the arrest of a noted professor on the suspicion of uxoricide and that of a noted actor on suspicion of trafficking in drugs — it appears they have been quite reluctant to do so.

The Government has presented to Parliament a plan for a complete revision of the code of criminal procedure, on which as this edition goes to press, Parliament has not acted. Among the proposed innovations are the introduction of cross examination and the abolition of the verdict of Not Proven. No basic revision of the criminal code has been undertaken as of 1971, but impatience with Parliament's procrastination on this matter led activists in the fall of 1971 to collect signatures for a referendum that would delete all purely Fascist crimes from the criminal code.[24]

The police are said to get most of their information from informers. When dealing with the lower classes, particularly in the south of Italy, it is commonly believed that the police use third-degree methods. Although certain classes of southern Italians are notoriously uncooperative with the police, this hardly excuses such practices.

As is the case with the judges, the police in Italy seem to be confused as to the basic philosophy in accordance with which they should operate. It is difficult, however, for even a well-intentioned policeman to become in mid-career a servant of the people and to cease acting as the agent of Fascist oppression, i.e., of a state that considers its subjects mere instruments for realizing the glory of the nation.

Conclusion

The antiquated laws are not fully responsible for the weaknesses in the Italian legal system; much of the fault lies in the administration of justice. The courtrooms are overcrowded, the territorial jurisdiction of the courts needs to be overhauled, the judges deserve higher salaries and, above all, more clerical assistance. Civil cases normally take over five years to settle. In 1960 the Constitutional Court judges, who rank among the highest officers of the state, were writing their decisions in longhand for want of stenographic assistance. Legal aid for the poor is a farce in Italy. In one out of every four cases before the High Court of Justice in Great Britain counsel is provided and paid by the state. In Italy legal aid is received by one in about 200 litigants, and no provision is made for paying the attorneys.[25]

A peculiarity of the Italian legal system is the amnesty. Every few years the government finds some occasion, usually an anniversary of some kind, to present an amnesty bill to Parliament, proposing a reduction in the sentences of various classes of prisoners. Generally the amnesty also applies to the numerous defendants who are awaiting trial. The frequent amnesties are a way to relieve the intolerable overcrowd-

[24] For a suggested minimal reform of this code see E. Ferrara, R. Libertini, P. Onorato, and A. Saba, "Progetto di riforma stralcio del codice penale," *Il ponte,* XXIV (1968), pp. 569–577.

[25] See Mauro Cappelletti, "Il processo come fenomeno sociale di massa," *Il ponte,* XXV (1969), pp. 1234–40, and Mauro Cappelletti, "La giustizia dei poveri," in Mauro Cappelletti, *Processo e ideologie* (Bologna: Il mulino, 1969), pp. 547–556.

ing of the prisons and the court dockets, but they are not a good way. They allow the state to continue to enforce outmoded and unjust laws and to give it the satisfaction of feigning always to be right when it is often wrong. It makes the partial rectification of an injury not a right of the citizen but an act of grace of the state.

There are at least three features of Italian criminal law, however, that appear preferable to the usual American practice. These features are: (1) the abolition of capital punishment, mentioned above; (2) the practice of combining the civil and criminal actions concerning the same facts; and (3) a system of damages to be paid persons convicted of crimes who are later discovered to be innocent.

The arguments against the death penalty are generally known to Americans, and capital punishment may well be on the way out in the United States. It is already abolished *de iure* in some states and *de facto* in others. The advantages of combining civil and criminal actions based on the same facts are the obvious ones of saving time and avoiding duplication. A 1960 law authorizing the award of damages to persons unjustly imprisoned removes in part a major injustice in the Italian legal system. Damages are to be paid either in a lump sum or as a pension.[26] Radical amendments that would have included time served in jail pending trial were defeated.

The British or American observer, however, should reflect that by adopting three Anglo-American procedures much could be done to alleviate this situation. One would make a single-judge court competent in all cases in the first instance and reserve plural benches for appeals. Another would relieve the appellate courts of the power to review the facts of the court of primary jurisdiction when the evidence was properly introduced and a reasonable man could adduce the facts from the evidence. The third would deprive the prosecuting attorneys of the power to appeal criminal cases.[27]

[26] Law of May 13, 1960.

[27] For further information on the Italian legal system, see Mauro Cappelletti, John Henry Merryman, and Joseph M. Perillo, *The Italian Legal System* (Stanford: Stanford University Press, 1967).

$$\approx \quad 11 \quad \approx$$

The Party System

Introduction

The basic function of a constitutional political party in a democracy is to act as a broker between the public and the state. The party is an instrument through which private interests are detected and public opinion is formed and translated into public policy. This essential role of the political party in the democratic process seems to be recognized in the Italian republican Constitution, which states in Article 49: "All citizens have the right to associate freely in political parties in order to contribute through democratic procedure to the determination of national policy."

Italy did not have a generally representative party system in the pre-Fascist period. A modern Socialist Party had been formed under the leadership of Filippo Turati in 1892, and in 1919 the Sicilian priest, Don Luigi Sturzo, organized the *Partito popolare*. Although these parties were destroyed under Fascism, each had a certain fund of experience and a skeleton organization with which to start operation after the defeat of Fascism. In this respect the Catholic groups were in a better position than the Socialists, as the Catholic Action had been operating freely throughout the Fascist period, and the parish priests and the local church organization gave both a *locus* for and a focus to Catholic political activity.

The parties that should have represented the other major social forces of pre-Fascist Italy remained in a relatively amorphous state. There was a vaguely defined right and a moderate center group, neither of which, however, was organized into a modern party but rather was composed of an informal association of parliamentarians whose political power was based on their personal local influence more than on their party label. The top politicians, including Italy's most effective professional politician of the period, Giovanni Giolitti, were in much the same relationship to the lesser deputies that they in turn were to their constituents. Both relations were personal and based on the ability and willingness of the superior to grant or withhold favors. Both were destined to disappear as Italy adapted itself to its newly instituted "universal" suffrage.

After the fall of Fascism many political groups came to light in Italy. Those first to appear on the scene were the anti-Fascist groups that had been acting as revolutionary forces during the Fascist period. Most prominent among these groups were the Communist Party and the Action Party (*Partito d'azione*). The Communist Party, which had been split from the Socialists in 1919, had been driven underground during the Fascist period, but it alone had maintained a cohesion and a consistent anti-Fascist position during the twenty years of Mussolini's power. The Action Party had had no pre-Fascist existence. It was composed primarily of the anti-Fascist intellectuals who did not accept Communism.

Two other anti- and pre-Fascist groups, the Republicans and the Liberals, also reemerged after the fall of Fascism, although neither had played an active role on a national scale in the anti-Fascist underground or in the *Resistenza*. Various political leaders, particularly in southern Italy, who had refused to cooperate with Fascism, set about to reestablish their local political influence, and many of these banded together as the Labor Democrat Party (*Partito democratico del lavoro*), truly a misnomer.

These were the major political groups and factions that tried to fill the political void left by the fall of Fascism. That their success has been limited is not surprising when one considers the almost total lack of practical experience with the democratic process possessed by these early democratic leaders, who during the Fascist period were in exile, in prison, in the underground movement, or politically inactive. Many of them were trained as conspirators and as revolutionists; some of those in exile learned journalism; but only the Communists had an opportunity to gain experience in party organization. The leaders of the other parties were no further advanced than they had been in 1924, when they were virtually excluded from the Fascist Parliament. They were only older, and therefore less prone to mend their erroneous ways and to learn new techniques. The leaders of the Action Party, which was composed in the main of younger men, lacked even this inadequate pre-Fascist experience.

During its first quarter century the party pattern of the Italian Republic has been remarkably constant. This pattern is characterized by the following conditions:

1. The dominant party throughout this period has been the Christian Democracy, which has consistently polled between 35 and 50 per cent of the national vote.

2. The Communist Party, which has polled 20 to 30 per cent of the votes, has consistently been the second largest party. The Italian Communist Party is the largest Communist party on this side of the Iron Curtain. France is the only other Western democratic state where the Communist Party is a significant political factor.

3. The major Italian Socialist Party has consistently held third place among Italian parties, polling 8 to 15 per cent of the votes.

The Christian Democracy

The Catholic party, the *Democrazia cristiana* (Christian Democracy), has ruled the country, in coalition or alone, continuously from December 10, 1945, to the date of writing (1971). During this period it has muddled through on compromise policies. It has been quick to succor vested interests, slow to initiate basic reforms, and lethargic to the challenge of the liberal Constitution of republican Italy.

The Christian Democracy had the advantage of having as its first leader one of the few experienced professional politicians active in Italy in the immediate postwar period. This man, Alcide De Gasperi, had represented Italian interests as a member of the Austro-Hungarian Parliament before World War I, and had later served in Don Sturzo's *Partito popolare*. He had had a respectable though inactive record as an anti-Fascist, spending much of the period working in the Vatican library. Although De Gasperi's intellectual powers were not extraordinary, and although he had little feeling for basic economic problems, he was an able parliamentarian who succeeded in governing the country uninterruptedly and on the whole effectively from the fall of the Parri government in December, 1945, until July, 1953. His less able successors have carried on the tradition of uninterrupted Christian Democrat rule in Italy, but they have not been able to hold the party together as De Gasperi did or to elicit the support of the other center parties that was generally afforded to De Gasperi.

The various presidents of the Council of Ministers that have succeeded De Gasperi have been either factional leaders, like Amintore Fanfani, Mario Scelba, Fernando Tambroni, Aldo Moro, Mariano Rumor, and Emilio Colombo, who were obnoxious to rival factions within the party, or figureheads with little personal political following, like Giuseppe Pella, Adone Zoli, Antonio Segni, and Giovanni Leone. In recent years the factions within the Christian Democracy have become outspoken in their attacks on each other and have actually succeeded in overthrowing Catholic governments on a national scale in Rome and on a regional scale in Palermo and Aosta, through an unwillingness to support the leaders of rival factions. The same rivalries and weaknesses in party cohesion made it impossible to elect a Catholic President in 1964.

The factional strife within the party is based in part on personal rivalries and in part on irreconcilable differences in political aims. This is not the place to discuss the vicissitudes in the personal rivalries of the party leaders, but it is proper to mention here the major ideological divisions within the party. The right wing represents ultra-conservative economic interests and is intolerant of any activities on the part of the government or the private citizen that might by any stretch of the imagination be displeasing to the Vatican or might seem to question its supreme authority. This wing is supported by the *Azione Cattolica* (Catholic Action), an official Vatican political action group. The right wing is intransigently opposed to Communists and even Socialists, but displays a Christian charity in forgiving Fascists past and present. The left wing is socially conscious and seeks to offer the common man the material advantages promised by the Marxists along with the spiritual benefits offered by religion. In the center is a less doctrinaire group, interested primarily in keeping the party in power and composed principally of the party *notabili* (notables), prominent, and experienced politicians with little factional backing.

The Christian Democracy is an amorphous party, and this quality is both its strength and its weakness. Of the major European parties this is perhaps the one that most nearly resembles the Democratic and Republican parties of the United States, in both organization and cohesion. The Christian Democracy is a loosely knit organization of local bosses who represent various, discordant, and mutually incompatible interests. This makes it difficult to formulate and practically impossible for the party to put into execution any coherent and positive program. In all the regions of Italy except Emilia, Tuscany, and Umbria the Christian Democracy is Italy's major party. Its greatest strength, however, is in the rural districts.

The cement that has traditionally held the Christian Democracy together has been anti-Communism and an ultimate subservience to the Pope, but by 1971 even this meager consensus seemed to be evaporating. While the right and much of the center of the party were still faithful to these principles, there was considerable wavering among those left wing Catholic politicians most sensitive to the sentiments of the rank and file. The young voters in particular showed less fear of the Communists and less respect for the Pope. The Catholic workers' movements, the trade union, *Confederazione italiana dei sindacati dei lavoratori* (CISL), and the workers' assistance organization, *Associazione cristiana dei lavoratori italiani* (ACLI), claim complete independence from both the party and the Vatican.

The Communist Party

During the entire history of republican Italy the *Partito comunista italiano* (PCI) has been Italy's second largest party. Since 1947, when it was forced out of the government coalition by a series of circumstances among which pressure from Washington was popularly believed to be decisive, it has been Italy's major opposition party. Although it gets a number of votes all over Italy, its strongholds are the prosperous rural provinces of Emilia and Tuscany. North of the Po, however, it is strongest in industrial centers.[1]

There are many reasons for Communist success in Italy. The party had effective leadership from Palmiro Togliatti and his immediate associates. In addition, the Italian Communists were virtually the only anti-Fascist movement that had maintained constant communication with the people under Fascism. The vast majority of the postwar Catholic and Socialist leaders were politically inactive during the Fascist period. The present Communist leaders, on the other hand, were regularly engaged in underground political activity. The party leaders were much like priests in that they devoted their full energies to the realization of an ideal and submitted to a discipline that permitted their full efforts to be channelized and coordinated with those of their fellow workers. In return for this dedication and obedience the militant Communist was assured a high measure of security. The party satisfied his material needs, and his Marxist faith was supposed to satisfy his spiritual needs. The man who accepted communism in this way might well lose his birthright as a free man, but he lost nothing in efficiency. When he was not actually working on his party job, he was going to party meetings, reading party newspapers, or dreaming of the better world which he believed his efforts were helping to establish. Even the bed of the militant Communist was generally shared with a comrade. The subservience of the militant Communists to Russia was often heightened by a deep sentiment of personal gratitude, for in their days of tribulation and prison it was the Russian government that had come to their rescue, smuggling their children into Russia and giving them a good education. Much of the vote-getting power of these men was based on the fact that each was known in his own community as a

[1] For an intelligent account of Italian communism in English, see Sidney G. Tarrow, "Political Dualism and Italian Communism," *American Political Science Review,* LXI (1967), pp. 39–53.

thoroughly dedicated and honorable anti-Fascist who had risked his life to help the poor.

The PCI, like all Communist parties of an earlier day, had the habit of indulging in fairly free debates among the leadership behind closed doors, but at the termination of the discussion the minority in any debate was always expected to close ranks with the majority and present a united front to the outside world, and Russian policy was always supported. Since the death of Togliatti, however, the PCI has broken with this general Communist practice, and now the party has not only gone on record against the Russian invasion of Czechoslovakia, but two factions are openly known to exist within the party. One group, led by Giorgio Amendola, favors the creation of a single radical party of the left, like the British Labor Party, which could offer a viable alternative to the continuing Christian Democrat hegemony. The other group, led by Pietro Ingrao, seeks to maintain the purity of the PCI but is willing to govern in coalition with other groups. The major difference between these factions appears to be less one of policy than of the strategy for attaining political power. Amendola envisages a two-party system on the British formula, with the Communists joining other lay groups to the left to form an effective opposition to the traditionalist and essentially conservative Christian Democrats. Ingrao envisages the continuation of a multiparty system and foresees a possible future alliance between the Communists and the left wings of the Christian Democracy.

That the Communist party is Italy's major opposition party is obvious to anyone who can count votes; what is less obvious is whether Communist opposition is loyal or disloyal, whether the Communists wish to work within the system or to destroy it. The number of convinced Communists in Italy — those who want to model the Italian government after Russia — is not thought to be large. It may not comprise more than 2 or 3 per cent of the population (about 10 per cent of the PCI vote) and can hardly be a determining factor in Italy's immediate future.

Far more important is the attitude of the rest of the Italian voters toward the PCI and the accuracy with which they judge the party's aims. Many Italians have the hysterical but not necessarily irrational fear of Communism which seems endemic to the lower middle classes everywhere. For these people the only good Communists are dead ones, and a Communist victory at the polls would spell the probable end of liberal democratic government. For many other non-Communists in Italy, however, the radical reforms proposed by the Communists and the undoubted honesty of the PCI leaders represent the only hope for the preservation of liberal democracy in Italy. Italians are encouraged to reach this latter conclusion by the fact that in spite of its revolutionary tag the PCI has always been careful to act in a thoroughly democratic way. It has sought power by ballots rather than by bullets, and of all the Italian parties it has most vociferously supported the liberties guaranteed by the Constitution. The close personal relations that Togliatti had with the Russian leaders and the high esteem in which Stalin and others held him not only enhanced his prestige in Italy but appeared to give him greater freedom of action vis-à-vis the Russians than that accorded other Western Communist leaders. This freedom was clearly expressed in the strong stand the PCI took against the Russian invasion of Czechoslovakia and in the consistency with which it has maintained that position ever since. If the PCI continues its present policy of moderation and accommodation, it seems destined to reach the goal sought by both Amendola and Ingrao, that of acceptance within the Establishment no longer as a pernicious but rather as a revivifying radical influence.

The increasing interest that the PCI leadership shows in joining the Government and the less intransigent attitude toward Communist participation displayed by some Socialists and Catholics have together been instrumental in causing a serious split within the party. In 1970 a group of dissident Communists led by Luigi Pintor and Rossana Rossanda, both deputies to Parliament, and centered around the review *Manifesto*, were expelled from the party. They have been joined by other Communists of some prominence and by a number of leaders of the furthest left Socialist party, the PSIUP (see *infra*, p. 161) but by no top Communists. The point of contention is over the question of whether to join the Establishment or to remain essentially a revolutionary movement.

The minor national parties

Except for the Christian Democracy and the Communist Party, the Italian political spectrum consists of confused and nebulous images. One would expect to find in a country like Italy at least three more distinct parties, 1) a strong Socialist party representing the radical left, 2) an anticlerical center party, and 3) an ultraconservative and reactionary rightist party. Most of the other Italian parties have set up business with one of these three types of voters in mind, but none has succeeded in organizing these voters into a compact, cohesive, and comprehensive party.

The Socialist Parties. A major factor in Italian politics of the twentieth century has been a negative one: the failure of the Socialist party to unite and to represent the radical and labor elements in Italian society.

This failure can be attributed primarily to the inability of the Socialists to agree whether to seek their ends by revolutionary or evolutionary means, or more precisely, whether to work within or against the system (in the latter case not necessarily with violence). As a consequence, the history of the Italian Socialist party has been that of continual expulsions, scissions, and reunifications that bewilder and bemuse most Italians and virtually all foreigners who have been aware of them.

This history dates back 100 years to the establishment of the revolutionary Paris Commune of 1871, an action applauded by such idols of Italy's radical left as Giuseppe Garibaldi, Karl Marx, and Mikhail Bakunin, but decried by the leader most beloved by Italians eager for social justice, Giuseppe Mazzini. When Mazzini died the following year Bakunin gained the upper hand among Italy's radical left, but this essentially traditional and compassionate group soon had enough of his violent words and deeds. In 1874 a general strike was crushed, and the moderates were able to form a labor party (*Partito operaio*) in time to take part in the 1882 elections. This party, which disappeared a few years later, was replaced in 1892 by Italy's first Socialist party (*Partito socialista italiano*). Its founder, Filippo Turati, like Mazzini was more of an evangelist than a politician. He represented the extreme right of the labor movement in the sense that he distrusted violence and believed progress resulted from cooperation, compromise, and patient determination. His hatred of violence led him to take a pacifist stand in World War II, and his party was the major Socialist party in Europe to oppose the war consistently throughout its course.

The proponents of revolution, however, caused the party many difficulties. In 1908 Arturo Labriola and his friends were expelled from the party for their revolutionary doctrines. Four years later the right-wing Socialists who supported Italy's colonial war against Turkey were in turn expelled, and the leader of this faction, Leonida Bissolati, then founded the *Partito socialista riformista* (Reformed Socialist Party). Prominent among those who advocated the expulsion of Bissolati was a young upstart, Benito Mussolini, who had just completed a prison term for acts of political violence. When the evolutionary Socialists were again safely in power some left-wingers, including Mussolini, were expelled; others, such as the founders of the Communist party, Antonio Gramsci, Palmiro Togliatti, and Amadeo Bordiga, left of their own accord.

When the Fascists came to power they proceeded to crush all the Marxist opposition groups (except the Communists, who operated underground during the entire Fascist period). In 1930 the remnants of most of the Socialist factions except the Communists succeeded in reuniting in exile in France and in forming the PS(SIIS) *Partito so-*

cialista [*Sezione italiana dell'internazionale socialista*] — Socialist Party [Italian Section of the Socialist International]), which on reentering Italy after the liberation became the PSIUP (*Partito socialista italiano di unità proletaria* — Italian Socialist Party of Proletarian Unity) by fusing with Lelio Basso's *Unità proletaria* groups. Unification, however, did not resolve the old revolutionary-evolutionary dilemma. As a result, in January, 1947, the right wing of the party, not sharing the anxiety of the party leaders over deviation from the Communist line and having obtained the financial support and the blessing of the American Federation of Labor and of the United States government, split from the party over the issue of a continued alliance with the Communists, and formed the PSLI (*Partito socialista dei lavoratori italiani* — Italian Workers' Socialist Party) under the leadership of Giuseppe Saragat. Just before this split occurred, the PSIUP had changed its name back to the PSI in order to prevent the right-wing dissidents from adopting this traditional name and acquiring its prestige. In April, 1947, another group of anti-Communist Socialists, including the author who calls himself Ignazio Silone, left the PSI and in concert with other anti-Communist leftists, including Piero Calamandrei, formed a splinter group called *Unità socialista* (Socialist Unity). In the following year still other evolutionary groups broke away from the PSI and joined *Unità socialista* to form the PSU (*Partito socialista unitario* — Unitary Socialist Party), with the *Unità socialista* group as a nucleus. In 1951 the PSU fused with the PSLI to form another PS(SIIS). In 1952 this party adopted the name of *Partito socialista democratico italiano* (PSDI — Italian Social Democratic Party). During all these formal metamorphoses, however, Pietro Nenni remained head of the philo-Communist party and Saragat head of the anti-Communist party, and few socialist leaders at any time changed their personal allegiance from one faction to the other.

Nenni's fellow-traveler policies made it impossible to form a loyal radical opposition to the essentially conservative traditionalist Christian Democratic majority and led to a series of losses on the party's right, particularly in the period of 1947 to 1953. Nenni's admirers point out that, on the other hand, this policy was responsible for maintaining the proletarian basis of the party and containing the Communist vote. Their argument is that the discipline and rigidity of the Communist Party are basically distasteful to the Italians, and that the Socialists will inevitably beat the Communists in the long run if they do not let the Communists outdo them as the representatives of the workers' interests. The Russian suppression of the Hungarian revolution of 1956, however, greatly shocked all classes in Italy, and from that moment Nenni began freeing his party from the Communist embrace. In this task he was helped by the return of prodigal sons from the Socialist right, by the recruitment of many of the best elements from the former Action party, and by the assistance of such renegade Communists as Antonio Giolitti.

By 1962 Nenni was ready to cross the Rubicon and give his support to a bourgeois government headed by the Christian Democrat Amintore Fanfani without, however, letting members of the PSI assume ministerial responsibility. After the elections of 1963 Nenni announced the Socialists' intention to join the government. This move brought about another serious split among the Socialists and led to the formation in January, 1964, of a new party, using the old name, PSIUP, on the left of the PSI and perhaps even to the left of the Communists.

The departure of the strongly anti-Establishment faction led to a *rapprochement* with Saragat's Social Democrats, and finally in 1968 to the formal reabsorption of the PSDI in the PSI, which then took the name of PSU (*Partito socialista unitario* — Unitary Socialist Party) but soon after changed back to PSI. The new marriage, however, was not a happy one, and there was another split in 1969, when substantially the same elements that had previously been part of the PSDI formed a new party, which also took the name of the *Partito socialista unitario,* only to change it back the following year to PSDI. This new party appears to be well financed, and it is commonly believed that the sources of much of this support are American. The excuse the party offers for its existence is militant anti-Communism, but the major results of its existence have been a serious weakening of the center-left coalition caused by the rivalries and antagonisms between the Socialist groups and a general deceleration of social reform as a consequence of the PSDI's almost total lack of interest in policy and almost total preoccupation with politics.

With the departure of the right wingers, now in the PSDI, the time appears ripe for a reconciliation between the PSI and the PSIUP. In the first five years of its existence the PSIUP, with only meager financial assistance from internal or external sources, managed to build itself up to a position from which it attracted almost 5 per cent of the national vote. In the regional elections of 1970 and the local elections of 1971, however, it fared badly. It originally attracted the ultraradicals who were dissatisfied with the moderate Socialist position and with the rigid Communist bureaucracy. The new revolutionary movements of the left, however, have siphoned off some of this vote and the party leadership and the core of its followers appear to see eye to eye with the *Manifesto* group of Communist dissidents.

Almost one voter in five in Italy casts his vote for one or another of Italy's Socialist parties. In the 1970 regional elections the PSI elected sixty-seven Councilors, the PSU forty-one and the PSIUP sixteen, making a total of 124 out of 690 Councillors elected. As the Communist party becomes increasingly respectable and as evolution rather than revolution becomes more obviously the road to social reform preferred by the Italian voter, there seems to be little reason for the continued existence of more than one Socialist party. For this reason the prognosis for the PSIUP is negative. It is more difficult to predict the future of the PSDI. If there is truth in Harry Truman's maxim, "Whenever the public is asked to choose between two conservative parties, it will prefer the genuine article," then there is no place for the crypto-conservatism of the PSDI. It is possible, however, that the Truman maxim is valid in the United States but is invalid in Italy.

The Action Party. Another party that attempted to represent the radical left was the *Partito d'Azione.* The leaders of this party, who had played such a courageous and dominant role in the partisan movement, were unprepared to cope with the practical problems of party organization, and the party broke up in 1946, less than a year after the termination of the war and less than two months after the fall of the government in which the leader of their party, Ferruccio Parri, had served as President of the Council of Ministers. Former Action Party members who are politically prominent in the seventies include Riccardo Lombardi and Tristano Codignola (both PSI), Ugo La Malfa (PRI), Vittorio Foa (PSIUP), and Ferruccio Parri (Independent).

The Liberal Party. The *Partito liberale italiano* (PLI) is a constitutional party of the right with a glorious past and a modest present. In the nineteenth century the liberal movement under Cavour united Italy. During the first half of the twentieth century before and after fascism its strength lay among the large industrial interests of the north, a considerable number of virtually independent southern political bosses, and some of Italy's most distinguished professors, such as Luigi Einaudi, Benedetto Croce, and Gaetano Mosca. Since the middle 1950's, however, the large industrialist has been losing political power, and the old-fashioned southern Italian political boss surrounded by his faithful favor-seeking clientele has been dying out; as a result, the PLI under its able secretary, Giovanni Malagodi, has been gradually becoming the party of the small business man. By catering to this class, which is anti-socialist, anti-welfare state, anti-government planning, and anti-government interference with business, and aided by the alliance between the Catholics and the Socialists, Malagodi built the PLI into Italy's fourth largest party, with about 8 per cent of the votes in 1963. Since then it is again declining. In the 1968 parliamentary elections the PLI received a little over 5 per cent of the vote, and in the regional elections of 1970 it received less than 4 per cent of the seats. The Liberals have served in only three of Italy's twenty-three governments from 1948 to 1971, and have been consistently in opposition since 1957.

The Republican Party. The *Partito repubblicano italiano* (PRI), an anticlerical center party, is composed of the followers of the political philosophy of Giuseppe Mazzini, a nineteenth century Italian patriot and visionary who, although deeply religious, strongly opposed the temporal power of the Roman Catholic Church. After World War II its leaders were for the most part highly respectable and politically inept scholars and poets, and only in certain parts of central and southern Italy, where the party had maintained grass roots support, was it able to gather enough votes to win seats in parliament. By 1970 the party had been for two decades the personal fief of Ugo La Malfa, a Sicilian by birth and a Milanese by education, and one of Italy's most able and respected politicians. The Republican Party under his leadership holds a place on the political spectrum similar to that of the so-called Eastern or Liberal wing of the Republican Party in the United States, as evidenced in the policies of Charles Goodell, Jacob Javits, and Nelson Rockefeller. If one looks merely at election results, the PRI, with its 2 per cent of the national vote, appears insignificant; but this conclusion is somewhat belied by the reality. Unlike other parties of comparative size in Italy or elsewhere, the PRI is a consistent vote-getter, with a faithful following, which appears to be gaining rather than losing votes. Furthermore, the PRI has been asked to serve in virtually all the postwar governments in Italy, and has actually served in ten of the first twenty-three governments since 1948. It was the only minor party to gain votes in the 1970 regional elections, where it appeared to have increased its total vote by about 50 per cent.

The Neo-Fascists. The neo-Fascist *Movimento sociale italiano* (Italian Social Movement) represents the former Fascist little shots, who for lack of sufficient political acumen or for other causes, remained to the bitter end in the Fascist fold. Fortunately for Italian democracy, this group is remarkably sterile and disgusting to most Italians. Its main strength is in Rome, and it hardly exists in the north. In Rome, and on occasion in a few other cities, bands of neo-Fascists have proved themselves adept at throwing stink-bombs and at clubbing their unarmed opponents. The MSI has never been invited to join a Government. When the reactionary Catholic Tambroni Government tried to maintain itself in power with neo-Fascist votes in Parliament in 1960, it was forced out of office as a consequence of riots in most of the principal cities of Italy. In the 1968 parliamentary elections the MSI received about 4 per cent of the vote. In the 1971 local elections the MSI appeared to have made significant gains, getting about 15 per cent of Italy voting in these elections included such neo-fascist strongholds ever, was less spectacular than it might seem on first sight, as the parts of Italy voting in these elections included such neo-fascist strongholds as the cities of Rome and Bari and the entire region of Sicily, whereas the only city of appreciable size to vote in the anti-fascist north was Genoa.

The Monarchists. Another group on the right is the Monarchists, who call themselves the *Partito democratico italiano di unità monarchica* (PDIUM), and who are an amalgamation of the *Partito nazionale monarchico,* headed by Alfredo Covelli, and the *Partito monarchico popolare,* headed by the Neapolitan shipowner and former mayor, Achille Lauro. The PDIUM has no apparent principles and little or no grass roots organization. The sources of its voting strength are (1) the elderly people who have emotional prejudices in favor of the monarchy and who look with dismay at all social change, and (2) a number of the politically immature lower classes in parts of the south. The party elected twenty-five deputies in 1958 but fifteen of them left the party before the next elections.[2] In the 1963 elections the PDIUM returned only eight deputies and in 1968, six. In the 1970 regional elections, out of a total of 690 Councilors elected, only one was a Monarchist.

The regional parties

Besides the parties of national significance described above, there are two Italian parties with strong local influence. Each of these operates exclusively in one of the semiautonomous regions of Italy. They are the *Südtiroler Volkspartei,* which operates in the region of Trentino-Alto Adige; and the *Union valdôtaine,* in Val d'Aosta.

The *Südtiroler Volkspartei* represents the nationalist elements in the German-speaking population of the Tirol. It is a rigidly conservative, strongly Catholic party, and is usually allied politically with the Christian Democracy.

The *Union valdôtaine* is a regional party of the French-speaking inhabitants of the Val d'Aosta. This center left party, in alliance with the Communists and the Socialists, wrested power on a regional basis from the Christian Democracy in 1959. The Christian Democracy and its allies have represented the conservative interests of the valley, while

[2] See Fausto De Luca, *La stampa,* February 19, 1963, p. 12. Four went to the Christian Democracy, one to the PSDI, four to the PLI, six became independents.

the *Union valdôtaine* has tended to occupy a central position between the Christian Democracy on its right and the Communists and Socialists on its left. Neither the *Südtiroler Volkspartei* nor the *Union valdôtaine* has served in any national Government, although the former has consistently and the latter frequently been represented in Parliament.

The anti-parliamentary groups

The student unrest in Italy, the resurgence of anarchist, trotskyite, and maoist groups on the left and fascist squads on the right would seem to suggest that there are large alienated groups in Italy that have lost confidence in all the traditional parties. As one observer suggests, however, the most surprising thing about the 1970 regional elections was the stability in party strength that it reflected. In fact, the party that suffered the heaviest losses in percentage was the most revolutionary party represented in Parliament, the PSIUP. The estimated more than two million alienated citizens, when called to the polls, voted much as they and their elders had voted in pervious elections. The revolutionaries and the discontented did not express revolution and discontent in the ballot box.[3]

Membership and organization

Party membership in Italy is relatively low. The Christian Democracy and the Communist Party have an estimated membership of about one and one-half millions each.[4] The Socialists have about 600,000,[5] and the Social Democrats perhaps 100,000. The four other parties with anything approaching a permanent nationwide organization, the PSIUP, the Republicans, the Liberals, and the MSI, count their membership from 100,000 to 200,000.[6]

Membership in a political party in Italy is a more serious affair than it is in the United States. Both for its procedure and for the quality of commitment it entails, membership in an Italian political party is not dissimilar to membership in an American church. Joining a major party in the United States is a unilateral act. A person becomes a Democrat

---

[3] Jacques Nobécourt, *L'Italie à vif* (Paris: Editions du Seuil, 1970), pp. 131–141.

[4] Ada Cavazzani, "Organizzazione, iscritti e elettori della democrazia cristiana," in Giordano Sivini, *Partiti e partecipazione politica in Italia* (Milano: Giuffrè, 1969), pp. 169–188, at 179. See also Telesio Malaspina, "Chi paga i partiti," *L'Espresso/colore*, February 25, 1968, pp. 5–9, at 6.

[5] Franco Cazzola, "Elettori e iscritti del partito socialista italiano dal 1946 al 1968," in Sivini, *op. cit.*, pp. 189–212, at 204.

[6] Malaspina, *op. cit.*, p. 7.

or a Republican by declaring himself such, and the party has no effective way of ridding itself of an unwanted member, as any student of the Democrats' losing battle for the maintenance of white primaries in the South is aware.

The Italian who wants to join a party must have his name proposed and seconded by active party members. On admission he must profess his sympathy with the basic tenets of the party and agree to follow the party line during the contortions of its evolution. He also obliges himself to pay monthly and annual dues. Party flags are carried in funeral processions of ordinary party members.

Both men and women may become party members. The minimum age of admission in most of the parties is eighteen. The Republicans and the Social Democrats place the minimum age at twenty-one, while the MSI accepts members who are fourteen years old, which is about the mental age to which this party's program appeals. The MSI does attract teenage hoodlums, particularly in Rome.

There is similarity among the Italian party organizations. Each is based on local units, called sections. In addition to the section, which is a territorial unit comprising a commune or, in the case of the larger cities, a part of a commune, the Communists and the Socialists set up groups at the members' places of work, called respectively cells and nuclei. The sections normally elect their own officers and are united into provincial or regional bodies, with limited powers.

The sovereign body of the party, in the formal sense, is the National Congress, which meets annually, or every few years. Delegates to the National Congress are elected locally or provincially and have a number of votes equal to the number of dues-paying members they represent. As in the case of American labor conventions, however, no serious attempt is made to count noses, and it may happen that local leaders pay dues and cast votes for mythical members.

The National Congress elects a permanent committee, called the National Council or the Central Committee, which then elects an executive committee, called by various names depending upon the party concerned. The party secretary, at the top of the heap, is elected by this committee or by the National Council.

Party finances

Italian parties are ostensibly financed by the dues collected from their members, but this source accounts for no more than 10 per cent of the income of the larger and for even less in the smaller parties. The rest of the income comes from various individual and collective sources, including the following:

1. Party-sponsored entertainment
2. A tax of about 50 per cent on the salaries of deputies and senators
3. The profits from the party-controlled cooperatives
4. Subsidies from interested groups.

Party-sponsored entertainment as a source of revenue is somewhat similar to the $50-a-plate dinners to which the major American parties resort. In Italy the major exploiter of this source of revenue is the Communist Party, with its popular outings, called the *Feste dell'unità*, in honor of the Communist newspaper, *L'Unità*. The salaries of the Communist and Socialist deputies are paid directly to the parties' parliamentary groups. A percentage of this salary, based on the deputy's or senator's needs, is turned over to him, and the rest is kept by the party. As a result, the salaries become an indirect state subsidy for the parties. The profits the parties take from their cooperative organizations divert the cooperatives from their basic purpose of reducing costs for producers or consumers and turn them into regular capitalistic enterprises. Subsidies from interested groups have always been a suspect source of party finance, but they are of predominant importance in Italy.

Giulio Andreotti, the Christian Democrat party boss in Rome, is credited with saying that talking about party finance has been as much tabu as talking of sex education. Be that as it may, there are few hard facts on party finance. Only the Communist Party publishes figures that could by any stretch of the imagination present an accurate picture of the situation. This party claims to collect two billion lire ($3,200,000) annually in dues from its 1,500,000 members and to get another two billion out of them through such activities as the *Feste dell'Unità*. A fifth billion comes from rebates averaging 50 per cent on parliamentary salaries. Miscellaneous sources are said to bring in another 750,000,000 lire.

A recent estimate suggests that over 70 per cent of Communist Party revenue is derived from these sources, while the estimate for the Christian Democrats is over 95 per cent. The other parties' reliance on these sources is thought to be less than that of the Christian Democracy and greater than that of the Communist party. The category of subsidies is a large one, however, and the different practices elicit varying degrees of disapproval. As in the United States, wealthy interests, seeking to influence government policy, may make substantial campaign contributions to various parties, directly or indirectly, and party leaders holding office in the central government or in the municipalities who are personally incorruptible may look with greater favor on, let us say, a public works contract, if the bidder makes a party contribution. There is increasing talk of state subsidies for the parties as in Germany, Norway, and Sweden, but the Government has presented no such bill to Parliament.

Partitocrazia

The formal separation of the party hierarchy and the party's parliamentary group, and the formal subordination of the latter to the former, are major points of attack from those quarters that complain of *partitocrazia* in Italy, by which is meant the rule of the parties rather than of Parliament. This term is usually one of opprobrium and often comes from the pen of a former Fascist or Fascist sympathizer with little insight into or sympathy with the democratic process. In practice, however, the parliamentary groups in Italy are not in the subordinate position within their parties that a glance at the party organization might lead one to suppose. The general rule is for the parliamentary leaders and the party hierarchs to be the same persons.

That Italy, as well as the rest of the democratic world today, tends to operate through a new technique of representative government unknown to the classical liberal and democratic philosophers is obvious to those who are aware of the political reality. In the aristocratic past when there was restricted suffrage, democracy operated through a parliamentary system. In the modern world the party has to a considerable extent replaced the legislature as the agent of the sovereign people. Those who recognize and accept this new role of the party display an insight into the facts of politics. Those who decry the influence of parties lack this insight. It is not the power but the weakness of Italian parties; it is not the Machiavellian machinations of Italian party leaders, but their professional incompetence, that are causes of the weakness in the democratic process in Italy.[7] *Partitocrazia* is not a political malady; rather it is a name for the present stage of development of Western democratic government. But if it were a malady, the Italian parties would still not be strong enough to infect Italy with it.

There is, however, a sense in which Italy does suffer from *partitocrazia;* it has to do with the traditional factionalism of Italian public life. The parties may lack the strength to bring about efficient and responsible government, but they are strong enough to reduce the independent citizen who refuses to accept party discipline to a position

[7] See Luigi Salvatorelli, "Partiti e governo," *La stampa,* June 9, 1964, p. 1. "Contrary to what certain theorists say, who without wishing to do so exert a defeatist (*qualunquista*) influence on public opinion, the evil in Italian public life is not *partitocrazia* but rather the lack of cohesion within the parties. In a democratic parliamentary regime based on coalition governments two elements are necessary: internal discipline within the parties and loyalty toward the coalition."

of political impotence. The nonpartisan expert who could make an effective member of a British Royal Commission or the American Supreme Court, has little chance to make himself heard in Italy. It is precisely in those realms of public life where partisan politics are least appropriate that the Italian parties seem most insistent on placing their men. This is the spoils system at a level where at the least it robs the state of the counsel of many of Italy's least prejudiced and most competent minds and where at the worst it may seriously interfere with the proper functioning of the state.

Conclusion

The Italian party system is normally classified as multipartied. The accuracy of this diagnosis is attested to by the number of parties that are competing on the Italian scene.

A more sophisticated analysis of party systems would suggest that it is not the number of parties in the field that most accurately describes the party system but rather the presence or absence of a democratic alternative to the existing government. According to this analysis, countries like Great Britain, the United States, Belgium, Denmark, Canada, Norway, and West Germany, where parties or coalitions of parties alternate in power, are distinguished from most of the continental democracies, where the government coalition remains essentially unvaried. Under this classification Italy falls within the common European pattern of a country where there is no effective loyal opposition.

This situation left the Christian Democracy as the essential government party, and the only plausible variants were for the Christian Democrats to govern alone, in coalition with the minor constitutional parties to the left (the PSDI and the PRI), in coalition with the minor constitutional party to the right (the PLI), or with all three of them at once. When the minor parties were in the government coalition, their leaders were flattered by a generous assignment of cabinet positions, but effective power remained with the Christian Democracy, a giant among dwarfs.

Many Italian intellectuals and anticlericals, aware that under the present circumstances the Christian Democracy will be perpetually in power, have sought to establish a third force (*terza forza*) between the Christian Democracy and the Communists, which would constitute a loyal radical opposition and would bring together all the Socialists, the Radicals, and the Republicans, and would win a significant number of votes from the Communists and from the left wing of the Christian Democracy.

A significant step in this direction appeared to have been made with the formation of the fourth Fanfani Government in 1962. This Government, composed of Christian Democrats, Republicans, and Social Democrats, had as its distinguishing feature the "external" support of the PSI, heretofore frequently indistinguishable from the Communists in policy. The new alliance was made possible by the hard work of Aldo Moro, secretary of the Christian Democracy, and of Fanfani himself, who together succeeded in convincing their party of its potential benefits. Pietro Nenni deserves credit for his statesmanship during the long negotiations, as does Pope John XXIII for restraining his reactionary cardinals, opposed to the alliance; but the underlying economic cause of the Socialist shift was the improvement in the living conditions of the Socialist voters, that turned them from agitators, distrustful of the existing order, to constructive critics of that order.

When after the 1963 elections the PSI was ready to share government responsibility, republican Italy seemed finally to have an alternative to the centrist Catholic governments that had been in power for fifteen years. The new center-left coalition — the *centro-sinistra* — was composed of the Catholics, the Republicans, the PSDI, and the PSI, i.e., all the constitutional parties except the PLI. After the first year of center-left government the Socialists appeared seriously discouraged with the progress made. They believed that they had done most of the compromising and were not convinced that the Catholics had made much of an effort to meet them halfway. After the 1963 and 1968 elections, however, a center-left government still seemed virtually the only one that could hold Italy together. In the regional elections of 1970 the electorate continued the trend of giving slightly increased support to the center-left at each round and of shifting the vote within the coalition slightly to the left, upping the Socialist and Republican percentages at the expense of the Catholics. Yet by 1970 the center-left no longer seemed an alternative government, but merely a continuation of Christian Democratic hegemony.

The failure of the *terza forza* in Italy, and the similar failure of the same forces in France, to offer a viable alternative to the conservative governments in power have placed before the democratic left of both countries the choice between remaining anti-Communist and impotent, and joining the Communists and perhaps thereby losing for themselves and their country those aspects of liberal democracy that the conservative governments support. In both countries, then, the choice is now between a conservatism that has alienated a considerable part of the public and a radical coalition that would bring to power a Communist leadership that is feared and distrusted by another and probably equally large number of voters.

12

Elections

The Italian election laws offer an unusually rich field to the student of parties and elections. The Italian laws are complex, varied, and ingenious. Almost every type of election system known in other countries is in use somewhere in Italy for some kind of council. Proportional representation, preferential voting, single-member districts, run-off elections, *panachage,* and limited voting are all found here. The ingenuity with which these various ingredients are combined, along with some original Italian refinements, could perhaps have more profitably been expended elsewhere. In most cases, however, the laws result in a reasonably equitable procedure for proportional representation, but in two cases the regional election laws have been badly written.

The Italian voter is at present concerned only with electing legislators at various levels — national, regional, provincial, and local. All the executives, including the President of Italy, the presidents of the regions and of the provinces, the mayors, as well as the President of the Council of Ministers, and the presidents of the regional governments are elected indirectly by the popularly elected legislators. Italian judges are normally career civil servants; they are never elected directly.

Voters

According to the Constitution, voting is personal, equal, free, and secret; it is a civic duty, and all Italian citizens who have reached their majority must vote with the exception of those who lack legal capacity, who are condemned criminals, or who are morally unfit as determined by law (Art. 48). According to present legislation "personal" voting seems to be interpreted so as to require the voter to present himself personally at the polls, and absentee ballots are not provided. The duty to vote bears no penal sanction, although failure to vote, if unexcused, is recorded for five years on an official document, a copy of

171

which must be presented on many occasions in a citizen's life. Men and women reach their majority at the age of twenty-one in Italy.

Referenda

The Constitution provides for a popular referendum (Arts. 75, 132, and 138). Referenda are also approved in the constitutions of the special regions of Sardinia (Arts, 32, 43, 54), Val d'Aosta (Art. 30), and Trentino–Alto Adige (Art. 53), and in the law on the normal type of region (Arts. 3 and 4).

A referendum may be called to abrogate a law on a petition signed by 500,000 voters or approved by five regional councils. In order to be effective, over half the electorate must vote on the proposal, and the majority of those voting must approve abrogation. A referendum is not permitted on money laws, on amnesties, or on authorizations for treaty ratification. The Constitutional Court determines the legality of a proposal for a referendum.

A similar referendum is permitted for amendments to the Constitution, except that in this case the referendum must be proposed within three months of the approval of the amendment by Parliament and that to defeat the amendment it is sufficient that it be opposed by a majority of those voting (even if a majority of those eligible to vote do not participate in the election).

Sardinia and Trentino–Alto Adige have also enacted enabling legislation for referenda. Sardinia permits this form of direct democracy on petition by one-third of the regional councillors or by 10,000 voters for the abrogation of regional laws. The referendum is successful if approved by a majority of the voters in an election in which at least one-third of the voters participated. It further authorizes referenda when there is contemplated an alteration in the boundaries or functions of provinces or when one house of Parliament has approved a modification of the Sardinian constitution with which the regional assembly is not in agreement (Sardinia law of May 17, 1957, No. 20). Sardinia has also enacted enabling legislation for referenda on the creation of new communes or for altering the boundaries of present communes (Sardinia law of May 3, 1956, No. 14). Trentino–Alto Adige has enacted enabling legislation for calling referenda for the abrogation of both regional and provincial legislation. The petition must be signed by 8000 voters and approved by a majority of the votes cast in an election in which a majority of the voters participated (Trentino–Alto Adige law of June 24, 1957).

Provision is made for a communal referendum on the question of whether or not the commune should take over a public utility (Royal

Decree of October 15, 1925, No. 2578, Art. 12). A referendum is called after the common council has voted to take over the utility and the *giunta provinciale amministrativa* has approved the council's decision, if either one-third of the councillors or one-twentieth of the voters request it. The authors know of no instance in which a referendum has been called on this question. Only time will show the use that will be made of the referendum.

A referendum is to be held in the spring of 1972 on the Fortuna divorce law. This referendum has been instigated by right wing Catholics and Neo-Fascists. The radical elements in Italy were gathering signatures in the fall of 1971 for referenda (1) to abrogate the Lateran Treaties and (2) to eliminate a series of Fascist-inspired articles in the criminal code.

Chamber of Deputies

A constitutional amendment of 1963 states that the Chamber of Deputies is elected by direct universal suffrage and shall consist of 630 deputies. Any person entitled to vote who has reached the age of twenty-five may be elected deputy. Deputies serve for five years (Arts. 56 and 60).

Italy is divided into thirty-two electoral districts, and a list system of proportional representation is used in all but one of them. With the exception of the eleventh district, which includes provinces in the Veneto and in Friuli–Venezia Giulia, and the eighteenth district, which includes the region of Umbria and the province of Rieti, each district consists either of an entire small region or several provinces within the same region. Each electoral district elects a number of deputies in proportion to its population. Each party prepares a list of its candidates for each district and may nominate as many candidates as there are seats to be filled. It is not necessary that the candidates reside in the district, and the same candidates may run in as many as three districts. They may also run for the Senate in the same election. If a candidate is elected in more than one district, he must opt for one seat, and the next person in line in the same party takes the seat he vacates in the other district or districts.

Each party selects a symbol (in several election districts a large number of voters are illiterate). The party symbol and the lists of candidates are then posted on signboards throughout the district, where the voters may consult them. On election day, which is a Sunday, the voter goes to the polling place of his residence and receives a ballot consisting of a piece of paper with the various party symbols on it and a blank space in the middle.

The party symbols often contain the name of the party within them. This is particularly true with the parties which are primarily interested in the literate vote, such as the Socialists and the Republicans. The Communists, however, use merely the hammer and sickle, and the Christian Democrats use a shield with a cross and the word *Libertas* written on the cross. (This has led the foes of the Christian Democracy to suggest that the Catholics want to crucify liberty.) The PSI uses a hammer, sickle, and a book along with the name of the party. The PSDI uses a rising sun and the word *socialismo,* and the Republicans rely on their name and their traditional ivy leaf. The Liberals use the Italian flag, the MSI uses a flame, and the Monarchists, a five-pointed star and a crown.

After having marked the symbol of the party of his choice, the voter may express a preference for from one to four candidates (maximum of three if the total number of deputies to be elected from the district is less than sixteen) who represent the party for which he has voted. This action is voluntary, and the ballot is valid whether or not the voter has availed himself of this prerogative. As the names of the candidates are not on the ballot, the voter who casts a preference vote must write in either the name or names of his preference in the space on the center of the ballot set aside for this purpose, or, if he is lazy or illiterate, the candidate's number. This number represents the candidate's numerical position on the party's electoral list. In parts of the highly illiterate south, the candidates actually pass out stencils to the voters so they can stencil in that candidate's number. As not all voters express preferences, a relatively few preference votes (roughly 20 per cent of the votes cast for the party) are enough to put a candidate near the top of the list.[1]

When the voting is completed, all the votes within the district are totaled by party. The sum of the party totals is divided by the number of seats assigned the district plus two. The quotient thus obtained is called the electoral quotient. The party totals (*cifre elettorali*) are then divided by the electoral quotient, and the number obtained from this division becomes the tentative representation granted that party from that district. When this process has been completed for each party the number of seats tentatively assigned each party are added, and if the sum is not greater than the number of seats assigned the district, the tentative allocation becomes final. If the sum is greater than the number of seats allowed the district, a new electoral quotient is found by dividing the total number of votes by the number of seats assigned plus one, and the same procedure is followed. If again too large a

[1] See Luigi D'Amato, *Il voto di preferenza in Italia* (Milan: Giuffrè, 1964).

number of seats is allocated, the process is repeated, dividing the total vote this time by the total number of seats assigned plus zero.

After the number of seats to be assigned to each party has been determined, the preference votes for each candidate are counted and the candidates are elected in the order of their descending number of preference votes. These lists are kept until the next general election, and if deputies die or resign, their places are filled by the next in line in the list of preference votes for their party in their district. In this manner by-elections are dispensed with.

The Val d'Aosta, because of its small size, constitutes a single-member district, where each party is limited to a single candidate and there is no preference vote. In order to be elected, a candidate must secure an absolute majority. If no one achieves this vote in the first election, a runoff election between the two leading candidates is held a fortnight later.

It normally occurs that all the seats attributed to an election district are not assigned to the parties even when the lowest electoral quotient is used, that derived from dividing the total vote by the total seats plus two. These additional seats are assigned by a national election office (*Ufficio centrale nazionale*) in the following way:

Each of the election districts (except the uninominal district of Val d'Aosta) informs the national office of the following: (1) the number of seats unassigned in its district, (2) the remainders belonging to each party resulting from the division of the party vote by the electoral quotient, (3) the electoral quotient of the district, and (4) the number of candidates elected by each party in the district. On receipt of this information the national office (1) discards the remainders of all parties who have not both (a) elected at least one candidate in one electoral district and (b) compiled a total of at least 300,000 votes, (2) totals (a) the list of unassigned seats and (b) the remainders of all the parties not eliminated in step (1), (3) determines the national electoral quotient by dividing the total votes (2b) by the total seats (2a), (4) divides the total of each party's remainders by the electoral quotient, (5) attributes seats to the parties in accordance with the number of times the electoral quotient is contained in the total of each party's remainders, (6) attributes any additional seats to the parties according to the system of major fractions, i.e., to the size of the remainders derived from step (5), (7) determines the percentage of the electoral quotients of each district represented by the remainders within that district of each party to which a seat was attributed by steps (5) and (6), (8) assigns the seats to the electoral districts in accordance with the results of step (7). Then the party's so far unelected candidate who has received the most preference votes is given the seat.

The Senate

The Constitution stipulates that the senators shall be elected for five-year terms by regions. There are 315 elected senators, divided among the regions according to population except that all but two regions have a minimum of six senators regardless of population. One senator is allotted to Val d'Aosta and two to Molise. Three regions — Trentino–Alto Adige, Umbria, and Basilicata — benefit from the provision assigning a minimum of six senators to them. Voters must be twenty-five years old to vote in the senatorial elections and candidates must be forty. (Arts. 57–60, Constitutional Amendment of December 27, 1963, No. 3.)

According to the present law on the senatorial elections (No. 29 of 1948), the regions are divided by the Ministry of the Interior into as many senatorial districts as there are senators to elect. The various parties then put up their candidates in the electoral districts, but only one per district. No man can run for senator from more than one region, but within the region he can run from as many as three districts. The voter casts a single vote for the party and candidate of his preference. If a candidate receives 65 per cent of the votes cast within the district, he is elected. Only a few candidates, representing the Christian Democracy in the Veneto or either the Christian Democracy or the *Südtiroler Volkspartei* in Trentino–Alto Adige, are elected in this way. When no candidate receives such a majority, the D'Hondt system is used.[2]

[2] The D'Hondt system of proportional representation can be applied in three ways.

Method No. 1: (1) Divide the total vote of each party successively by every whole number from one to the number of seats to be filled. (2) Arrange these quotients in descending order of magnitude. (3) Consider that quotient which occupies the place in the list of quotients obtained in step 2 equal to the number of seats to be filled, as the electoral quotient. (4) Divide the total vote for each party by the electoral quotient, disregarding fractions. (5) The quotient thus obtained represents the number of seats assigned to each party.

Method No. 2: (1) Same as Method 1. (2) Same as Method 1. (3) Assign one seat to the party from whose total vote the highest quotient was derived. (4) Continue this process with the successive quotients until all the seats have been filled.

Method No. 3: (1) Divide the total vote of each party by one, and assign one seat to the party obtaining the highest quotient. (2) Derive a new quotient for the party to which the first seat has been assigned, by increasing the divisor of the total party vote by one (i.e., $\frac{\text{party vote}}{1 + 1}$), compare this quotient with the other quotients previously derived, for which no seats have been assigned, and assign the second seat to the party presenting the

A further procedure is necessary in order to determine which of the party candidates is to be elected. This is done by finding the percentage of the total within his district obtained by each candidate. In the case of men running in more than one district the highest percentage obtained is used. The seats are then assigned to the party candidates in the order of these percentages. As was the case with the electoral law for the Chamber of Deputies, special provisions were necessary for the Val d'Aosta, which elects a single senator. The solution, however, differs from that applied to the election for deputy, where there is a run-off election a fortnight after the first election in the event no candidate receives a majority of the votes on the first balloting. For election to the Senate a simple plurality is sufficient.

As in the case of the Chamber of Deputies, whenever it is necessary to replace a senator, the next candidate in line of the same party in the same region takes his place.

There are two other categories of senators besides the elected senators. The Constitution provides (1) that all ex-Presidents of Italy shall be senators for life and (2) that the President of the Republic may appoint five senators for life for outstanding services in the fields of art, letters, or science (Art. 59).

Both houses are elected for five-year terms on the same day. The system of representation is only slightly less proportional in the Senate, as a result of the five life senators appointed by the President of the Republic, the *ex officio* membership in the Senate of the former Presidents of the Republic, and the few additional seats given to the three regions with a population that does not automatically entitle them to six senators (Trentino–Alto Adige, Basilicata, and Umbria). The higher age requirement, both for voting and for nomination, is unimportant. The difference of size between the two houses (630 deputies and 315 elected senators plus less than a dozen *ex officio* and appointed senators) is not important because the Senate itself is too large a chamber to make it an intimate deliberating assembly capable of proceeding in a manner significantly different from that of the lower house. The major parties, however, do have a slight advantage in the Senate, as the greater number of votes required to elect a senator works to the disadvantage of the minor parties. This advantage becomes important

---

highest quotient. (3) Derive a new quotient for the party to which the second seat was assigned by increasing the divisor of that party vote by one and proceed as in step (2) until all seats have been assigned.

The results obtained by each of these methods are identical. An advantage of the D'Hondt system is that fractional remainders need not be considered.

when, as in the national elections of 1958, the Christian Democracy obtained 50 per cent of the seats in the Senate and only 41.2 per cent of the popular vote.

The regions

The regional councils are unicameral. In the special regions they are elected for four-year terms and by proportional representation. Except for Val d'Aosta, which has not had such power delegated to it, the regions enact their own electoral laws subject to the general provisions laid down in their constitutions.

Val d'Aosta uses the Hare system of proportional representation, by which each voter has one vote and the number of votes is divided by the number of seats in the council (thirty-five). This quotient, after disregarding fractions, is divided into each party total. The resulting quotients indicate the number of seats assigned to each party. If all seats are not filled in this process, the extra seats are given to the parties with the largest remainders. (Law 1257 of 1962).

The regional council of Sardinia is composed of seventy councillors. The three provinces of Sardinia are the election districts. The voting is similar to that for the Chamber of Deputies. The voter votes for a party and has three (in Nuoro), four (in Sassari) or five (in Cagliari) preference votes. Seats are assigned to parties by dividing the total number of votes within the province by the sum of the number of seats assigned the province plus three. The result is the electoral quotient, and the number of seats won by each party is the number of times the electoral quotient is contained in the party vote. Leftover seats, if any, go to the parties with the largest remainders (system of the major fractions). If this operation elects more councillors than there are seats, it is repeated, using as the new first divisor a number one less than the previous first divisor (i.e., for the second try, number of seats plus two, and for the third, number of seats plus one). The Friuli–Venezia Giulia system is similar except that (1) units smaller than the provinces are used as election districts, (2) the voter is permitted fewer preference votes, and (3) the electoral quotient is determined by dividing the number of votes cast by the number of seats assigned the district plus one (instead of plus three) (Friuli-Venezia Guilia Law No. 3 of 1964).

A system of proportional representation is used for the elections to the regional councils of Sicily and Trentino–Alto Adige, but the laws are so badly written that it is mathematically possible (1) for more deputies to be elected than there are seats in the assembly, and (2) for a party with fewer votes than another party to get more seats. No good purpose would be served by explaining this "system" in detail.[3]

The regional councils of the normal regions are elected by proportional representation for five-year terms according to a procedure that is almost a duplicate of the procedure adopted for electing the Chamber of Deputies (Law 108 of 1968).

Provincial councils (Consigli provinciali)

The elections for the provincial councils[4] are somewhat like the senatorial elections. The province is divided into single-member districts;[5] no candidate can run in more than three districts. To determine the electoral quotient, the total number of votes cast within the province is divided by the number of councillors to elect plus two, and the fraction is disregarded. The number of seats assigned each party is determined by dividing the province-wide party vote by the electoral quotient. In case all the seats are not assigned in this way, the remaining seats are assigned one each to the parties with the largest remainders from the division of the party vote by the electoral quotient. As in the case of the Sardinian regional elections and those for the Chamber of Deputies, in the unlikely but mathematically possible event that this operation results in assigning more than the legal number of seats on the Council, a new electoral quotient is obtained by reducing the divisor by one and this process is continued until a properly functioning quotient is found.

The candidates of each party are classified according to the percentage of the votes they receive of those cast in their district, and are declared elected in that order. A candidate running in more than one district is rated according to the highest percentage he obtains. As in the case of the senatorial elections, the method of counting ballots turns a system based on the use of single-member constituencies into a system of proportional representation.

[3] Sicilian regional law of March 30, 1951, No. 29, Art. 54; Trentino–Alto Adige regional law of August 20, 1952, No. 24, Art. 59. The article of the Trentino–Alto Adige law is copied almost verbatim from the Sicilian law. In both there is an ignorant misapplication of the Droop and D'Hondt systems of proportional representation. See John Clarke Adams, "Enigmatica elettorale," *Il mondo,* October 25, 1960, pp. 5–6.

[4] Law of March 8, 1951, No. 122, as modified by the law of September 10, 1960, No. 962.

[5] For the 1960 elections, Article 14 of the Law of September 10, 1960, permits the use of the electoral districts established for the implementation of the Law of March 8, 1951, which authorized the creation of two-thirds as many districts as there were seats. In case any party elects more councillors than there are districts, the additional seats will be assigned to additional candidates running at large.

This system is likely to lead to results that would appear shocking to Americans. Thus it is possible for no one to be elected in some districts and for two or more persons to be elected in others. It is also possible for the candidate who gets a plurality of the votes in his district to be defeated and for another candidate receiving fewer votes to be elected.[6] The system, however, does guarantee representation of the parties in proportion to the votes they receive.

Provincial councillors are elected for five-year terms, but since the new elections can be held only as the result of a governmental order, there is no assurance as to just when they take place. (The same weakness is found in the system of municipal elections). Since provincial (and municipal) councils are frequently dissolved by the central government before the expiration of their mandate and since the election of a new council (for a five-year term) is supposed to follow quickly (but does not necessarily do so), local elections do not fall on the same day in Italy. It is common, however, for a large number of them to take place at the same time.

Provincial councils in the special regions

The provincial councils of the two provinces (Trento and Bolzano) that form the region of Trentino–Alto Adige are composed of the members of the regional council that have been elected from each prov-

[6] The reader who wishes to see for himself can do so by assigning the seats according to the following simplified example. Given a province with five districts and four parties and with five councillors to elect:

Party			Districts		
	A	B	C	D	E
F	6000	250	250	250	150
G	2500	2400	2000	500	250
H	1250	2200	5000	5250	4350
L	250	5150	1250	5000	4250

The candidates elected are: Party F — none
Party G — Candidate in District A
Party H — Candidates in districts C and E
Party L — Candidates in districts B and E

The two candidates with the highest number of votes are not elected (Party F's candidate in district A, because Party F fails to amass total votes equal to the electoral quotient, and Party H's candidate in district D, because his percentage of votes in his district is lower than the candidates of his party in districts C and E). No one is elected from district D, and two candidates are elected from district E although 2000 votes less were cast in E than in D. Party G's candidate in district A is elected with 2500 votes, while two candidates in district D with 5250 and 5000 votes respectively are defeated.

ince (Constitution of Trentino–Alto Adige, Art. 42). The region of Val d'Aosta is composed of a single province and therefore the regional council performs the function of a provincial council. In Sardinia and Friuli–Venezia Giulia the councils are elected in the ordinary way.

In Sicily the provincial councils are elected by the members of the municipal councils. Each province is divided into one or more election districts and the seats vary in number from forty to twenty-four according to the population of the province. Each district is allotted its proportion of seats according to its population, and the number of votes cast by each municipal councillor is determined by the percentage of the provincial population within the commune, divided by the number of councillors. The councillors vote for a party list and are allowed one or two preference votes for individual candidates, depending on whether five or less, or six or more, provincial councillors will represent the district. The distribution of seats according to parties is determined by the D'Hondt system of proportional representation, and the individual candidates that will represent the various parties are those who have received the greatest number of preference votes (Sicilian regional law No. 16 of 1957). The Sicilians have not managed to get this system in operation.

Municipal councils (Consigli comunali)

The election procedure for communal elections in Italy varies with the size of the commune. In those with a population of 5000 or less each party may nominate and each voter may vote for a number of candidates equal to 80 per cent of the number of members in the council (which is fifteen for the communes with a population of 3000 or less and twenty for those from 3001 to 5000). This is known as the system of the limited vote, which virtually assures the majority party of 80 per cent of the seats and the representation of a single minority group. In these elections *panachage* (i.e., split ticket voting) is allowed.

In the communes with a population of over 5000 the local elections resemble the elections for the Chamber of Deputies. The list system of proportional representation is used and each voter votes once for a party by means of an X and in addition has preference votes to the number of four (in communes with no more than 500,000 population) or of five (in larger communes). The number of seats assigned the parties is determined by the D'Hondt system.[7]

---

[7] D.P.R. (Decree of the President of the Republic) of April 5, 1951, No. 203, as modified by law of March 23, 1956, No. 136, and law of August 10, 1964, No. 663.

Election campaigns

The Italian election campaigns have traditionally been based on a large number of *comizi,* public gatherings normally addressed by party leaders, and a great deal of billboard advertising. The parties spent so much money printing posters and pasting them on the walls of buildings, preferably over the posters of rival parties, that they agreed to the passage of a law that limits this kind of publicity to certain spaces designated and reserved for this purpose by the government. Each designated area has a space marked off for each party.

The intellectual level of the parties' appeal is generally low. The MSI and the PDIUM make little attempt to appeal to the intellect and offer no clear program. The Christian Democracy runs on its record and raises the bogey of Communism. The Communists attack the government and support the Constitution. Neither party, however, campaigns on a program. In its campaigning the PSI probably devotes more time than the other parties to discussing issues.

Starting with the 1960 *elezioni amministrative,*[8] the government-controlled radio and television network has presented a program, *Tribuna politica,* in which each party is given the chance to state its views through a leader of its choosing, usually the national secretary, and this leader is then subject to questioning by a group of journalists.

Participation in elections

The Italian voters take elections more seriously than the more blasé voters of many of the democracies. The percentage of turnout for the parliamentary elections is high (92–94 per cent). The fact that voting is technically compulsory may have some influence on the turnout, but more than anything else the interest in voting is probably due to the reaction to the twenty years of Fascist dictatorship, when voting was a sham.

The prestige of Italian elections has undoubtedly been enhanced by the way the government has twice accepted defeat by a small number of votes. In the plebiscite of 1948 on the "institutional" question of whether Italy was to remain a monarchy or become a republic, although the king lost his throne by less than two million votes out of a total of over twenty-three million, he accepted the decision in good

[8] This term, whose literal translation is "administrative elections," is normally used in Italy to designate local and provincial elections. The reasoning is that local government is only a branch of the administration and lacks legislative and judicial powers.

grace and left the country, remaining thereafter out of politics. In the elections of 1953 the Christian Democrats and their allies in power failed by less than 60,000 votes (out of a total of over twenty-seven million) to get the majority that under the election law known as the *legge truffa* (the fraud law) would have entitled them to 380 of the 590 seats. These instances give the voter reason to believe that not only is his vote actually counted, but that in some cases the voting is so close that it makes a difference.

There is, however, a not inconsiderable danger for the proper functioning of the democratic process in the present plethora of elections and election systems. The Italian voter is legally obliged to vote at least every five years for a senator (unless the voter is under twenty-five years of age) and an average of over a dozen deputies, at least every five years in a different election for a provincial councillor (unless he is from Val d'Aosta, Trentino–Alto Adige, or Sicily) and a lot of municipal councillors, and for a number of regional councillors. It is asking much of the voter to expect him to take all these elections as seriously as they deserve; it is certainly asking more of him than do many older and better established democracies.

Preference voting

One of the peculiarities of the Italian election system is its combination of proportional representation and preference voting. Most Italians, however, are content to vote for a party and do not bother to select the particular party candidates of their choice. Less than 20 per cent of the possible preference votes were cast in northern Italy (continental Italy, Emilia Romagna, and Tuscany) in 1963 while in southern Italy over 45 per cent were cast. As might be expected, the largest per cent of possible preference votes was cast by Christian Democrat voters,[9] for it is in this party that the greatest variance among the candidates occurs. In fact, the Christian Democrat preference vote is the vote that so far has determined the kind of government Italy is going to have. The party returns about four out of ten deputies. If the majority of the preference votes goes to rightists in the party, the government will go right of center. If enough preference votes go to the candidates of the Catholic labor movement and to the Catholic political leaders who at any given moment represent the party's various

[9] D'Amato, *op. cit.*, pp. 119, 125–132. The percentage of preference votes cast in the north decreased steadily from 1946 to 1963, while in the south there was a slight increase in preference voting over this period.

left-wing groups, Italy has a mildly left of center government. All this might be quite confusing to persons not cognizant of the activities of the warring leaders in the Republican and Democratic parties in the United States, where the policies of many leaders zigzag abruptly from right to left as they jockey for positions of power within the party hierarchy and for positions of favor among the voters. Just as it may be more important to pick the right candidate in a primary election in the United States than to vote in the final elections, so the exercise of the preference vote in Italy may have more effect on the policies of future Italian governments than the selection of the party for which one votes.

The methods employed for gaining preference votes often display the ingenuity of the candidate better than the common sense of the voters. Raffaele De Caro, a liberal and one of the last great local bosses of the south, used to have a helper in each community of his Benevento stronghold whose sole duties were to know every professional man, artisan or white collar worker in the community by name and to accompany De Caro on his visits to the locality and whisper the name of everyone who approached him, adding when possible some information about his family or his public life. De Caro was thus able to greet everyone by name who was likely to be literate enough to cast a preference vote.

The Christian Democrat Ugo Angiolilli used a variant of this method. Taking advantage of the fact that Roman Catholic ceremonies are open to the public and that his political stronghold, Civitavecchia, was near Rome, he managed to attend most of the weddings, baptisms, and funerals in the environs of Civitavecchia. This gave him the chance to kiss the brides, fondle the babies, and weep at the funerals. To be sure he would be identified and his presence remembered, he would always leave a visiting card and in the case of weddings and baptisms would follow this up with another card for each anniversary. Two other deputies, Francesco Colitto and Salvatore Foderaro, built up large and faithful followings through the use of letters of recommendation and questions in Parliament. Colitto's position was so strong that he was able to switch parties (from the *Uomo qualunque* (Common Man) party to the Liberals) without any loss of power in Molise. Foderaro maintained his position of leadership of the Christian Democracy in Catanzaro by the astounding achievement of averaging ten parliamentary questions a day over a particularly active five-month period and by writing over 100,000 letters of recommendation annually, and then carefully reproducing copies of the letters and the answers to them and sending them back to the constituents.[10]

[10] Telesio Malaspina, "Il portafoglio dell'onorevole," *L'Espresso,* March 3, 1963, pp. 7–8.

I. *Example of election to the Chamber of Deputies*

Electoral district: Liguria
Seats: 20
Total votes: 1,122,529

Electoral quotient: $\dfrac{1,122,529}{20 + 2} = 51,024$

Party	Votes		Electoral Quotient		Seats		Remainder
DC	446,493	÷	51,024	=	8	+	38,301
PCI	275,957	÷	51,024	=	5	+	20,837
PLI	46,412	÷	51,024	=	0	+	46,412
PSI	193,143	÷	51,024	=	3	+	40,071
MSI	43,612	÷	51,024	=	0	+	43,612
Comunità della cultura, degli operai e dei contadini d'Italia	5,571	÷	51,024	=	0	+	5,571
Partito monarchico popolare	7,869	÷	51,024	=	0	+	7,869
Partito nazionale del lavoro	1,048	÷	51,024	=	0	+	1,048
PSDI	67,875	÷	51,024	=	1	+	16,851
PRI-PR	18,752	÷	51,024	=	0	+	18,752
Partito nazionale monarchico	15,797	÷	51,024	=	0	+	15,797

Seats assigned: 8 + 5 + 3 + 1 = 17
Seats still to be assigned: 20 − 17 = 3
The national office

(1) disregarded the remainders of the *Comunità della cultura* party and of the *Partito nazionale del lavoro* because they elected no candidate in any district;

(2) added the remainders for the other parties in each electoral district;

(3) added the number of unassigned seats in each district;

(4) divided the total remainders for all parties by the total number of unassigned seats to obtain the electoral quotient;

(5) divided the total remainder for each party by the electoral quotient and assigned to that party the number of seats equal to the quotient thus obtained;

(6) assigned any remaining seats to the parties with the major fractions derived in Step 5;

(7) assigned the seats to the electoral districts in which the percentages of the electoral quotient represented by the party's remainders were highest.

In this way in Liguria four additional seats were assigned, one each to the DC, the PLI, the PSI, and the MSI. This meant that with the use of the remainders Liguria had one more deputy than its population entitled it to and some other district had one less.

II. *Example of election to the Senate*

Region of Trentino–Alto Adige, divided into six single-member districts.

1. In districts 1 and 2 the Christian Democrat candidates received over 65 per cent of the votes cast and were elected.

2. In district 3 the SV candidate received over 65 per cent of the votes and was elected.

3. The total party vote for the other 3 districts was:

PLI	10,672
MSI	15,487
PSI-PSDI	43,191
DC	97,341
SV	44,625

4. Seats to fill: $6 - 3 = 3.$

PLI

$$\frac{10,672}{1} = 10,672 \qquad \frac{10,672}{1} = 10,672 \qquad \frac{10,672}{1} = 10,672$$

MSI

$$\frac{15,487}{1} = 15,487 \qquad \frac{15,487}{1} = 15,487 \qquad \frac{15,487}{1} = 15,487$$

PSI-PSDI

$$\frac{43,191}{1} = 43,191 \qquad \frac{43,191}{1} = 43,191 \qquad \frac{43,191}{1} = 43,191$$

DC

$$\frac{97,341}{1} = 97,341 \ (1) \qquad \frac{97,341}{2} = 48,671 \ (2) \qquad \frac{97,341}{3} = 32,447$$

SV

$$\frac{44,625}{1} = 44,625 \qquad \frac{44,625}{1} = 44,625 \qquad \frac{44,625}{1} = 44,625 \ (3)$$

5. Two additional seats assigned to the Christian Democracy and one to the SV.

6. Electoral quotient of individual candidates (percentage of total vote in district obtained by candidates):

DC	Spagnolli	59.17%	(elected)
	Benedetti	57.72%	(elected)
	Rosati	18.90%	
SV	Sand	41.66%	(elected)[11]

[11] The above examples contain the actual figures for the 1958 parliamentary elections. The same system is still in effect.

13

The Economy

The study of the politics of a country is not very enlightening to those who do not have at least an elementary understanding of its economics. In the case of Italy such an understanding is more obviously necessary than in some other countries because the Italian economy presents a number of unusual features not only in the problems with which it is faced but also in the tools by means of which it operates.

Economic geography

From the viewpoint of economic geography Italy is a poor country. It is long, narrow, and mountainous. The fact that the country is at the periphery rather than the center of a market is an added disadvantage.

Italy has only one large fertile plain, that of the Po Valley (*Val padana*), a triangle that extends roughly from Turin and Venice southeast to Rimini. Seven of Italy's twenty regions are all mountainous (Val d'Aosta, Liguria, Trentino–Alto Adige, Marche, Umbria, Abruzzi, and Molise), and only two, Veneto and Puglie, are over 50 per cent plain. The Veneto is principally in the *Val padana,* and the Puglie plain in the heel of Italy is the only other plain of any importance in the country.

Italy's subsoil wealth is unimpressive. There are exportable quantities of sulphur and marble, but other and more important materials (iron, copper, precious metals, coal, oil) are found, if at all, in insufficient quantities to supply the internal market. A valuable subsoil product recently discovered in large quantities under the Po Valley is methane gas, which although not exported in quantity, has become a principal fuel in northern Italy.

Hydroelectric power is abundant in the north because of the Alps. It is also abundant in certain seasons in central Italy, when the snows of the Apennines melt. It is in short supply in much of the south.

Italy is in two climatic zones. Northern Italy has a temperate climate with a humid winter, rain and fog in the plains and snow in the mountains, and a warm, relatively rainy summer. Only the Ligurian coast around Genoa, protected by the sea and the mountains, has a noticeably different climate, milder and wetter in the winter. As one proceeds down the peninsula, the winters become milder and the summers drier until in some parts of Sicily and Sardinia the summer is a period of arid stagnation in agriculture rather than of growth.

Demography

The population of Italy is somewhat over 50,000,000. The population is still increasing, although the natural increase is slight in northern Italy except for the staunchly Catholic rural sections of the Veneto and Trentino–Alto Adige. The lowest regional rate of natural increase for 1968 was .07 per cent for Friuli-Venezia Giulia and for Liguria, and there was a greater number of deaths than births in six northern provinces (Vercelli, Cuneo, Asti, Alessandria, Pavia, and Trieste).[1]

Emigration to foreign countries has normally been a safety valve for Italy's expanding population, and in fact much of the stock in the Americas originated in Italy. As the various American states have been less willing or less able to absorb large numbers of immigrants, the Italians from the south and from the prolific northern farm country have turned to northern Europe and to the industrial centers of northern Italy in search of work.

Because of this heavy internal migration, the resident population of the provinces and the regions follows a different pattern from that of the natural increase. In fact, seven regions — Friuli–Venezia Giulia, Umbria, Abruzzi, Molise, Basilicata, Calabria, and Sicily — lost population in 1968.[2]

Production

(a) *Agriculture.* Italy leads the world in grape and wine production and in olives and olive oil. She leads the western European countries in the production of rice and lemons and is second to France in wheat. The main food imports are beef, corn, and coffee. Tomato paste, citrus fruits, other fresh fruits and vegetables, and wine are exported. The salt demand is met locally by a government monopoly, which sells an inferior product at a high price. The sugar beet industry more than meets the demand for sugar, but it is protected by tariffs, and consumer's prices are high.

Italy's agricultural produce increases annually. At the same time the

[1] *Annuario statistico italiano, 1969* (Roma: Istituto centrale di statistica, 1969), pp. 23–24.
[2] *Ibid.,* p. 19.

farm population is diminishing, marginal farm land, particularly in the mountainous regions, is being abandoned, and the young adult population is deserting the country to seek work in the cities. By the early 1960's less than 30 per cent of Italy's employed (roughly 5,500,000 out of 20,000,000) worked in agriculture. By January, 1969, the number had dropped below 4,000,000.

In 1961 about 80 per cent (3,500,000) of Italy's farmers farmed their own land, and they cultivated about half (30,000,000 acres) of the farm land in production.[3] This system is particularly prevalent in continental Italy north of the Po. These independent farmers (*coltivatori diretti*) are the backbone of the Christian Democracy in the north, as well as of Paolo Bonomi's powerful pressure group within the party.

At that time about 12 per cent (50,000) of the farms were extensive, but they contained about 30 per cent (eighteen million acres) of the farm land. Such farms in the north are generally highly efficient and are operated according to modern methods. Living conditions on the industrialized units are not bad, but they are necessarily restrictive and yield little of the satisfaction the worker finds in tilling his own soil or the plot of ground he has rented. Young people particularly resent the regimentation imposed by management on these farms, where, for instance, it is necessary to have special permission to go out at night as the gates to the buildings are locked at a certain hour. A variety of produce is grown on the north Italian farms, including meat, dairy products, wheat, corn, fruits, and vegetables.

In central Italy the traditional farm system has been *mezzadria*, a form of sharecropping. Originally the farms were virtually self-sufficient units, each of which was tilled by a large farm family under the supervision of the owner or his agent. In the plains of Emilia the system is still economically feasible, but in the hill lands that predominate in the Marche, Tuscany, and Umbria the system is no longer profitable, and the land is being abandoned. The *mezzadria* system, which if left alone would die a natural death, is being hastened to its demise by a 1964 law prohibiting any new tenant farming agreements.

A principal result, however, seems to have been the abandonment in the 1960's of over a million hectares of farm land formerly operated on the *mezzadria* system, and the changeover from *mezzadria* to tenant farming on about 1,400,000 hectares, which constitutes a loss to farm use of over 40 per cent of the land.[4]

[3] These and subsequent agricultural statistics are from *Annuario statistico,* 1963, pp. 160–162, 345. (Later figures will be available after the next census, presumably in 1971.)

[4] See *La stampa,* January 10, 1971, p. 17. See also Luigi Einaudi, "Superata la mezzadria? Ammazziamola!" in *Il corriere della sera,* August 24, 1961.

The traditional farm in the south was the *latifondo,* a large, generally absentee-owned holding farmed haphazardly by *braccianti* (day laborers) paid only for the days they worked. There were also small sub-marginal farms, owned by the farmers themselves, where conditions were often worse. Poverty was further increased by the fact that the crops in the south are normally not diversified, and the independent farmer must pay cash for many of his necessities.

Through its extensive *riforma agraria* (agricultural land reform program) the government has radically altered the farm picture in large sectors of the south, as well as in two other small depressed areas, the mouth of the Po River in north Italy, and the district known as the Maremma in the Tuscan province of Grosseto in central Italy. Much of the land of the *latifondi,* which for centuries had been used for grazing or for extensive as opposed to intensive farming, has been expropriated and converted into small farms suitable for farming by single families. The government has built houses on these properties, so that the future owners can live on the land they will till, instead of living in clusters, often miles away, as was frequently the case with the *braccianti* in the past. The farms have been turned over on easy terms to individual farm families.

(*b*) *Industry.* Italy is not self-sufficient industrially, in part because of its lack of raw materials. Among the chief exports are Fiat automobiles and Olivetti typewriters and calculating machines, and Necchi sewing machines. The textile industry (located in good part in eastern Lombardy and the Veneto but also important in the cities of Biella [Piedmont] and Prato [Tuscany]) produces an exportable surplus of artificial fibers, cloth, and wool cloth. Leather goods, particularly shoes but including tons of gloves, also constitute sizable exports. Other chief industrial exports are fertilizers, gasoline (refined in Italy), refrigerators, and tires. The major industrial imports are raw materials, including iron, copper, fuels, rubber, wood, and wool.

Italian industry is concentrated in a small triangle in northwest Italy, the points of which are Turin, Genoa, and Milan. About 30 per cent of the nation's 700,000 industrial concerns in 1961 were located in the three regions of Piedmont, Liguria, and Lombardy. They employed over 54 per cent of all the industrial workers.[5]

In Turin are located the headquarters of the great Fiat works, and in nearby Ivrea is found the Olivetti business machines company. Italsider is centered in Genoa, and Milan is the headquarters of the Montecatini chemical and mining company, the Pirelli rubber company, Snia Viscosa, producer of synthetic textiles, and the two large department

[5] *Annuario statistico, 1963,* pp. 210–211.

store chains, Standa and Rinascente-Upim. Although the nominal head-quarters of the publicily owned industries are in Rome, the industrial plants are usually within the Turin-Genoa-Milan triangle.

Table 3

Italy's Nineteen Largest Industrial Concerns (1968)[6]

Name	Location	Ownership	Product	Sales in Millions of Lire
Fiat	Torino	Private	Automobiles	1,334,715
Agip	Roma	Public (ENI)	Oil	680,378
Italsider	Genova	Public (IRI)	Steel	570,058
Montecatini Edison	Milano	Private	Chemicals	567,640
Esso Standard Italiana	Genova	Private (USA)	Oil	544,586
Shell Italiana	Genova	Private (Great Britain & Netherlands)	Oil	395,294
Sip-Italiana Eser. Telef.	Roma	Public (IRI)	Telephones	389,411
Magazzini Standa	Milano	Private (Montecatini)	Department stores	253,903
Pirelli SpA	Milano	Private	Rubber	208,653
BP Italiana	Milano	Public (Great Britain)	Oil	208,563
Snia Viscosa	Milano	Private	Textiles	196,086
Alfa Romeo	Roma	Public (IRI)	Automobiles	189,279
Alitalia	Roma	Public (IRI)	Airline	182,493
La Rinascente	Milano	Private	Department stores	180,522
Total	Milano	(France)	Oil	169,000
Ing. C. Olivetti & C.	Ivrea	Private	Business machines	159,271
Mobiloil Italiana	Milano	Private (USA)	Oil	156,784
Anic	Roma	Public (ENI)	Chemicals	155,584
Snam	Roma	Public (ENI)	Methane gas	152,681

(c) *"Hidden exports" and balance of payments.* Italy suffers from an apparent chronic imbalance in foreign trade; no economy can remain solvent for long with an annual deficit of hundreds of thousands of millions of lire.

Italy's apparent deficits, however, are covered by "hidden exports,"

[6] From Claudio Risé, "Imperi vecchi e nuovi," *L'Espresso/colore,* No. 45, Nov. 9, 1969, pp. 10–25, at 15.

of which the most important is the tourist trade. Thus Italy's most valuable resource is the beauty of her land and the beautiful things with which she has adorned it. The Italian lakes, the lagoons of Venice, the fertile plains of Lombardy and Emilia, the rolling hills of Tuscany and that peculiarly clear atmosphere which makes the landscapes in Tuscan painting seem unreal to persons who have not lived there, the Bay of Naples, Amalfi, Taormina — each has a unique natural beauty. But the Italians have not idly contemplated their beauty. The Sistine Chapel of Rome and the galleries of Florence and Venice, the medieval treasures of Ravenna, the cathedrals of Tuscany and of Milan are revered by all lovers of the visual arts. La Scala is the shrine of Italian opera. These and countless other treasures are found in Italy for the delight of the tourist, and consequently, although it is true that the Italian land has not been prodigal in produce to be sent the foreigner for gold, it is in recompense rich in those qualities which bring the foreigner and his gold to Italy.

Another valuable "hidden export" are the remittances from Italians working abroad. Millions of Italians, at work in all parts of western Europe and in the Americas, send money back to Italy to their parents, their wives, their children, and their more distant kin. The remittances sent to the Vatican from Roman Catholic organizations around the world are to a large degree spent in Italy and constitute another important hidden export.

The dual economy of the north and the south

Mention has already been made of the economic cleavage between the north and the south. According to many orthodox economists, a condition such as Italy's cannot continue. The economic growth of Italy's north should lead to greater production, higher wages, and more employment, and the economic benefits of this growth should, they say, seep down to the south and gradually transform it into the image of the north. It is now realized that this does not necessarily happen and that under certain conditions (economists suggest that rising wages and oligopoly are determining factors) the increased production due to economic growth in the dynamic sector will be consumed by the same sector without improving the situation in the static sector, which will continue at the subsistence level.[7]

The Italian economy would appear to bear out this theory. Large oligopolistic combines, often government-controlled (see *infra*) operate Italy's large capitalist enterprises, which are found almost exclusively in the north. This sector of the Italian economy is prosperous and is ex-

[7] Luigi Spaventa, "Dualism in Economic Growth," *Banca Nazionale del Lavoro Quarterly Review*, XII (1959), pp. 386–434.

panding, producing more goods and more employment. As it expands it takes over more and more of the products that used to be made by the small independent artisan and semiartisan units. But this economic growth has hardly touched the agricultural mass in the south.

It was inevitable that under these conditions the state should try to do something for the south. The first major step was the creation of the *Cassa per il mezzogiorno* (Fund for the South) by law No. 646 of 1950. The *Cassa* is administered by an interministerial committee presided over by a minister without portfolio called the *Ministro per gli interventi straordinari nel mezzogiorno e nelle aree depresse del centro-nord* (Laws 717 of 1965 and 614 of 1966).[8]

The expenditures of the *Cassa* and of the ministries (with the exception of that of State-Controlled Enterprises) go primarily for public works and land reclamation. The government's encouragement of the industrialization of the south has been expressed in the requirement that the largest combines of state-controlled industries (IRI and ENI, described in the following section) make at least 40 per cent of their investments in the south, and in a series of laws offering various financial inducements to private business for the establishment of industries there.

There is no doubt that the government has succeeded in doing things to the south. The medicine has been strong, but it is not certain that it will have the desired effect. In the first place, much of the money spent by the *Cassa per il mezzogiorno* does not go to the south. Most of the materials come from the industrial north, as do many of the technicians. The land reforms have settled tens of thousands of families on their own farms, but these families are hardly able to market at a profit, owing in part to the power of greedy middlemen.[9]

The attempts to bring private industry to the south fall for the most part in one of two categories. One category comprises the "social capital" being poured into the south by the *Cassa:* roads, bridges, water, sewers, railways, flood control, gas, electricity, vocational training. The other category comprises the tax exemptions or reductions granted new industrial plants (and to a degree plant expansions) in the south. But the economic results of this impetus toward industrialization have not been particularly promising. Only a few of the large private concerns have set up plants in the south, among which are Olivetti, Fiat, Montecatini-Edison, Italcementi, and Pirelli. A major reason for the relative failure of the *Cassa* is the human element. A culture cannot be

---

[8] There is, however, no ministry for this minister to direct. For a discussion of this anomaly see Roberto Lucifredi, *Elementi di diritto pubblico,* 24th ed. (Milano: Dante Alighieri, 1968), p. 249.

[9] Ninetta Jucker, "The Italian State and the South," *Political Quarterly,* XXXI (1960), pp. 163–173.

changed overnight, and it will take a long time before the mass of southerners can function efficiently in a modern capitalist society.[10] The following anecdote illustrates one phase of the problem. An international
student work camp was set up in Calabria with all (or most) of the
proper government authorizations, to clean up an abandoned monastery
and turn it into a much needed school. After three weeks of hard work,
scanty food, and no pay, the students had the project well in hand and
the end in sight. Only at this time did the local engineer get around to
inspect the building and to declare it unsafe for occupancy. The engineer's delay thus robbed the south of any benefit of the students' good
will and hard work.

Put in other words, Italy is in the position of a colonial empire with
its colony incorporated within itself, where north Italy acts as the
imperial power and south Italy as the colony. The cost of administering
and policing the colony is paid out of public funds and ultimately by
all the taxpayers; the profits are absorbed by private enterprise. Thus
the money that the government pours into the impoverished south finds
its way into the pockets of the northern industrialists and farmers much
as the major portion of the billions that the United States spends on
foreign aid never leaves the homeland, where it is consumed in paying
for American products, for their transportation in American ships and
planes, and for American technicians. To the degree that state-owned
enterprises succeed in setting up plants in the south, this will be less true.
A huge state-owned steel plant, for instance, was opened in Taranto
in 1964.

The dual economy of private enterprise and state socialism

Whatever the Italian economy may be called, it is certainly not that
envisaged by Adam Smith and David Ricardo. To a degree never
known in the United States, the private sector is dominated by wealthy
and powerful families, whose heads are generally both the owners and
the managers of vast economic empires. In many ways they resemble
the enlightened monarchs of the eighteenth century. If the report is true
that Giovanni Agnelli, the owner of most of Turin, refers to Leopoldo
Pirelli as "my friend of Milan" and that Pirelli, who owns much of

[10] *Comitato dei ministri per il mezzogiorno, Relazione al parlamento*
(Roma: Istituto poligrafico dello stato, 1960), pp. 171–172. See also, for a
pessimistic view, Paolo Sylos Labini, "Riflessioni sul problema dello sviluppo
industriale in Sicilia," *Il ponte,* XV (1959), pp. 642–656. For the more opti-
mistic argument, that after all something finally is being done, see Luigi
Einaudi, "Il mezzogiorno e il tempo lungo," *Il corriere della sera,* August
21, 1960, p. 1. The difficulties encountered in setting up a plant in the south
are described in a novel written by the personnel director of the Olivetti
plant. See Ottiero Ottieri, *Donnarumma all'assalto* (Milan: Bompiani, 1959).

Milan, pays the reciprocal courtesy to the head of the Agnelli family, it is probable that these cultured and intelligent men are aware of the analogy between this form of address and that of the kings who referred to each other as "my cousin of France" and "my cousin of Spain."[11]

Family holdings of this type are diminishing (as did the monarchies of the past) as they fail to produce highly competent offspring. The Olivettis lost control of their family business after the death of Adriano the Great, and the upstart Motta family lost Motta when their self-made king and his designated successor both died. Even the famous and infamous Krupps in Germany were forced to abdicate. The Agnellis and the Pirellis, like the Fords, the Houghtons, the Gettys, and Howard Hughes, are still going strong.

The economic interests of these barons of Italian industry are protected by the Italian Confederation of Industry (*Confederazione italiana dell'industria,* shortened to *Confindustria*), which seeks to formulate a common policy for the members of the group. Confindustria also functions as one of Italy's important pressure groups. In recent years it has not been signally successful in Parliament and has lost several major battles, such as the forced withdrawal from Confindustria of all government-controlled enterprises and the nationalization of the electrical industry. It still retains a good deal of *sub rosa* influence, particularly in the ministries in which it is interested.[12]

Underneath these giants there is a substratum of the Italian economy where thousands of small companies find the competition far too stiff. These companies normally operate in industries, such as textiles, where capital outlay is not heavy, and they cut corners by underpaying labor.

State-controlled enterprises

The Italian state has entered the field of economics in a different manner from that of other countries and for different purposes. As in other countries, the early interventions were in the establishment of publicly owned utilities. Shortly after World War I, however, the government instituted a new practice, a practice which, incidentally, is nor-

[11] The Agnelli family controls over a hundred Italian corporations, including Fiat (automobiles), Cinzano (vermouth), *La stampa* (newspaper), Ercole Marelli and Magneti Marelli (electrical supplies), Florio (Marsala wine), and the toll road from Turin to Milan; and the Pirellis' power stems from their rubber monopoly. Other family empires that are still managed by the family include the Marzotto textile empire located in the Veneto and the Pesenti cement empire with headquarters in Bergamo. See Claudio Risé, "I padroni dell'industria," *L'Espresso/colore,* December 24, 1967, pp. 8–25.

[12] See Joseph LaPalombara, *Interest Groups in Italian Politics* (Princeton: Princeton University Press, 1964).

mally illegal in the United States: that of buying shares in private companies.[13]

With the advent of Fascism, Benito Mussolini as payment for capitalist support professed to take Italy out of business; he actually went as far as selling the state-owned telephone companies to private investors, but he kept the postal service and the state railways.

When the depression hit Italy in the thirties, however, the Fascist government did a *volte face*. The major banks of Italy had lent large sums to many of the country's industrial concerns, taking shares of stock as collateral. As these shares dropped in value the banks reached the verge of total collapse. At this point the government intervened by taking over the shares from the banks and turning them over to a newly created agency, IRI (*Istituto per la ricostruzione industriale* — Institute for Industrial Reconstruction). Thus practically overnight the Italian government became a major shareholder, often the majority shareholder, in many of Italy's larger corporations as well as in its bigger banks. In this way state socialism was instituted in Italy as a drastic cure for the ailing capitalist system.

Even after the fall of Fascism the Italian government did not change its methods for acquiring control over industry. There was no nationalization of key industries comparable to the program of the British Labor Party, nor was there confiscation of pro-Nazi collaborationist concerns as in France in the case of Renault, but there was a continuation of the investment banking functions of the IRI.

After a few years the holdings of the IRI, including those held over from the Fascist period and those acquired after the war, became a bewildering maze of more than a thousand interrelated companies,[14] most of which were actually of the type of the mixed enterprise, where the state held the controlling interest but where private investors still maintained a minority interest.

It had not been the primary purpose of the IRI to impose a coordinated plan of operations on its empire. Management was left mainly to its own devices to get on as best it could, but in order to assure some coordination the IRI founded some private holding companies to take over the control of the state-controlled industries in certain economic sectors.

The first of these, STET (*Società torinese esercizi telefonici*) was formed in 1933 to take over those of the five private companies that

---

[13] The first example is said to be the secret acquisition of shares in the *Südbahn*, the railway linking Trieste to Vienna, by the Minister of the Treasury, Stringher, in 1919. See Sabino Cassese, "Partecipazioni statali ed enti di gestione," *Rivista trimestrale di diritto pubblico*, VIII (1958), pp. 907–938, at 908.

[14] Ernesto Rossi, *Il malgoverno* (Bari: Laterza, 1955), p. 123.

had bought the government telephone system a decade earlier and that were already close to bankruptcy. In 1936 the second of this series of holding companies, Finmare (Società finanziaria marittima) took over control of four major shipping companies (Italia, Adriatica, Tirrenia, Lloyd Triestino). Finsider (Società finanziaria siderurgica) was formed for the steel industry in 1937. Finmeccanica came along in 1947 for the metallurgical industries.

The IRI unfortunately was mainly interested in those sectors of the national economy in the poorest financial condition, which were supported by Fascism in its presumptuous attempt at making Italy an autarchy, and therefore the IRI was often faced with the task of salvaging the salvageable in basically uneconomic enterprises. The IRI was also troubled by the fact that although it still controlled the majority of state-owned economic enterprises, a considerable number of other enterprises were the jealously guarded property of various other government agencies.

IRI, however, overshadowed all other business enterprises in the hands of the state until by the law of February 10, 1953, No. 136, the ENI (Ente nazionale idrocarburi) was formed. IRI can be likened to a non-self-liquidating RFC (Reconstruction Finance Corporation) that has gone into management instead of accepting repayment with interest on its loans. The ENI, on the other hand, is similar to a government-owned corporation like the TVA.

The major state-controlled operating companies turned over to ENI included AGIP (Agenzia generale italiana petroli — gasoline) and AGIP mineraria (oil wells), SNAM (Società nazionale metanodotti — methane gas pipelines) and ANIC (Agenzia nazionale idrogenazione combustibili — oil refining). Unlike the majority of the IRI holdings, which were in poor financial condition, the ENI holdings were solvent. Of the major units controlled by ENI, only ANIC has a substantial minority interest in private hands.

The original purpose of ENI was to exploit the oil and gas resources of the Po Valley, including methane gas, which has become a major source of fuel in Italy. Under its highly dynamic founder, Enrico Mattei,[15] ENI expanded greatly. After six years ENI was composed of sixteen mining companies, three nuclear energy companies, ten gas distributing companies, seven refining companies, ten oil distributing com-

---

[15] The late president of ENI is not the same man as the influential journalist Enrico Mattei, the editor of La nazione (Florence), until 1970, when he became editor of Il tempo (Rome). The ENI Mattei was killed when his private plane exploded. Some of the press suggested that the explosion was OAS sabotage; others blame the Mafia. For an account of Mattei's public life see Dow Votaw, The Six-legged Dog (Berkeley and Los Angeles: University of California Press, 1964), and Claire Sterling, "Mattei, the condottiere," The Reporter, March 20, 1958, pp. 20–23.

panies, four chemical companies, and seven miscellaneous concerns.[16] It was also deeply involved in the oil business in Africa and Iran and had control of a leading Milan newspaper, *Il giorno*.

By the law of December 22, 1956, Parliament took a big step in the direction of creating order out of the chaos of the state-controlled economic enterprises. This law created a new Ministry of State-Controlled Enterprises (*Ministero delle partecipazioni statali*) and gave it control over IRI, ENI, and most other state economic enterprises, but not the postal service and the railways.

With the creation of the Ministry of State-Controlled Enterprises, Italy has established an original system for dealing with the state's business holdings. There appears to be no other ministry like it in any other country. The most obvious originality is to place virtually all state enterprises under a single minister. The organization and the policy of the Ministry, however, are also worthy of note.

Control is exercised through a hierarchic structure with the Ministry at the apex and the operating companies at the base. In the middle are *enti di gestione*, holding companies that supervise the operating companies in a single economic sector. In the case of IRI-controlled companies, IRI itself occupies a place in the hierarchy between the *enti di gestione* (STET, *Finsider*, etc.) and the Ministry.

The Ministry is responsible for the overall policy as determined by the government, the *enti di gestione* are responsible for the efficient division of labor among the concerns in their sectors, and the operating firms are given the greatest possible independence at the operating level so that they and the private firms, their competitors, can compete under conditions of equality.

In carrying out this reorganization the Ministry has a free hand to consolidate or liquidate existing bodies and to create new ones. It has already set up three new *enti di gestione* for (1) the mining industry, (2) the film industry, and (3) the spas.

The Italian state also runs a series of economic enterprises (often called *aziende autonome*) independent of IRI and ENI. These enterprises are entirely government owned. The *aziende* of major importance include:

Amministrazione autonoma monopoli di stato. Salt and tobacco monopoly (in Ministry of Finance)[17]

Azienda autonoma delle poste e dei telegrafi. Postal and telegraph service (in Ministry of Postal Service)

[16] *Annuario parlamentare,* 1959–60, pp. 1202–05.

[17] In 1970 the government proposed to reorganize this agency, giving it complete financial and managerial autonomy. The agency will be rebaptized IFITAS (*Istituto finanziario delle industrie del tabacco e del sale*).

Azienda autonoma delle ferrovie dello stato (**FFSS**). State railroads (in Ministry of Transportation)

Azienda nazionale autonoma delle strade statali (**ANAS**). State roads authority (in Ministry of Public Works)

Azienda delle foreste demaniali (**ASFD**). Public forest authority (in Ministry of Agriculture and Forests)

Azienda dei servizi telefonici. Telephone authority (in Ministry of Postal Service)

Azienda di stato per l'intervento nel mercato agricolo. Farm price control agency, established in 1963 to meet Common Market requirements (in Ministry of Agriculture)

Cassa depositi e prestiti. Government bank (in Ministry of the Treasury)

Ente nazionale elettricità (**ENEL**). Electricity monopoly (in Ministry of State-controlled Enterprises)

Istituto poligrafico dello stato. Government printing office (in Ministry of the Treasury)

By far the most important of these bodies is ENEL, which represents the single significant act of nationalization effected by republican Italy. The electrical industry of Italy, headed by the giant Edison Company of Milan, had vast economic power that was not always used in the public interest. Nationalization of this industry was part of the price that had to be paid for Socialist support of the fourth Fanfani government. The creation of ENEL was a serious defeat for big business interests, and for years thereafter the pros and cons of establishing it were debated. The procedure used for taking over the electricity services, however, was in itself a half victory for the business interests. Instead of following the British example and merely transforming the electrical shares into bonds bearing interest comparable to the dividends of the former shares, a method by which the state gets control of an industry without any money changing hands, the Italians adopted a complicated method that has left the former electrical companies in control of their capital, which they are diverting to other industries.

Private enterprise

The sectors of the Italian economy that are not under the financial control of the government are subjected to various types of legal control. Some of these controls apply to specific industries and others are general.

Typical examples of the special controls applied to specific industries are the methods used with respect to the silk, paper, and rice industries.

It is doubtful if any of these industries would be profitable under the conditions of a free economy. In each case, therefore, the government has established an agency (*ente*) that in effect artificially creates a condition of monopoly in the sole interest of the private producers as against what would normally be thought of as public policy.[18] The controls take the form of taxes, foreign currency restrictions, import and export permits, and social security payments, all of which are complex, costly, and time-consuming. The paper work involved is incredible, and the benefits derived (except to the civil servants, who are kept moderately busy in this wise) are minimal. Unfortunately, these controls weigh particularly heavily on small business, not only because the unit cost of all this paper work is many times greater but because the small businessman is at the mercy of every dishonest tax collector who comes to inspect his books, as well as of every dishonest labor or sanitary inspector who cares to fleece him. Big corporations are not afraid of these people; they can fight them in the courts or appeal over their heads. The little fellow, however, is at their mercy.[19]

Conclusion

There is a divergence of opinion concerning the degree to which the Italian economy is under state control. Italy's is certainly an unplanned

[18] See Rossi, *op. cit.,* pp. 291–301, for an account of the mischief done by these agencies.

[19] Just before starting to write this chapter one of the authors received a statement from an Italian publisher to the effect that 6720 lire (about eleven dollars) was due him for royalties. The publishers, however, had first to deduct the 3 per cent IGE turnover tax (200 lire), reducing the sum owed the author to 6520 lire. They subsequently deducted five separate taxes, each of which is figured as a percentage of two-thirds of the total royalty after the deduction of the IGE. One is called a personal property tax and is 8 per cent of two-thirds of the royalty. Another is a municipal tax of 2.4 per cent of two-thirds of the royalty. The provincial tax is 1.2 per cent of two-thirds of the royalty. Charitable agencies get .5 per cent of two-thirds and finally an unspecified supplementary tax takes 4.2 per cent of two-thirds of the royalty. The total taxes paid add up to 16.3 per cent of two-thirds of 97 per cent of the original 10 per cent royalty, plus 3 per cent of the royalty, or about 13.5 per cent of the 10 per cent royalty. In the case in point the various taxes were:

		lire	dollars
IGE	3% of 6720 lire	200	.32
Personal property tax	8% of ⅔ of 6520 lire	347	.56
Municipal tax	2.4% of ⅔ of 6520 lire	104	.16
Provincial tax	1.2% of ⅔ of 6520 lire	52	.08
Charity tax	.5% of ⅔ of 6520 lire	25	.04
Supplementary tax	4.2% of ⅔ of 6520 lire	182	.29
		910	$1.45

economy, and in this sense it is signally free. Government action to encourage or direct economic development, to avoid depression, to protect consumers, is rarely taken and when taken, feebly executed. On the other hand, the government burdens the economic system with complex, unnecessary controls, ineffective for the achievement of socially desirable goals but harmful to efficient management.

The anomalous and paradoxical condition of the Italian economy does not seem to indicate stability and makes prediction particularly precarious.

Italy's paucity of natural resources and her geographical position on the periphery of the European market place her at a disadvantage in competing with the large economic units of continental Europe. Her lack of capital and her excess of unemployed unskilled labor are additional drawbacks.

In the postwar period, to the delight of the liberal economists, who see in Italy a prime example of the unplanned economy, the country enjoyed a spectacular and prolonged boom. Wages, employment, and the standard of living all rose sharply. One element in this economic growth was the creation of the European Common Market, which reduced tariff barriers and encouraged trade among the member nations (Belgium, France, Germany, Italy, Luxemburg, and the Netherlands). In the early 1960's, however, Italy faced a depression characterized by serious inflation, increased unemployment and a highly unfavorable balance of payments. Although the steps the government took to curtail the depression were, according to many economists and practically all socialists, both tardy and puny, nevertheless by early 1965 the crisis seemed to have passed.

The wave of strikes that has disrupted the economy in 1969, 1970, and 1971, many of which were of a political nature, i.e., aimed at the government and not the employer, appears to be seriously weakening the economy, increasing costs and lowering production. This, added to the other factors mentioned above, has put Italy more or less on a par with Great Britain and France, but well under the rank of Germany and the Netherlands on the economic scale.

The Common Market exposes the Italian economy to shock that may disturb or destroy its uncertain equilibrium. On the other hand, the fluidity of the economy and the rapid change it is undergoing give it a resiliency and adaptability that a static and traditional economy would find it difficult to emulate. These considerations do not make prediction any easier, but they may serve as arguments in support of a positive prognosis.

14

Labor and Social Security

The unions

With the rise of liberal democracy in the Western world labor has become for perhaps the first time in history a major political force.

This result has occurred through no design of the theorists or practitioners of politics. Not a few scholars, including Karl Marx, foresaw the rise of this new force, but labor's arrival on the political scene was the inevitable and unconscious result of the economic evolution of the West, and its efforts at organization and its struggle for recognition were in good part improvisation of the early labor leaders. As a result there is no single pattern of development; instead, most of the major countries have a labor history that in many of its phases is unique.

Thus the main trend of the American labor movement has concentrated on economic power rather than political power. American labor has never had a powerful political party of its own. The British trade unions, on the other hand, while never neglecting the need of establishing their economic power, built up a political party strong enough to oust the Liberals as the second party in the British two-party system, and have consistently held that the ascension to political power and the control of the state machinery by a labor party should be a major goal of the trade unions.

The tradition of the French labor movement is anarcho-syndicalist. As in the United States, labor leaders in France rarely hold public office, and although the French unions are now more closely related to the various left and Catholic parties, there is little interchange between the party and the union personnel. Although the apolitical position of the French and American labor movements is a point of similarity between them, the American unions far surpass the French unions in their economic strength. While the American unions rely preponderantly on economic pressure in their struggle for improving the lot of the working man, the French unions devote a significant part of their energies to political maneuvers.

In its political action the Italian labor movement resembles the British, but its economic position is far weaker than that of British and American unionism. As a result of their economic weakness and in the absence of a strong anarcho-syndical tradition, the Italian unions maintain close political ties and operate principally in the political arena. In a multiparty system, particularly in a state where a Communist party and a Catholic party compete for the labor vote, labor cannot unite politically; therefore the Italian unions are weak in the political field as well as in the economic field.[1]

The origins of the movement are closely allied with the rise of socialism in Italy. The political orientation of labor, as well as its weakness, favored the development of horizontal rather than vertical unionism, and thus the labor chambers (*camere del lavoro*), in which all organized workers within the provinces were represented, tended to be more important than the vertically organized national unions (*federazioni di categoria*).

The first national trade union of importance in Italy was the CGL (*Confederazione generale del lavoro*), affiliated with the major Socialist party. In the period immediately following the First World War the CGL was competing against three rival federations: the Catholic CIL (*Confederazione italiana del lavoro*), the anarcho-syndicalist USI (*Unione sindacale italiana*), and the strongly nationalist UIL (*Unione italiana del lavoro*). Little concerted action was possible among these unions, known respectively as the red, white, yellow, and black unions.

The CGL was Marxist and internationalist; its leadership, however, was not revolutionary. In fact, its foremost men, Rinaldo Rigola and Ludovico D'Aragona, even cooperated with Fascism. The CIL was strongly anti-Marxist. The USI was particularly strong among the

---

[1] There is more material available in English on the Italian labor movement than on most other aspects of the Italian political scene. See, for example, Joseph LaPalombara, *The Italian Labor Movement* (Ithaca: Cornell University Press, 1957); John Clarke Adams, "Italy," in Walter Galenson, ed., *Comparative Labor Movements* (New York: Prentice-Hall, 1952); Humbert L. Gaultieri, *The Labor Movement in Italy* (New York: Vanni, 1946); John Norman, "Politics and Religion in the Italian Labor Movement," *Industrial and Labor Relations Review*, V (1951), pp. 63–91; Maurice F. Neufeld, *Italy: School for Awakening Countries* (Ithaca: New York State School of Industrial and Labor Relations, 1961); Daniel L. Horowitz, *The Italian Labor Movement* (Cambridge: Harvard University Press, 1963); Walter Galenson, *Trade Unions and Democracy in Western Europe* (Berkeley: University of California Press, 1961); and Walter Galenson, *Labor in Developing Economies* (Berkeley: University of California Press, 1962).

railway workers. The ultranationalist UIL was the group most closely related to Fascism, and after 1922 it became the basis of the Fascist labor movement, and the other unions passed out of the picture. The UIL leader, Edmondo Rossoni, became the major figure in labor under Fascism.

After the fall of Fascism and as a result of the political alliance in the national liberation committees (CLN — *Comitati di liberazione nazionale*) of the seven anti-Fascist parties (PLI, PDL, DC, PRI, P d'A, PSIUP, PCI), a single labor federation was founded and given the name CGIL (*Confederazione generale italiana del lavoro*). The Catholics, Socialists, and Communists were supposed to have an equal voice in this federation, and a minority representation was accorded the Republican and the Action parties. The Liberals and the Labor Democrats, as rightist parties, were not included.

The organization of the CGIL closely resembled that of the parties that created it; it was suspended in midair. The general secretaries were appointed by the parties, as were most of the secretaries of the labor chambers and the national federations; they were not chosen by the union members they claimed to represent. In this early period, therefore, the CGIL resembled an organizing committee for a union more than it did a union.

The men chosen by the parties to head this organizing committee were perhaps the best available to them at the time. The Communists appointed Giuseppe Di Vittorio, a man of outstanding ability and considerable experience, who had been head of the CGL in exile during Fascism. The Socialists had expected to appoint an equally capable and experienced man, Bruno Buozzi, former secretary of the FIOM (*Federazione impiegati operai metallurgici*), the metalworkers' union, but the Germans captured him a few days before they evacuated Rome and killed him as they were retreating. The Socialists chose as a substitute Oreste Lizzadri, a Neopolitan who had distinguished himself in the partisan war but who turned out to be no match for Di Vittorio. The Catholic choice was Achille Grandi, the most experienced and capable of the former CIL leaders, but Grandi was dying of cancer, and he had little influence on the CGIL.

The first job of the CGIL was to get contact with the workers and to build up its membership, starting from zero. By and large it was not successful in doing this, although a few unions, such as the printers' union (*Federazione italiana lavoratori poligrafici e cartai*), the port workers (*Federazione italiana lavoratori dei porti* — FILP), the electrical workers (*Federazione italiana dipendenti aziende elettriche*), and the seamen (*Gente del mare*) — the latter two under their pre-Fascist leaders Vasco Cesari and Giuseppe Giulietti — acquired an appreciable degree of popular backing. Of the provincial labor chambers, that of Turin under Luigi Carmagnola was one of the first to begin operating with efficiency and with the solid backing of dues-paying members.

Under this system of political unionism, labor unity was possible only so long as the coalition of anti-Fascist parties on which it was based remained intact. When in June, 1947, the Communists were forced out of De Gasperi's government, probably with American and Vatican connivance, a split in the labor front became inevitable.

The theory of the CGIL was that the major mass parties, the PCI, the PSIUP, and the DC, would have equal representation. It was possible to maintain this equality, however, only so long as the CGIL remained merely an organizing committee. Just as in the political arena the period of equality of the seven CLN anti-Fascist parties was succeeded by a period of hegemony of the Christian Democracy as soon as the political elections were held, so a period of Communist hegemony of the CGIL commenced as soon as the union's chiefs were elected by the union members.

The Communist hegemony of the CGIL was not the result merely of the superior ability of Di Vittorio; this superiority went all the way down the line. With only a few exceptions, the most active and dedicated labor organizers were Communists, and at this period the Communist Party alone appeared to realize the importance of controlling organized labor and to be willing to subsidize its organizers. In many a provincial capital the Communist secretary of the labor chamber was the only secretary to be found on duty; the others were working on other part-time jobs to support themselves. Likewise the Communist organizers were the ones who could attend regional or national meetings, with their way paid by their party. So the spring of 1947 found the Communists with the majority of the votes in the CGIL, and when a split in the labor movement was inevitable it was the anti-Communists who had to leave and who had to start anew to organize another labor movement, from the top and without a firm foundation of active dues-paying members.

At this period in Italian labor history, foreign influences were bringing their pressure to bear on Italian labor. The Russians and the Americans, and to a lesser extent the British, all had their fingers in the pie. The Russian government invited the Italian labor leaders to Russia and carefully extended the invitation to Communists, Socialists, and Catholics alike, and most of those invited went, including the Christian Democrat leaders. The Americans refused to invite the Communists, and as a result most of the Socialists refused the American invitation, so that few but the Catholic leaders came to the United States. The AFL and CIO were also operating in Italy, often at cross purposes.

The AFL, through Luigi Antonini of the ILGWU (International Ladies' Garment Workers' Union), exercised primarily a political influence in the direction of anti-Communism, and primarily with the Christian Democracy and right wing Socialist (then PSLI, later PSDI) groups. The CIO and the British Labour Party took a less political attitude and were more concerned with strengthening the labor movement.

The formal breakup of the CGIL started in July, 1948, with the withdrawal of Giulio Pastore, its Christian Democrat secretary, and his followers. This defection was followed by those of the Republicans and two major waves of Socialists. After a time these forces coalesced in two new federations, the CISL (*Confederazione italiana dei sindacati dei lavoratori*) and the UIL (*Unione italiana del lavoro*).

The CISL was founded on April 30, 1950, as a fusion of Pastore's Catholic LCGIL (*Libera confederazione generale italiana dei lavoratori*) and the FIL (*Federazione italiana del lavoro*), composed of the Republicans and the first wave of Socialists to leave the CGIL. This fusion was strongly urged by the Christian Democracy and by various American sources, including the labor attaché at the American Embassy, on the theory that in this way a single non-Communist federation could be established that would not bear the stigma in anti-clerical labor circles of being dominated by the church. It was opposed by more than 90 per cent of the membership of the PRI, which held a plebiscite, and by the labor section of the PSDI.

The UIL, which has nothing to do with the pre-Fascist (and pro-Fascist) UIL, was founded in March, 1950, a month before the fusion that created the CISL was effected. It was composed of the rank and file and most of the leaders of the FIL as well as a second wave of Socialist labor leaders to leave the CGIL.

A fourth federation, the CISNAL (*Confederazione italiana dei sindacati nazionale dei lavoratori*), with Fascist leanings, was also founded in March, 1950. It is of little consequence but receives some Christian Democrat support in order to lessen CGIL influence in any inter-union committees. One CISNAL representative, for instance, is on the CNEL (*Consiglio nazionale dell'economia e del lavoro*).

All four of the labor federations (*confederazioni*) are organized in the same manner. Each dues-paying member is twice represented, once through his national union (*federazione*) and once through the provincial labor chamber (*camera del lavoro*). The former is called vertical representation, the latter horizontal. The only actual contact the average worker has with his union is through the labor chamber, which, as a local headquarters for all workers with a common political faith, by its very nature is politically oriented. Few Italian unions have their own locals, and although the only unions with large memberships in

Rome are the civil service unions and the printers, the political orientation of the unions is such that with a few exceptions, headquarters are in Rome.

In 1971 the Italian labor movement remained in the doldrums. The Christian Democracy still dominated the CISL, the PCI dominated the CGIL, and the Fascists the CISNAL. The UIL was badly split by PSI, PRI, and PSDI factions. In recent years, however, there has been increasing talk of reuniting the unions. Reunification is a partial reality on the practical level of strikes and contract negotiations, but it is far from a reality on the structural and political levels. Perhaps the strongest support for unification comes from the metalworkers' union, which represents the workers who in the United States might belong to either the steelworkers' union or the UAW. The metalworkers are probably the strongest vertical union in Italy.

Nothing is more indicative of the weakness of the Italian unions than a view of their financial structure. Dues are collected in a rather haphazard manner and do not appear to be the major source of union funds. The CGIL rejects the checkoff system for dues collection in favor of collectors who go around to the workers selling stamps, which are then pasted in their membership booklets to show they are paid up. The Communists like this system, and it keeps up personal contacts between workers and organizers. On the other hand, the CISL uses the checkoff. The CGIL system makes it particularly hard to judge active membership, as workers may skip a few months' dues without officially losing membership. The other sources of union income are similar to those of the parties and cooperatives — entertainments, and subsidies from management, from foreign labor movements, and from foreign governments. This condition is in sharp contrast to that of the CIO, the AFL, the British TUC, and the German DGB, which latter is said to own the fourth largest bank in Germany. Italy thus has one of the weakest labor movements in Europe. Of the major countries only France is thought to have a smaller percentage of organized workers.

The position of the Italian unions is further weakened by the strength of the employer organizations. Collective agreements are normally industry-wide and not, as in the United States, between a national union and the management of a single concern. The *Confindustria* (*Confederazione italiana dell'industria*), a sort of glorified NAM, is the normal bargaining agent with which the industrial unions are faced. Only after the withdrawal of the government-controlled industries from the *Confindustria* has a substantial breach been made in the unity of management representation. The farm owners are also united in the *Confederazione generale dell'agricoltura italiana*, a solid and not particularly enlightened organization, and by Paolo Bonomi's powerful association of independent farmers (*Confederazione nazionale coltivatori diretti*), which forms a solid and influential bloc at the right of the Christian Democracy.[2]

What American or British labor can gain from economic pressure on management the Italian worker seeks through political pressure Labor laws rather than collective agreements are the main source of his benefits.

During 1969 and 1970 the Italian economy was disturbed by virtually continual strikes. Some of them were economic strikes that the unions undertook against the major industries. These strikes, of a kind frequently met with in the United States, were combined with sporadic strikes of most of the public services, including the postal and transport services, the public utilities, social security services, and even the tax collectors. In addition, numerous general strikes for purely political purposes were called. These were evidence of the frustration of large segments of the population as a result of the inability or the unwillingness of the government to face the social problems which beset Italy (such as inadequate housing and schools, ineffective, and irresponsible administration). Every year in the sixties Italy lost a larger percentage of man hours per employed worker than the average of the other five Common Market countries. The amount of increase rose from 30% in 1960 to over 1275% in 1969.[3]

These manifestations of labor unrest in Italy have had serious consequences. They have been a divisive force, increasing the tension between economic classes, and they have strengthened the forces of reaction. They have seriously weakened the Italian economy, sharply increasing the cost of living.

On the other hand, the political strikes seem to have increased the power of the unions, which in spite of their differing party affiliations have learned to act together harmoniously. Regardless of the weakness of the unions in Parliament the Colombo Government has been treating directly with the unions on questions of overall government policy and has gained their support, i.e., their agreement to soft-pedal political strikes in exchange for "medicare" and low cost housing reforms.

Labor legislation

The Italian Constitution has a good deal to say about labor. Article 4 in the section on fundamental principles establishes the right to

---

[2] See Joseph LaPalombara, *Interest Groups in Italian Politics* (Princeton: Princeton University Press, 1964).

[3] Sergio Devecchi, "Il tempo perduto," *La stampa,* May 30, 1971, p. 9.

work and the duty to contribute to the material or spiritual well-being of society. Later articles speak of the right to an adequate wage, to a maximum hours law, to a weekly holiday, and to paid vacations (Art. 36); the right of equal pay and maternity benefits to women, and to child labor legislation (Art. 37); the right to social security (Art. 38); the right to organize (Art. 39), and the right to strike (Art. 40). Article 39 further states that unions can be required by law only to register and to maintain a democratic organization. It further provides that the registered unions together can make collective agreements binding on all workers and employers in a given field.

In 1970 the Italian Parliament enacted a labor charter (*Statuto dei lavoratori,* Law 300 of 1970) that granted certain rights to workers by defining and proscribing unfair labor practices. The result seems to be an Italian Labor Relations Act without a Labor Relations Board to act as an enforcing agency. Enforcement and interpretation of the provisions of the Act are left to the regular courts, and only time can tell how effectively they may perform this task.

The rest of the present labor legislation dates for the most part from the Fascist period. This legislation is complex and uncoordinated. The intricate distinctions in pay and other benefits that it creates render a large amount of Italian economic and labor statistics difficult to interpret.

The basic minimum wage is set in the various collective agreements. These agreements are generally national in scope, but the practice has been to supplement them by provincial agreements that establish the basic wage for the province. Labor is trying to eliminate these distinctions between provinces, and the tendency now is to approach a single national minimum basic wage for each industry.

Besides the basic monthly wage, the worker receives a cost of living bonus (*indennità di contingenza*) and a Christmas bonus (*gratifica della tredicesima mensilità*). The cost of living bonus is triggered to the government's cost of living index. The Christmas bonus is equal to a full month's pay.

A family allowance (*assegno familiare*) is further added for each dependent. This is paid from a fund collected entirely from management. It is the percentage of the national payroll that it is calculated will cover the family allowance payments across the nation. The individual employer contributes to this national fund any tax in excess of what he pays out to his own employees and receives from the national fund any deficit he incurs by employing personnel with larger than average families.

Another significant factor in employer-employee relations in Italy is the high severance pay that must be given to each employee who is dismissed without cause. For white collar workers the severance pay is equal to a full month's salary at the latest rate, for each year of employment. Thus a worker with thirty years' seniority receives a severance bonus of two and a half years' salary. The treatment afforded manual laborers was far less advantageous under Fascism but is now approaching that of the white collar workers.

Italy also has elaborate factory legislation and a labor inspectorate with regional and provincial offices, a principal function of which is the enforcement of these laws. The system is not particularly effective, as the laws are complex and the inspectors too few to permit careful enforcement. It is extremely difficult for the employer, even with good intentions, to live up to the letter of the law and therefore he is at the mercy of the inspector, who almost invariably can find some reason to exact a fine. The employer naturally resents the intrusion of the inspector, whom he fears and distrusts. The British-American type of union through its grievance committees or its legal offices can handle many of the cases that devolve on the labor inspectors, not only at less expense to the state, but in a manner conducive to less animosity and friction.

Social security

Although take-home pay in Italy is relatively low, labor costs are high because of a poorly organized social security system. In industry, in fact, management normally pays premiums for the various types of obligatory insurance that often equal over half the worker's take-home pay.

Little purpose would be served in describing the present (1971) Italian social security system in detail. One of the unpleasant and difficult tasks facing the Parliament and the Government is the complete overhauling of a system that has given remarkably little satisfaction. There are more than a hundred social security agencies in Italy, but much of the work is done by the three major agencies, INPS (*Istituto nazionale per la previdenza sociale*), INAM (*Istituto nazionale per l'assicurazione contro le malattie*), and INAIL (*Istituto nazionale assistenza infortuni lavoro*).

The INPS administers old age pensions, unemployment benefits, and twelve other compulsory insurance plans, some of which insure against specific diseases (e.g., tuberculosis), and others of which insure a specific category of workers (e.g., sailors). The basic old age pension premiums are paid by the employer by means of stamps he buys and places in the worker's work record book. Old age pensions are paid to retired males of sixty years of age and females of fifty-five who have made payments to INPS for fifteen years.

Unemployment benefits are also handled through INPS. The basic benefits are disbursed from funds paid in by management by buying special stamps. Benefits are paid for a maximum of 180 days, and the amount received depends on the number of dependents of the unemployed worker.

INAM and at least fifteen other agencies administer compulsory health insurance. Insurance benefits are of two kinds, free medical care, including hospitalization and drugs, and wages. Free medical care will normally be given for a maximum of 180 days, but in certain cases it is permanent for retired workers. INAM pays wages to only certain categories of workers, of which non–white-collar industrial workers are the most important. Maternity benefits are paid by INAM to workers who are covered for wage payments. These benefits for non–white-collar industrial workers are 80 per cent of the wage for the three months before and the eight weeks after childbirth. In cases where INAM does not make this payment, the employer is obliged to pay directly. In 1967 INAM disbursed about one billion lire to pay medical costs and wages.

INAIL insures Italian workers against injury. Over three million industrial workers are covered by this insurance. All premiums are paid by management. The workers receive two-thirds of their wages during temporary disability and a lump sum payment of 120,000–180,000 lire ($200–$300) for permanent disability.[4]

[4] The following example shows how unsatisfactory the system can be in practice.

On May 6, 1952, a worker in his thirties with a wife and three young children was run over by a truck while bicycling to work. The injuries were such that two years later the workman was still unable to go back to his job. The company that owned the truck carried private insurance, and the insurance company was ready to pay the injured man 1,500,000 lire, a sum equivalent to about $2250. This would have made it possible for the man to buy a little bit of land and to cultivate it with the help of his wife and children.

INAIL refused to allow the private insurance company to indemnify the injured workman, since it claimed the exclusive right and obligation to indemnify him. Presumably, however, it required the private insurance company to pay the 1,500,000 lire into INAIL's own coffers. Then, on October 30, 1953, almost eighteen months after the accident, INAIL informed the injured man of the terms of its settlement. It should be noted that no provision had been made for maintaining the family during this eighteen-month period, during which they presumably had no income. After the eighteen months' delay INAIL decided that the man's work capacity was reduced 60 per cent. Actually, since he was unemployed, the 40 per cent work capacity remaining to him was of little value. Next INAIL determined that the worker's pay had been 1000 lire a day. Actually it had been more than this. Then it multiplied 1000 lire by 300 days to get the worker's annual wage. The product of this multiplication was 135,000 lire instead of 300,000. Then it calculated that 60 per cent of 135,000 lire was 48,600 lire instead of 81,000,

A general overhauling of the system, including an integration of the various agencies and a streamlining of their administration, is necessary. The task, however, will run counter to the vested interests of powerful blocs of bureaucrats.

If Italy is to compete successfully in a European common market, however, the labor costs must be reduced, as they are generally higher than in the other member countries. It is in fact in part because of their desire to be freed from some of this burden that many Italian businessmen have favored Italy's participation in the Common Market. In 1964 the Moro government came up with a partial solution to the problem more palatable to the civil servants involved. This solution was to socialize the costs of social security by raising general taxes to subsidize the social security system, relieving business of some of the burden of supporting the present cumbersome and incompetent agencies and placing an additional burden on the general taxpayer. In October, 1964, a first step in this direction was made that was expected to transfer annual costs of two hundred billion lire from business to the public. Needless to say, the business interests are quite willing to submit to this type of socialization. In 1970 the Colombo Government approved an extensive reform of "medicare," which would place Italy substantially on a par with Great Britain (and far beyond the United States) in respect to this basic social service. The reform would offer free medical care and hospitalization to all, would make INPS the collecting unit for all "medicare" taxes, and would abolish most of the minor "medicare" agencies, but not INAM.

---

or rather of 180,000 which is 60 per cent of 300,000 lire. The result was that the worker received a monthly pension of 4000 lire (about $6), with an annual supplement of 9720 lire (about $15) for the support of his four dependents. With this supplementary pension each of his dependents could buy about four small rolls of the cheapest bread each week. Thus INAIL has presumably collected 1,500,000 lire from the private insurance company, which it is keeping for itself, and is paying the injured worker less than 4 per cent interest on the money which is rightfully his, but which he will never receive. (Letter from Monsignor Don Giovanni Lacidonia to Ezio Vigorelli, Minister of Labor and Social Security, reprinted under the title "La beffa senza cena," in *Il ponte,* X (1954), pp. 841–42.)

15

Italy as a
Liberal Democracy

Whether viewed as a form of government or as a political philosophy, liberal democracy will probably be recorded by historians as one of the most noble, important, and original contributions of Western civilization. By liberal democracy is meant a government by popular majority in which the power of that majority is limited by a belief in the supreme interest of individual growth and by the legal and moral rights of minorities, including minorities of one, to the free expression of their dissent.

Liberal democracy has developed out of many factors of Western culture, and the humanism of the Italian Renaissance is not the least of these. Italian philosophers and reformers have made major contributions to its development. Cesare Beccaria in the eighteenth century, Giuseppe Mazzini in the nineteenth, Luigi Einaudi and Piero Calamandrei in the twentieth are luminous examples of the liberal democratic tradition in Italian thought that inspired both the *Risorgimento* and the *Resistenza.* From unification to Fascism Italy operated under a liberal democratic constitution that reflected the philosophy of Cavour and his supporters. Twenty years of Fascism gave Italy a taste of the antithesis of this philosophy. The republican Constitution is among other things an attempt to return to the principles of liberal democracy and to devise new and modern instruments through which this political philosophy can better be expressed.

Civil liberties

The Constitution provides Italy with a detailed bill of rights that specifically guarantees many substantive rights which in the United

214

States are only indirectly protected through the interpretation of such traditional catch-all phrases as due process of law and equal protection of law. On the other hand, the procedural rights that are spelt out in the United States Constitution are less clearly defined in the Italian one.

Freedom of speech and press in Italy is much as it is in the United States, with two exceptions. Theatrical performances and the sale of books can be banned only on the grounds that they are contrary to *buon costume* (i.e., obscene), and for no other reason. Only films are subject to precensorship, and only for minors or on the grounds of obscenity. In Italy, however, unlike the United States, a police permit is necessary to operate a printing press, and there is a crime called *vilipendio*. *Vilipendio* is a disrespectful statement or action toward certain public institutions and the persons who direct them. The Constitution does not mention *vilipendio*, but the penal code has a good deal to say about it (Arts. 278–279, 290–293, 297–299, 302–303, 402–404, 406, 408, 410.)

The hypothesis on which the crime of *vilipendio* rests is that persons and institutions have a kind of honor that can be damaged by the public statement of uncomplimentary opinions or facts. Under Italian law a court might consider it a crime to express such opinions as the following:

1. "A major factor in determining the pronouncedly lesser antagonism felt in the United States during World War II against Italy than against Germany and Japan was the fact that the United States did not fear Italy and actually considered the Italian army a little ridiculous." (*Vilipendio* of the Italian army)

2. "President Gronchi is unfit to hold public office in republican Italy because he served in the first Mussolini government." (*Vilipendio* of the President of the Republic)

3. "In Italy, as in many other countries, the dregs of society are attracted to the police force and therefore a number of Italian police officers are a disgrace to the country they claim to serve." (*Vilipendio* of the police)

4. "The Romish doctrine concerning purgatory and pardons, worshiping and adoration as well of images as of relics, and also invocation of saints, is a fond thing vainly invented, grounded upon no warranty of scripture but rather repugnant to the word of God." (*Vilipendio* of the Roman Catholic Church, taken verbatim from the Articles of Faith of the Church of England)

Americans would feel quite free to make statements of this kind about the United States. The only restraints would be the canons of good taste; the criminal law does not enter the picture. In Italy, however, the former secretary of the Milan section of the Radical party, Mario Besana, was sentenced to four months in jail for sending a telegram to the Minister of the Interior Fernando Tambroni criticizing him for congratulating the police on "capturing a murderer," thereby prejudicing the arrested man's case before his trial. Besana's telegram read: "Your telegram to police on Fenaroli case expression your lack of sense of political and legal propriety."[1] This statement is less strong than those made by a large part of the United States press when President Nixon repeated Tambroni's injudicious behavior during the Manson trial.

Legal restrictions, however, are not the sole enemies of freedom of expression. It has been said that Italy has freedom of the press but no free press.[2] Journalism, like medicine and the law, can and should be a mission, a public service that supplies a fundamental ingredient of liberal democracy. Most of the provincial press and a significant part of the big city press in Italy, as in the United States, is owned and operated by persons who show no awareness of this mission, and the papers they publish serve little or no useful purpose. Among the exceptions are the two papers with the largest circulation in Italy, *Il corriere della sera* of Milan (estimated circulation 550,000) and *La stampa* of Turin (estimated circulation 500,000). *Il corriere* has good coverage but is generally fearful of political or economic change. It is owned by a wealthy and conservative Milan family. *La stampa,* part of the Agnelli empire, takes a more central position on public affairs. The other newspapers worthy of note in Italy include *Il giorno* and *La voce repubblicana. Il giorno,* published in Milan, a government-owned newcomer (through ENI), with an estimated circulation of 300,000, has perhaps the fourth largest circulation in Italy (after the Communist *L'Unità* with an estimated 350,000).[3] *La voce repubblicana,* the organ of the Republican party, published in Rome, has a long history of sober political reporting.

Freedom of religion is guaranteed by the Italian Constitution, but

---

[1] See *Il ponte,* XVI (1960), pp. 432–433. See also Paolo Barile, Mauro Calamandrei, Giancarlo Marmori, Francesco Russo, and Lucio Villari, "Vilipendio?" *L'Espresso/colore,* April 27, 1970, pp. 7–17. On December 6, 1960, a policeman was arrested for the crime of not arresting a man who insulted him, although the man was known to the policeman to be suffering from a nervous illness. See *La stampa,* December 7, 1960. Later the judge dismissed the case.

[2] Jacques Nobécourt, *L'Italie à vif* (Paris: Editions du Seuil, 1970), p. 185. Nobécourt is Rome correspondent of France's most prestigious paper, *Le monde.*

[3] The estimates on circulation are from Nobécourt, *op. cit.,* p. 337.

the special position of the Roman Catholic Church under the Lateran Pacts and the remnants in the law of other acts of the Fascists in the cause of religious intolerance have led to a somewhat equivocal practice in this matter. Freedom of assembly is well respected in Italy except when a timorous prefect or *questore* prohibits political rallies because of an exaggerated fear of disorder. As in the United States, the prohibition of unreasonable searches or seizures is not as earnestly enforced as one would wish.

The Italian Constitution specifically grants equal rights to women, but this provision is being tardily and reluctantly applied. Female suffrage is a fact. Equal pay for equal work is sanctioned by Italian legislation and by the ILO, and it is a requirement of the Common Market. All public careers except in the armed forces are now legally open to women, but the more conservative services (e.g., the judiciary and the diplomatic service) have shown no enthusiasm for putting this law into effect.

Problems peculiar to Italy

For the protection of civil liberties, however, a constitution can never be more than an instrument and a symbol. Liberal democracy itself is a thing of the spirit. As Learned Hand said, it must live in the hearts of men.

The liberty that is in the hearts of many Italians, that inspired the new Constitution, and that is an ornament of the Italian tradition does not always become an effective reality. (The same can of course be said for all liberal democracies, and the student who deludes himself into thinking liberty is safe in the United States should look at an annual report of the American Civil Liberties Union.) Italian liberalism, however, must overcome some particularly difficult obstacles, the major of which are state-citizen relations and state-church relations, and the mafia.

(*a*) *State–citizen relations.* A perceptive Italian once said that the reason so many foreigners were enamored of Italy was that they were in the fortunate position of being able to enjoy the physical beauties of Italy, to appreciate its history and culture, to meet its people, and even to indulge in the material comforts offered by its cuisine, its excellent servants, and its wide tolerance of personal foibles, all without having more than superficial contact with what for Italians themselves is the wrong side of the coin — the Italian state.

It is difficult for Americans to understand the Italian attitude toward the state. In the United States as in Great Britain, patriotism is closely linked to loyalty to the state and to the government. In Italy, as in France, patriotism brings out a loyalty to a national ideal but not necessarily to the presently existing state. The difference in attitude is caused in part by the lack of continuity of French and Italian states and governments.

Italy is a country with a European majority governed by a Mediterranean minority. The south dominates the administration and imprints on it two traditionally Mediterranean habits of mind: a profound suspicion of the public and a belief that public office is a benefice rather than a public service. There are, of course, among the mass of southern Italians in the public administration many individuals of high intellectual caliber and impeccable morality, and in fact the Mediterranean mind at its best is quick to grasp generalities and is essentially unbureaucratic, but for all their virtues these exceptional administrators are not strong enough in numbers to have changed the tone of the administration as a whole.

In a well-functioning democracy the public servants who operate the administration are responsive to parliament and to the public. The vast social reforms of the Labor party government in Great Britain after World War II were implemented by the predominantly conservative administrative class of the British civil service. The American presidents who do not trust the political mentality of the top civil servants appointed by the rival party are wont to make wholesale changes in personnel in top and middle management. The Italian career civil service, on the other hand, has been singularly unresponsive to the Constitution, to Parliament, and to the public, and has gone its own way, serving its own interests.

This attitude is well described by Ernesto Rossi in the following words:

> Every branch of the public administration, every public service, is today a feudal fief of a group of bureaucrats who like the medieval barons give only a purely formal recognition to the sovereignty of the power that invested them with their fief. Each group of bureaucrats has its own sphere of influence in certain agencies or offices or corporations subsidized by, controlled by, or dependent on the government, where its members can obtain salary supplements (for serving on the board of directors, for acting as accountants or inspectors) and where they can exercise arbitrary power in letting contracts, granting licenses. . . . No foreigner is allowed in these fiefs, and ministers, deputies, and senators, as well as bureaucrats from other fiefs, are all treated as foreigners. . . . Thus, for example, the Ministry of the Treasury has been try-

ing for years to get back millions of acres of good land that the Ministry of Defense took over for calvary horses during the war.[4]

Perhaps even more succinct is the statement attributed to one of Italy's most distinguished historians and influential anti-fascists, Gaetano Salvemini: "If they [the police] should accuse me of raping the little madonna on the top of the Milan cathedral, I would think first of escaping and only later of defending myself against the charge."[5]

Bureaucracies tend by nature to be cumbersome, egocentric, and oriented toward tradition, and it would be unfair to the Italian administration to single it out for condemnation for attributes endemic to bureaucracies in general.

There are, however, some procedures of the Italian administration that perhaps merit exemplification. The following information concerning the Ministry of Defense[6] relates practices that help explain the peculiarly chaotic and unfocused achievement of the Italian bureaucracy.

In 1967 Italy spent 3.3 per cent of the national income on military expenses, as against 2.9 for Belgium, 3.6 for Norway and West Germany, 4.4 for France, and 6.4 for Great Britain, but of the European nations for which data were available (for 1965 — France, West Germany, Great Britain, Italy, the Netherlands, and Russia) Italy was highest in the percentage of military costs that went into (a) salaries and (b) operations and maintenance, while it was lowest in the percentages spent on (a) construction and equipment and (b) research and development.

Under Italian law it is possible for the administration to spend moneys to be allotted to it in future years. The Ministry of Defense availed itself so consistently of this special privilege that as of December, 1967, it had already spent over 300 billion lire ($480,000,000) that were still unappropriated.

Again, as of 1967, the law provided for 192 generals, while the Ministry had promoted to ... rank 474 persons still on active duty. Parallel data for the Navy and the Air Force were respectively seventy to 202 and sixty-three to 228. The excuse for this quite illegal situation is that the pay of the officers is so poor that only by illegal promotions can sufficient numbers of relatively competent personnel be encouraged to remain in the service.

[4] "Le vie del Signore," in Rossi, *Il malgoverno,* pp. 403–412, at 405–406.
[5] Cited in Mino Monicelli, "L'italiano e i carabinieri," *L'Espresso,* September 7, 1970.
[6] Cited in Bonacina, *op. cit.* Unfortunately, the further chapters promised by the guide of this "tour" of the Roman ministries have so far (1971) not appeared.

Another method of getting around the low basic salaries of the armed forces (as well as of civil servants) is that of paying special bonuses. There are so many types of bonus in Italy that it is almost impossible to reckon what a specific government official is being paid. In the case of the armed services there are, according to the *Corte dei conti,* 119 special bonuses that are still paid on occasion. Among these are found a bonus "in place of firewood," one to pay for a servant and the keep of a quadruped (which presumably could be a dog, cat, or panda), another for blacksmiths, another called simply "professional bonus," and still another for military police buglers (*trombettieri corpo guardie di pubblica sicurezza*) but not for regular army buglers. (Readers who have been wondering about the contents of the nefarious *leggine* that occupy so much of the time and energy of Parliament may take this as an example.)

Furthermore, the Ministry does not appear to be above spending money for unauthorized purposes. Funds designated for USO type activities for enlisted men are spent on mountain and sea resorts for the exclusive use of officers and their families. There is also a National Association for the Protection of Youth, whose president is a Demo-Christian Senator and whose vice president is a priest. The purpose of the organization is "to provide for the protection of the physical integrity of young people and to educate them in the knowledge of the perils with which they are surrounded, as well as to encourage study and moral standards for the purpose of developing tomorrow's citizens." The Ministry has contributed two million lire without authorization to this association.[7] Faced with such Augean stables one wonders what Hercules could have effected.

It would not be fair to give the impression that the Defense Ministry is an anomaly among Italian ministries. The following facts chosen virtually at random contradict any such false impression.

(a) When he was President of the Council of Ministers Amintore Fanfani, believing that many top administrators were receiving supplementary pay from other government positions beyond their full-time salary, ordered all directors general in the various ministries to inform him immediately of all additional paid government positions they held. Only a seventh of them replied; the others failed to answer, and the Government fell before Fanfani could take further action.[8]

(b) In 1965 the Minister of Public Works, Giacomo Mancini, ordered the suspension of his subordinate, Giuseppe Rinaldi, the director general of ANAS, the state road building and maintenance monop-

---

[7] *Ibid.*
[8] Livio Zanetti, "Lo spreco di stato," *L'Espresso,* June 20, 1965, p. 7.

oly.[9] The result of this conflict is instructive. Mancini is the leading Socialist (PSI) politician from Calabria. Calabria has great economic need for the Milan-Reggio toll road that ANAS is building. As of 1970 the road is in operation from Milan to a point just within the region of Calabria, and although the road was completed in most of Calabria by 1965, ANAS has not finished the connecting lines — a matter of only a few kilometers — in the ensuing five-year period.

(c) In 1964 a public body, the National Association for Civilians who Suffered War Damages (*Associazione nazionale tra le vittime civili di guerra*) spent 66 per cent of its budget on operational expenses, and in the same year ANMIL (a workmen's compensation body) spent 442,000,000 lire of its 540,000,000 lire budget on operational expenses and only 48,000,000 lire on the victims of work accidents.[10]

(d) The administration is not only guilty of malfeasance and misfeasance; it is a past master of non-feasance as well. In 1969 *La stampa* reported that the *giunta provinciale* of Palermo, the executive authority of the province, had not met a single time during the preceding nineteen months.[11]

(e) Although the Ministry of the Interior receives 102,000,000,000 lire annually (about $175,000,000) to run some 40,000 charitable agencies, according to the Christian Democrat Deputy Maria Pia Del Canton the Ministry actually pays out pensions as low as 500 lire ($.80) a month to unemployed persons.[12]

(f) The Colombo Government announced in October, 1970, that it hoped to increase the pay of an army draftee from ninety to 250 lire ($.15 to $.40) a day starting in July, 1971.[13]

Strangest of all is the administration's inability to spend money. Parliament has often been quick and generous in coming to the aid of victims of natural disasters, as the recent cases of the burst dam at Vajont, the Florentine flood, and the Trapani earthquakes will attest. Yet the administration proved unable to disburse the sums appropriated.

The system for the administration of justice is also breaking down.[14] In 1969 half the prison population was awaiting trial, and roughly one

[9] Telesio Malaspina, "Il direttore che diceva sempre di no," *L'Espresso,* November 21, 1965, p. 12.

[10] Nello Ajello, "Nel paese di scandalusia," *L'Espresso,* March 20, 1966, p. 3.

[11] Antonio Ravidà, "Le giunte fantasma," *La stampa,* November 2, 1969, p. 11.

[12] Paolo Pavolini, "Tre poliziotti per un orfanello," *L'Espresso,* November 15, 1970, p. 3.

[13] *La stampa,* October 22, 1970, p. 2.

[14] See Enzo Enriques Agnoletti, ed., "La magistratura in Italia," *Il ponte,* XXIV (1968), pp. 715–928.

prisoner out of three would either be freed or given a shorter sentence than the time he had already served.[15] New rules of procedure for criminal cases granting greater protection to the defendants are sabotaged by judicial officials, who perhaps more than any other class of citizens should scrupulously obey the law.[16]

The dislike, not to say the scorn, of the average Italian for his state (but not for the concept of Italy, which he reveres) is increased by the countless small annoyances to which he is subjected. Little seems to be done to lighten his load *vis-à-vis* the state. It is difficult for him to take any action without wittingly or unwittingly putting himself in the wrong. Nuisance taxes in the form of stamps, often of a total value of less than one cent, must be affixed to many receipts. Official letters must be written in special forms on taxed paper and one must seek expert advice to discover just how much one must pay for the paper to be used for the particular letter one wants to write. The receiver of duty-free packages pays a fee to the customs for the trouble of examining the package, and at least in Florence the office where he must collect the package is open only six hours a week (Monday, Wednesday, and Friday from nine to eleven o'clock).

No one who is forced to use the salt and the matches sold by the government monopoly and who has seen an adequate match and matchbox and decently processed and packaged salt can have much respect for the interest the state displays for the welfare of the consumer. The impudence of the public services is such that the electrical company considers itself authorized to cut off service without warning for nonpayment of a single bill that was never received, and the telephone company requires full payment of whatever sum for which it cares to consider a subscriber liable before it will even consent to inform him of the destination of the long distance calls for which he is being charged.

A striking example of how askew the relations are between the administration and the public is found in the advice given to its readers on income tax matters by the official Vatican newspaper, the *Osservatore romano*. According to Italian practice the tax the individual is required to pay is based on a guess by a tax official of what the taxpayer's income is. It is assumed that the income the individual declares is false, and a higher income is almost automatically assessed to him. A citizen who felt a moral obligation to declare his actual income but who did not wish to be taxed afterwards on a considerably larger income wrote a letter to the *Osservatore romano* for guidance. A priest gave the paper's reply.

---

[15] Mino Monicelli, "Innocente che vuol dire?" *L'Espresso,* July 20, 1969, pp. 16–17. Law 195 of 1970, however, has reduced the maximum limit of pre-conviction incarceration to from six months to four years, depending on the seriousness of the crime imputed to the accused.

[16] Giovanni Conso, "I diritti trascurati," *La stampa,* May 29, 1970, p. 8.

It read in part: "So long as the present system persists, no moralist can conscientiously require a rigorously and scrupulously prepared declaration, which would inevitably result in grave loss to the declarer personally or to his business."[17]

Italy was and to a large extent still is a police state. During Fascism the police were under practically no legal restraint. They arrested at will and deported without trial, and their permission had to be obtained before the citizens could exercise such basic liberties as printing or distributing public announcements, forming groups, or holding meetings.

The Italian police have not willingly renounced their former power, and Parliament has done little to force them to do so,[18] although the Constitutional Court has abrogated some of the more obviously unconstitutional provisions of the Fascist law on public safety (*Testo unico di pubblica sicurezza,* Royal Decree of June 18, 1931, No. 773).

The low esteem in which the police are held, however, predates Fascism. Gaetano Mosca, writing in 1887, had this to say on the subject: "The main cause for this general inefficiency of the police stems principally from the repugnance the better elements feel toward entering the service."[19]

The power of the police in Italy is based in part on an exaggerated concern for public order. One writer has said, "The majesty that is lacking in the institutions and the laws, and that the principle of public interest fails to convey, in Italy is bestowed on the concept of public order,"[20] and public order is primarily a police matter. The importance placed on public order by the Italian government may not be so irrational as it seems. So long as public demonstrations remain a major weapon of the opposition, public order becomes a necessary condition for the continuation of the government, which may have more to fear from a demonstration than from elections.

[17] Reported in *La stampa* January 28, 1965, p. 15.

[18] For a history of the bills for the revision of the law on public safety see Silvio De Fina, "Testo unico di pubblica sicurezza e costituzione," *Giurisprudenza costituzionale,* IV (1959), pp. 964–993. The author is highly critical of Christian Democratic bills presented by Scelba, Fanfani, and Tambroni, all of which he considers unconstitutional in various sections and quite lacking in an understanding of liberal democracy. It is a sad commentary on Italian politics that the two Communist-sponsored bills (the Scoccimarro bill and the Terracini bill) are more liberal and more consonant with constitutional principles. For a criticism of the Tambroni bill see Marco Ramat, "Una legge retrograda," *Il ponte,* XIV (1958), pp. 1378–1382.

[19] Gaetano Mosca, *Teorica dei governi e regime parlamentare* (Turin: Loescher, 1887), Chapter IV, sect. 3.

[20] Nicola Chiaromonte, "I fatti e la cifra," *Tempo presente,* V (1960), pp. 453–455, at 453.

The superordination of public order has its obvious drawbacks. The career of a prefect or a *questore* can be seriously jeopardized by public demonstrations in his bailiwick, but gross infringements of civil liberties rarely cause a black mark to be placed after his name by the Ministry of the Interior. Under these circumstances the prefect who would not close meetings, ban parades, sequester posters, or arrest agitators when he had reason to expect disorder would indeed be a superman or a fool. Italian prefects are rarely either.

The question of bribery of public servants has reached such proportions that the Roman Catholic Church has come out with advice for priests who hear confessions, suggesting that it is not a sin to offer or pay a bribe to a public servant when it appears to be the only way a citizen can get a service to which he has a right, and it is not a sin to accept payment for assistance to the public that goes beyond the call of duty.[21] An evil but legal practice in some Italian ministries permits public servants to pocket the fees they collect for serving the public. The right to do so is called *diritto casuale*.[22]

There is thus an immense gulf between the governors and the governed and a traditional deep-rooted distrust. On both sides there is little realization of the mutual interests that should make collaborators rather than adversaries of the two groups. The fault does not lie entirely with the administration; from its position of authority, however, it is better able to take steps to break the vicious circle. The government is aware of the problems and has taken some steps in the right direction; nevertheless, to effect a lasting improvement not only old laws and regulations, but even more important, old mentalities must be renovated or eliminated.

There has been much talk about a drastic reform in the bureaucracy. Responsible government officials in and out of the career service agree that such a reform is needed, but bureaucracies that are determined to maintain their privileges are difficult to bring into line. Some improvement has been made. The tax structure has been reorganized, mechanization has been introduced, and directions go out now and then in the interest of decentralization and of better public relations. Not even the majesty of the laws, however, can reverse traditional attitudes overnight, particularly when the old attitudes are conducive to the personal comfort of the group that holds them.

(*b*) *State–church relations.* It is difficult for Americans, brought up under a system of religious freedom and separation of church and state,

---

[21] *Il ponte*, XV (1959), p. 1491.

[22] See Luigi Einaudi, *Lo scrittoio*, pp. 211–299, for a strong attack on the *diritti casuali*.

to understand state-church relations in Italy; yet these relations have played a dominant role in Italian politics for hundreds of years.[23]

The religion of the vast majority of Italians is the Roman Catholic, although it is estimated that only about 25 to 30 per cent of Italians attend mass with reasonable regularity.[24] The only Protestant group with roots in Italy is the Waldensian church, which has members primarily in Piedmont and which predates the Reformation by centuries. There is also a small traditional congregation of Sephardic Jews, located mainly in the cities of central Italy, such as Ferrara, Ancona, Livorno, and Rome. The Waldensians and the Jews because of their small number are of little political consequence; the centuries-old dispute is among the Catholics themselves — between the clericals and the anticlericals, or in medieval language, between the Guelphs and the Ghibellines.

The dispute is not basically a religious one, although the small numbers of Protestants, Jews, agnostics, and atheists in Italy are naturally on the anticlerical side; the dispute is over the temporal power of the Pope. It should be remembered that even Dante Alighieri, probably the greatest Roman Catholic poet, opposed the papal claim to temporal power and did not hesitate to consign a certain number of former Popes to damnation in his *Inferno*. Ever since his time the ranks of the anticlericals in Italy have been composed in the main of Roman Catholics.

The basic dispute is as follows: the clericals believe that the Pope as vicar of God and as a major and infallible source of divine inspiration is superior to all other powers and that Roman Catholics are bound to obey the teachings of the church and the specific orders of the church in all phases of life. The traditional Roman Catholic dogma teaches that the Roman Catholic Church is a divinely inspired institution that by the will of God is superior in quality to any other institution and that the truth it professes and propagates is God's own truth. It is the humanitarian mission of this institution to convert all mankind to its faith (the only true religion), to prohibit the propagation of other beliefs

[23] The student is referred to four excellent books on the history of state-church relations: Arturo Carlo Jemolo, *Chiesa e stato in Italia negli ultimi cento anni* (Turin: Einaudi, 1948); Luigi Salvatorelli, *Chiesa e stato dalla rivoluzione francese ad oggi* (Florence: Nuova Italia, 1955); Vittorio Gorresio *et al., Stato e chiesa* (Bari: Laterza, 1957); and Aldo Capitini and Piero Lacaita, *Atti della costituente sull'Art. 7* (Manduria and Perugia: Lacaita, 1959). Part of the Jemolo book has been published in English by Basil Blackwell at Oxford in 1956. See also Guido Calogero, "Church and State in Italy," *International Affairs*, XXXV (1959).

[24] *La stampa*, March 8, 1960, p. 9, interview with Mons. Gilla Gramigni, Archbishop of Novara, gives 30 per cent. Gaetano Salvemini made a reasoned estimate of 25 per cent in 1955. See Gaetano Salvemini, "Il cattolicesimo italiano," *Il ponte*, XI (1955), pp. 948–949. There is no indication that the percentage has increased during the sixties.

which are erroneous to the degree that they differ from Catholic dogma. The Roman Catholic Church believes in liberty but defines the word in a manner that deprives it of the meaning it has in the expression "liberal democracy." To the Catholic, liberty is the freedom to do God's will (as the church interprets it). This liberty does not give the right to propagate error. That liberalism in the modern political sense itself is an erroneous belief with which the Pope can have no dealings is in fact the culmination of the famous *Syllabus of Errors* (Arts. LXXVII–LXXX) issued by Pius IX in 1864.[25]

Even during the reign of John XXIII a further elucidation of the Papal doctrine on the political supremacy of the church appeared in the Vatican newspaper, *L'osservatore romano.* Although the article was unsigned, it was generally attributed to Cardinal Ottaviani.

The article can be summed up in the following points:

1. The church has full power of jurisdiction over all its members and therefore has the duty of guiding, directing, and correcting them. On all occasions the Roman Catholic must make his public and private conduct conform to the laws and the institutions of the church.

2. Politics cannot be separated from religion and therefore the church must intervene in politics.

3. The priests are to decide under what conditions Catholics may collaborate with agnostics.

4. The church cannot permit Catholics to collaborate with Communists or Socialists.

5. The church deplores the fact that persons calling themselves Catholics not only dare to act in politics against the position of the church but presume to take on themselves the right to think for themselves and to interpret and evaluate the rules and precepts of the church, which they do with patent superficiality and bravado.

6. Every Catholic must follow the political directives of the church.[26]

---

[25] Arts. LXXVII–LXXVIII specifically condemn freedom of religion, Art. LXXIX condemns freedom of speech, and Art. LXXX liberalism in general. For authoritative reaffirmation of these principles by Leo XIII, Pius XI, and Pius XII, see Ernesto Rossi, *Il sillabo* (Florence: Parenti, 1957), pp. 99–108. See also citation of Pius XI by Piero Calamandrei, "In a Catholic state freedom of conscience and speech must be exercised according to the doctrine and the law of the church." Cited by Piero Calamandrei during a session of the Constitutional Assembly on March 20, 1947, reprinted in Capitini and Lacaita, *op. cit.,* p. 366.

[26] *L'osservatore romano,* May 16, 1960. See *Il ponte,* XVI (1960), pp. 992–993, for résumé. A similar but less complete statement was endorsed by Pope John XXIII thirteen months earlier. See *Economic News from Italy,* XIV, No. 16, April 17, 1959. In May, 1971, Pope Paul VI announced that Catholic laymen, rather than the priests, should be responsible for

The anticlerical position is essentially negative; it is that matters of faith and conscience are private matters and that the church should not interfere in the political arena. This position is that of the American Constitution and of American practice. There is an ebb and flow in anticlericalism, depending on the political philosophy of the reigning Pope. Three of the most powerful and longest reigning Popes of the last hundred years, Pius IX, Pius XI, and Pius XII, were reactionaries whose attitude toward liberal democracy ran from hatred to scorn to a sort of malevolent disinterest. Under these Popes the struggle between the clericals and the anticlericals was exacerbated. Under John XXIII, on the other hand, the only Pope of the century to merit the respect and the affection of all men of good will, things took a decided turn for the better. John did not reign long enough to be able to put the reactionary forces in the church out of business. They were not silent during his Papacy, and under Paul VI they are reasserting themselves. The church, however, appears to be in an evolutionary phase, and it will be difficult to reverse John's trend. In fact, Paul broke with Catholic tradition in declaring that democracy was the best form of government.

Modern anticlericalism in Italy stems in part from the fact that the Roman church has been the enemy of united Italy. The *Risorgimento* was crowned in 1870 when the *bersaglieri* entered Rome, and Pius IX *motu proprio* became a "prisoner in the Vatican." The army defending the Pope from the King's attack contained no Italians. Only one country, Ecuador, protested against the King's violation of the Pope's territory.[27] Vittorio Emanuele II was excommunicated for this act of *lèse sainteté,* and the government of Italy remained in the hands of anticlericals until Benito Mussolini about-faced.

The Lateran Pacts are three documents, a treaty, a financial agreement, and a concordat, all signed February 11, 1929. They were negotiated between Benito Mussolini and Pietro Gasparri, the Papal Secretary of State. From the fall of Rome in 1870 until 1929 Italy and the Popes participated in a cold war. No government before that of Mussolini was willing to sell out the principles of liberal democracy and the Risorgimento to satisfy the Pope. The Roman Catholic Church, as befits an eternal organization, however, was both stubborn and patient, and at last the long-awaited "man sent by providence" (the words are those of Pius XI) arrived, who was more than willing "to trample on the putrid carcass of democracy" (the words are those of Benito Mussolini).

Catholic political and social policy, but he reiterated the condemnation of Marxism and liberalism. See *La stampa,* May 15, 1971.

[27] Ernesto Rossi, "Il nostro venti settembre," *Il ponte,* XV (1959), pp. 1069–1085, at 1077.

The resulting concordat (1) gave temporal sovereignty to the Pope over Vatican City and other territory (Art. 27),[28] (2) paid damages to the Pope,[29] (3) returned crucifixes and religious education to the Italian public schools (Art. 36), and (4) gave civil effect to Roman Catholic marriages (Art. 34). In exchange, the Pope offered to have an annual prayer said for the health of the King and the state (Art. 12), to give the government a veto over the appointment of priests to certain positions in Italy (Arts. 13, 19), to rearrange dioceses to conform to the Italian boundaries (Art. 16), to have bishops functioning in Italy take an oath to support the Fascist government (Art. 20), and to forgive the present owners of previously sequestered church property the sin of holding such property (Art. 28).[30] Seldom has one party to an agreement that during the negotiations held most of the trumps given so much for so little.[31]

The problem concerning the Lateran Pacts with which the Constituent Assembly was immediately faced was not whether or not they should be denounced or renegotiated, but whether or not they should be included in the Constitution. Only the Christian Democrats wanted them in the Constitution, and it took all the persuasiveness and fervor of two of their deputies to bring this battle to a successful conclusion. The deputies entrusted with this mission were two fanatics, a lay Franciscan brother, Giorgio La Pira, and a future priest, Giuseppe Dossetti, both college professors. They won not only by their persistence but also by agreeing that in the many cases where the Pacts were in contrast with the Constitution, the Constitution should prevail.[32] In order to get the bloc of non-Christian Democrat votes necessary for a majority, they made a pact with the only other major antiliberal force in the Assembly, the Communists. Thus the vote found the Catholics and the Communists united against the lay parties,[33] the Socialists, Republicans, and the Action party. The right parties were split. The final vote was 350

[28] The other territory includes the churches of San Giovanni in Laterano (Rome), Santa Maria Maggiore (Rome), San Paolo fuori le mura (Rome), San Francesco (Assisi), Santa Casa (Loreto), and Sant'Antonio (Padua).
[29] 750,000,000 lire ($37,500,000) cash and 1,000,000,000 lire ($50,000,-000) in bonds. *Convenzione finanziaria,* Art. 1.
[30] Property for which the Vatican was being compensated.
[31] See Luigi Salvatorelli and Giovanni Mira, *Storia d'Italia nel periodo fascista* (Turin: Einaudi, 1956), pp. 419–494.
[32] See Adams and Barile, "The Implementation of the Italian Constitution," pp. 69–71. For a more thorough discussion see Paolo Barile, "Concordato e costituzione," in Gorresio, *op. cit.,* pp. 50–94.
[33] See Gorresio, *op. cit.,* pp. 188–192, for an account of her vote by a former Communist member of the Constituent Assembly, Teresa Muzio Mattei.

yes (203 DC, 95 PCI, 52 other) to 149 no (103 PSI, 22 PRI, 7 Action party, and 17 others).[34]

In spite of the Christian Democrat assurance that the articles of the Pacts that were patently in contrast with the *corpus* of the Constitution were to be considered inoperative, some of them (those of greatest concern to the Vatican) were consistently applied. One obnoxious and patently unconstitutional provision denies the right of a defrocked priest to hold public office, including public-school teaching, that brings him in contact with the public (Art. 5). This has been applied regularly, even for an elective office such as mayor or deputy. In 1971, however, the Constitutional Court appeared to have put an end to such practices by denying constitutional rank to the Lateran treaties and consequently denying the validity of any provisions therein that were in contrast with the Constitution.[35]

The theory of the Roman church with respect to its relationship with the state has not changed since the Middle Ages. The *Syllabus of Errors* (Art. XLII) says it is an error to believe that in a conflict between the state and the church, the former should prevail. Pius XI expounded this theory,[36] as did Pius XII when he addressed Italian judges and told them that regardless of the law of the state they had sworn to uphold, they could not grant divorces "except for motives of great moment."[37]

A serious scandal concerning Italian-Vatican relations made the headlines in early 1965. The Vatican, with the connivance of Catholic cabinet members, was in arrears in taxes due the government to the tune of an estimated 40,000,000,000 lire ($600,000,000). A 1962 law passed by the Fanfani Government established a 15 per cent withholding tax on stock dividends. When the bill was being debated in Parliament

---

[34] If the 95 PCI votes had gone to the other side the vote would have been 255 yes to 244 no, but in this case it is almost certain that twelve additional no's would have lined up among the fifty-six absent members, of whom twenty-three were Communist, Socialist, or Republican, and only four were Christian Democrats. See Capitini and Lacaita, *op. cit.,* pp. 537–538.

[35] Decision No. 30 of 1971.

[36] ". . . l'homme appartient totalement à l'Eglise, doit lui appartenir, parce que l'homme est la créature du Bon Dieu. . . . Et le représentant des idées, des pensées et des droits de Dieu, ce n'est que l'Eglise. Alors l'Eglise a vraiment le droit et le devoir de réclamer la totalité de son pouvoir sur les individus; tout l'homme, tout entier, appartient à l'Eglise." Speech to *Confédération française des syndicats chrétiens,* September 18, 1930. Cited in Rossi, *Il sillabo,* pp. 76–77.

[37] *Discorso ai giuristi cattolici italiani,* November 6, 1949, cited in Rossi, *Il sillabo,* pp. 78–81. Pius XII's order would appear to require the immediate resignation of all Roman Catholic judges in jurisdictions where there is a right to a divorce.

a Christian Democrat deputy proposed an amendment that would exempt the Roman Catholic Church, which is considered to hold about 20 per cent of all Italian shares. The amendment was defeated. Nevertheless the church refused to pay the tax, and the banks were authorized not to withhold the tax. In 1965 the Moro Government proposed to put a special bill through Parliament that would exempt the Vatican retroactively, but the Socialists expressed opposition. It is difficult to decide which party was behaving more unethically in this situation, the church in trying to defraud the government or the government in trying to act the role of accomplice before the fact. In an attempt to explain the government's subservience to Vatican interests the press accused the Vatican of having threatened to knock the bottom out of the weak Italian stock exchange by dumping its holdings if it was forced to pay the tax.[38]

A main point of friction between state and church in Italy, as elsewhere, has to do with state support of Catholic schools. In Italy state aid to Catholic schools is unconstitutional, but nevertheless a regular practice of all the Catholic-dominated governments. It was in fact the discovery of a substantial increase in government grants to parochial schools by the Socialist deputy Tristano Codignola that led to the overthrow of the first Moro Government.

The traditional antagonisms between church and state in Italy were exacerbated by the fight over the mild divorce bill that became law in December, 1970. The consequent attempt of right-wing Catholics to abrogate the law by a referendum will increase the animosities on both sides.

While the Vatican is attacked from without and within[39] for its inability or unwillingness to adapt to a rapidly changing environment, it continues to operate even in small matters with unimaginative rigidity. A book review in the *Osservatore romano,* the official Vatican newspaper, announced the author's death. The author wrote the paper and asked for a rectification, to which he had a right under Italian law, but the editor of the *Osservatore* refused on the grounds that a rectification would jeopardize too greatly the credibility of the official Vatican paper,

[38] See Lino Jannuzzi, "La cedolare di S. Pietro," *L'Espresso,* February 14, 1965. The withholding tax was raised from 15 to 30 per cent in 1963.

[39] See, for example, the trials and vicissitudes of Don Lorenzo Milani in his *Le lettere* (Milano: Mondadori, 1970), and the revolt of the Isolotto, where the communicants, after their priest, Don Enzo Mazzi, had been removed, preferred to attend his celebration of mass in the streets to that of his successor in the church. For the Isolotto incident see "Il paradosso Isolotto," *Il ponte,* XXVII (1971), pp. 633–665.

and offered instead to review the author's next book and to refer to him in the present tense.[40]

In the Roman Catholic Church virtually every question that has in the past split the clericals and the anticlericals, that has made the church the official and traditional enemy of liberalism, is now in open dispute within the church itself. If the policies, and above all the spirit, of John XXIII should prevail in the settlement of this discord, then Cavour's dream of a free church within a free state might become a reality in Italy.

(c)   *The* mafia.   The *mafia* is a social disease endemic to western Sicily (the provinces of Palermo, Caltanissetta, Agrigento, and Trapani). It appears to have been successfully transplanted only to those parts of the United States where Sicilians have congregated.

It is fashionable to insist in certain Italian and Italo-American circles that the *mafia* does not exist. This appears for the *mafia,* as with the devil, to be the ultimate ruse, for evil can often work most successfully when the constructive forces are complacent, on the false premise that there is nothing to worry about. The rumor that the *mafia* does not exist is an old one. In fact, one of the etymologies suggested for this obscure word is that it is derived from the Arabic *ma fi* (there is not).

The facts are, however, that in 1964 in Palermo there were sixty-two blackmailing cases, four kidnappings, 170 cases of smuggling tobacco or drugs, three mass killings, forty criminal conspiracies, 159 murders, fifty-eight robberies, 108 cases of arson, seventy-eight thefts of cattle, 776 cases of property damage accompanied by violence or threats of violence to persons, and 558 cases of illegal possession of guns and explosives. In the ensuing seven years conditions have not improved. In 1970 a journalist investigating the *mafia* disappeared, leaving no trace. In 1971 the chief prosecuting attorney in Palermo was assassinated. This man, Pietro Scaglione, appears to have had close *mafia* ties. It is commonly believed that the *mafia* controls the de facto administration of the Palermo prison. The parliamentary report on the

---

[40] "Se sei vivo, non dirlo a nessuno," *L'Espresso,* February 16, 1969, p. 6. Cardinal De Retz, one of the Roman church's most astute political commentators, remarked, "I have more respect for a man who admits his error than for the man who never errs." (*"Car il est à mon sens d'un plus grand homme de savoir avouer sa faute que de savoir ne la pas faire."*) See Paul de Gondi, Cardinal de Retz, *Mémoires.* The citation is from the edition of the Bibliothèque de la Pléïade (Paris, Gallimard, 1956), p. 237. De Retz' *Mémoires* are one of the most insightful commentaries on political behavior found in western culture.

mafia found conditions so bad in the judicial system in Sicily that it recommended the assignment of no native Sicilians to judicial offices in Sicily.[41] This is tantamount to saying that Sicily is not able to govern itself.

The rules on capitalization are confusing and contradictory in English, but we can think of no time except in the unlikely event that it begins a sentence that the word *mafia* should be capitalized. The *mafia* is not only anonymous; it is amorphous. There is no single *mafia* organization, and its essence is not an organization but a way of life. Above all, the *mafia* is not an outlaw institution; it is a part of the establishment in Sicily. The art of the *mafia* is violence and corruption. One buys protection from the *mafia* against itself, for the state as it operates in western Sicily is often indistinguishable from the *mafia* and offers no legal protection.

Education

A presupposition, a *sine qua non* of liberal democracy, is a well-functioning school system. Speaking of the Italian schools, Piero Calamandrei observed, "No one in reviewing the supreme organs of government that give our Constitution its characteristic physiognomy feels it necessary to mention the schools. The schools are on a lower level (on the administrative level, as it were); they do not rise to constitutional importance. Yet there is no doubt that when one wishes to create, maintain, and perfect democracy, the schools are in the long run more important than Parliament or the courts. Parliament consecrates civil liberties in law, the courts protect these liberties, but the conscience of citizens is formed in the schools; the schools determine what Parliament will be tomorrow, what the courts will be, what the moral and intellectual caliber of the legislators, administrators, and judges of the future will be. . . . The blood that daily regenerates democracy comes from the schools, *seminaria republicae*."[42]

The quantity and quality of Italian schools are by common consent such that they are unable to perform adequately the function Calamandrei attributes to them.

---

[41] The figures are from a pre-publication account of an official parliamentary report on the mafia, prepared by Giovanni Elkan (DC) and Mario Assennato (PCI). It is not clear whether they refer to the city or the province of Palermo or to the Appellate Court district of Palermo. See "Antimafia" in *L'Espresso/colore,* May 23, 1971, pp. 8–39. See also Pietro A. Buttitta, ed., "Le tre mafie," *Il ponte,* XXVII (1971), pp. 551–630.

[42] Piero Calamandrei in "Introduction" to Ferretti, *Scuola e democrazia* (Turin: Einaudi, 1956), p. ix.

(*a*) *The quantity.* The quantity of education, or rather the lack of it, itself explains why Italy is behind France and Germany in many ways. According to the 1951 census one of every eight Italians over six years of age could neither read nor write. At that time some 7,000,000 could either read or write but could not do both and were therefore classified as semiliterate. Thus about three out of ten Italians were either illiterate or semiliterate. Continental Italy had a low illiteracy rate — 2 to 3 per cent in most of its regions. The rate rose as one proceeded south, to reach 31.84 per cent in Calabria (58.7 per cent if the semiliterates were included).[43] Thus it is estimated that 20 per cent of the six million immigrants that have come to the northern Italian cities in search of work since the end of World War II have been illiterate to the extent of being unable to read the numbers on the houses and street cars or the "*avanti*" (walk) signs that control pedestrian traffic.[44]

In 1955–56 the government initiated a pilot study in six of the most illiterate provinces of the south (Rieti in Lazio, Benevento in Campania, Foggia in Puglie, Materia in Basilicata, Reggio Calabria in Calabria, and Sassari in Sardinia). It reported that between 9 and 10 per cent of the children from six to eight years of age were not attending the elementary schools.[45] In 1959 the government announced marked improvement, claiming that 95 per cent of the young children went to school.[46]

In the 1960's almost one million children entered first grade every year, of whom about 10 per cent were repeaters. About 10 per cent of elementary school children failed each year and one in five never completed the fifth grade. At this rate it is estimated that about one child in ten of the new generation will be illiterate or semiliterate.[47] The economic effects of the continuance of this high illiteracy rate are obvious. Italy is the only major European state that has consistently had an unemployment problem. Of Italy's unemployed a large majority are permanently so, for lack of education.

The three-year lower secondary schools correspond to our sixth to eighth grades. As of 1968 about one-half of Italian children completed this course, although it is obligatory for all, according to the Constitution (Art. 34). About one-sixth of the eighth-graders fail each year.

[43] See Domenico Tarantini, "L'analfabetismo in Italia," *Nord e sud,* VI (1959), pp. 55–89.

[44] *La stampa,* November 18, 1970.

[45] Paolo Serini, "Analfabetismo e miseria," *La stampa,* July 20, 1957, p. 5.

[46] Statement of Giuseppe Medici, Minister of Education, in *La stampa,* September 1, 1959.

[47] See Felice Froio, *Una scuola da rinnovare* (Milan: Comunità, 1964), *Annuario statistico,* 1969, and the various articles by Paolo Serini and Felice Froio in *La stampa.*

About one-half of those who finish this type of junior high school fail to complete senior high school, and more than five-sixths of those with a senior high school diploma fail to get a university degree. A major factor in this situation is the lack of schools and of adequate teachers.

Inadequate scholarship funds make a higher education almost a monopoly of the higher income families. Over 80 per cent of college students have fathers who are white collar workers, professional men, or self-employed, which groups represent about 40 per cent of the population.

(*b*) *The quality.* The quality of education in Italy at its best is excellent. If the purpose of an educational system is to turn out a limited number of excellently trained minds, the Italian system can be ranked high. If the democratic function of education is the criterion, the quality of the Italian system is less. The problem that the Italians have to solve is how to give mass education in liberal democracy while maintaining and perfecting the obvious advantages of their *élite* educational system.

The system is based on that of France; specialization begins at an early age. Although the tendency has been to continue the common education of most pupils for a longer period, music students still leave the elementary schools for the conservatories after the third grade. For the others, the great majority, specialization begins after the eighth grade, at which time the pupil must select from among thirteen different types of senior high schools, of which ten prepare him to enter some kind of university course.

The pride of the Italian school system is the *liceo classico,* the most difficult of the secondary schools, which is entered after the third year of junior high school. The *liceo* is similar to the French *lycée;* nothing comparable to it is known in the United States. The student who manages to complete this grueling five years of mental discipline not only is educated but has a trained mind. The intellectual snobbery of France and Italy is based in good part on the pride of those students who succeed in passing their final examinations (*esami di maturità*). This is also a traumatic experience, and Italian psychiatrists say that a large portion of the anxieties of their patients are traceable to their fears of failure in the *liceo*.

The anticlerical tradition in the French public schools is not found in Italy. Large numbers of French public school teachers belong to the two traditionally anticlerical parties of France, the Socialists and the Radical Socialists, and French public education has been dominated by rationalist agnostic doctrines. Italian public school education, particularly since the Lateran Pacts, has been basically Roman Catholic. The

Italian school teachers come primarily from the lower middle classes where anticlericalism by and large has not penetrated, and the teachers in Italy are strongholds for the Roman Catholic trade unions of the CISL. There is therefore much less difference between the education received in the public and parochial schools in Italy than there is in France. There is also little difference in the financing of the two types of school in Italy, as the government (in spite of a constitutional prohibition, Art. 34) contributes heavily to the parochial schools. These latter have moved into the field of secondary education where the number of public schools is completely inadequate, and supply an education not essentially different from that given by the public schools. Over 90 per cent of elementary and secondary school pupils in Italy attend state schools.[48]

Many of the parochial and some of the public schools at the secondary level are boarding schools (*collegi* or *convitti*). They offer few of the charms of the British public (i.e., private boarding) and American preparatory schools. Italians are usually sent to them either because there is no school within commuting distance of home, or as a punishment for not studying hard enough at home. It is a rare Italian who looks back on such an experience with nostalgia.

The high standards of the *liceo* are compensated for by the low standards of many of the university faculties. After the *liceo* most students find the four-year law school easy; generally the economics course is still easier, while easiest of all is political science. History and literature are more serious, and the scientific subjects on the whole maintain high standards. This is particularly true of engineering and physical science.

All graduates of Italian universities receive the title of Doctor. This makes Italy in spite of the relatively few college graduates the most doctor-ridden country of Europe.[49] There is talk of a reform of this system that would permit the universities to give two degrees, a pass and an honors degree, similar to Great Britain. The Italian system of higher education needs many reforms, and this one seems quite in the right direction.

As a vehicle for training citizens of the Italian republic, the Italian educational system shows a serious weakness, the essential incompatibility between the indoctrination it imparts and the principles of the Constitution. The system is highly centralized, and power resides in a politically appointed Minister of Education and in a hierarchy of career

[48] *Annuario statistico italiano, 1969, op. cit.,* pp. 77–83.

[49] For an outline of the structure of the university system with indications of the seats of power therein, see Ettore Biocca, "Promemoria della struttura dell'università italiana," *Il ponte,* XXIV (1968), pp. 1775–1782.

civil servants, the upper echelons of which still (1971) had been trained civil servants, the upper echelons of which still (1971) had been trained and indoctrinated under Fascism. The system is authoritarian, and neither student nor teacher has adequate freedom.

Conclusion

Italy has been attempting for about a quarter century to operate a liberal democracy. The results have been mixed. Some of the factors that have had major influences on these results are international in scope; others are national. The same is true of the factors that may help or hinder the successful resolution of the problems that Italy faces at present. The major influences that are national or regional within the nation have been treated in this book. Before we summarize Italy's position and prognosticate Italy's future, a few international factors deserve mention.

Dissatisfaction with the present social order and in many instances alienation from it are endemic to virtually every western country and to Russia. In Italy this unrest is centered in student movements.

Like students of many other countries, a number of Italian students question the validity of their school system and many of this number, often including the most intelligent, sensitive, and idealistic, are profoundly disturbed by what they perceive to be the immorality and the inefficiency of the entire social system.[50] Political parties such as the PCI and PSIUP, which formerly contained (in both senses) virtually all Italian radicals, now find on the left new revolutionary groups that will not traffic with them.

Part of the problem may result from a profound change in the social structure. Throughout most of man's history government has been in the hands of a ruling class. The social system provided training for leaders, and the responsibility of leadership was clear to all. Only recently with the democratization of political power has the classical social system with a discernible ruling class disappeared, to be replaced by a new "feudal" system in which power lies in the hands of egocentric complexes (the labor unions, the military, etc.), and the so-called political leaders are merely the amoral brokers who make the accommodations between these selfish and socially irresponsible "barons". This sentiment of isolation and of lack of empathy with the establishment was increased by three almost simultaneous events, the death of John XXIII, the assassination of John F. Kennedy, and the retirement of Khrushchev, which were a shock to all idealists; the lack of leader-

[50] See Federico Mancini, "The Italian Student Movement," *American Association of University Professors Bulletin*, LIV (1968), pp. 427–434.

ship, responsibility, and integrity in government so noticeable in recent years has encouraged the alienation of the young. These events were a particular shock to Italians because Italians had little interest or confidence in their own leadership and to a considerable degree placed their hopes in these charismatic figures.[51]

An important factor in determining Italy's future that has been treated only peripherally in this book is the European Common Market. If this economic and political union is to progress as those who support it wish, all of Italy, because of its own backward south, will become the backward south of united Europe. In the process of adapting itself to Europe its economy, its public administration, and above all its fiscal system must undergo vast overhauling.[52] The peculiar genius of Italy, as well as France, will be sorely tried in this adaptation. It will be difficult for either government to compete with the greater efficiency and integrity of the northern European governments, just as it will be difficult for Italian and French citizens to learn confidence in their government or to give it the disciplined support on which the British, Dutch, German, and Scandinavian governments can still rely. De Gaulle's dislike and distrust of the Common Market, like that of Pierre Mendès-France before him, was perhaps based more on a realization of France's inferiority than on a desire to leave France's sovereignty unfettered. The Italian attitude toward the Common Market has been consistently more positive than that of France, and we suggest the reason is not that the problems European unity presents Italy are less serious or less obvious. It seems rather that Italians on the whole view the Common Market as a cure they are willing to undergo in the hope of relieving their ills, while the French display a greater reluctance for and fear of the cure.

Although the problems faced by liberal democracy in Italy have not, we believe, been exaggerated in these pages, it would be incorrect to

[51] For the theory of the ruling class see Mosca, *op. cit.* For the history of the theory, see Gaetano Mosca, *Storia delle dottrine politiche* (Bari: Laterza, 1965). For a brief account of the followers of Mosca see John Clarke Adams, *The Quest for Democratic Law* (New York: Thomas Y. Crowell, 1970), pp. 181–182. For the theory of government as brokerage see Arthur F. Bentley, *The Process of Government* (Indianapolis: Bobbs Merrill, 1908). For the theory that rulers who recognize no hierarchy among themselves have supplanted the ruling class see Renzo Sereno, *The Rulers* (Leiden: E. J. Brill, 1962). For an application of this line of reasoning to the Italian student movement see Eugenio Scalfari, *L'autunno della repubblica* (Milano: Etas Kompass, 1969), particularly chapters 7 and 8. For a presentation of the revolutionary picture in general see Jean François Revel, *Ni Marx ni Jésus* (Paris: Editions Robert Laffont, 1970).

[52] The Italian Parliament enacted a major fiscal reform in the summer of 1971.

leave the reader in despair. Postwar Italy is resilient, flexible, and rapidly changing. Perhaps its greatest asset at present is its adaptability, its capacity for improvisation tempered by a respect for tradition. Progress is being made faster than the understandable impatience of some Italians lets them perceive.

A liberal democracy, moreover, is never attained. The citizens of a free country can never sit back in disinterest on the assumption that their work is done, for democracy is constantly menaced. By 1971 the letter of the Italian Constitution had for the most part been implemented. The next task will be to imbue the Italian social system with its spirit. This will be neither a minor nor an easy task. The forces of reaction in Italy, however, are not as strong as they would appear. They have no alternative program and must rely on the corroding influence of cynicism and defeatism. Liberty is within Italy's reach, but it cannot be had for the asking, for liberty cannot be bestowed. Italy must will it and by her own efforts make that will a reality. If this cradle of our common culture cannot make liberal democracy effective, it is hard to believe that it can be successfully transplanted to the far corners of the earth.

BIBLIOGRAPHY

The major writers in English on Italian government and closely related fields include Samuel H. Barnes, Alan Cassels, Taylor Cole, Mario Einaudi, Robert Fried, Daniel Horowitz, H. Stuart Hughes, Ninetta Jucker, Norman Kogan, Joseph LaPalombara, Maurice Neufeld, John Norman, Massimo Salvadori, Renzo Sereno, Claire Sterling, Sidney G. Tarrow, and Elizabeth Wiskemann. The student should consult their books and articles.

The nearest Italian equivalents to the conventional American government textbook are the treatises on constitutional law or public law. The authors' preference among the many good books in this field goes to Costantino Mortati, *Istituzioni di diritto pubblico,* 8th ed., (Padua: CEDAM, 1969), and Paolo Barile, *Istituzioni di diritto pubblico* Padua: CEDAM, 1972). An overall view of Italian government can be found in Paolo Barile, Federico Mereu, and Marco Ramat, *Corso di diritto,* 3 vols. (Firenze: La Nuova Italia, 1970). This text is intended for use in the Italian high schools. For administrative law the authors relied heavily on Guido Zanobini (*Corso di diritto amministrativo,* 6 vols., Milan: Giuffrè, latest ed., 1958–59). For labor law they recommend Luisa Riva Sanseverino (*Diritto sindacale,* Turin, UTET, 1964). The works of Luigi Einaudi are of particular interest because of his official position as first President of Italy and because of his international reputation as an economist. They include *Il buon governo,* Bari: Laterza, 1954, *Lo scrittoio del presidente,* Turin: Giulio Einaudi, 1956, and *Prediche inutili,* Turin: Giulio Einaudi, 1957–59. The history of the Fascist period is treated authoritatively by Luigi Salvatorelli and Giovanni Mira (*Storia d'Italia nel periodo fascista,* Turin: Giulio Einaudi, 1956). Civil liberties are treated by Paolo Barile (*Il soggetto privato nella costituzione italiana,* Padua: CEDAM, 1953).

When discussing official Italian documents, such as laws and judicial decisions, the authors have cited law reviews and compilations of laws rather than official publications. In doing this they have followed the Italian custom. The law reviews are available more quickly than the official publications, and they present the commentaries of leading jurists, which are not found in the official publications.

The various reviews and *codici* cited in this book are almost all published by one of the two great legal publishing houses: that of Dr.

Antonio Giuffrè at Milan or that of Dr. Antonio Milani (*Casa editrice Dott. Antonio Milani*, CEDAM) at Padua. The law reviews of major importance to the foreign student are *Giurisprudenza costituzionale* (containing all the Constitutional Court decisions and excellent commentary), the *Rassegna parlamentare* (containing an account of parliamentary activities, and commentary), and the *Rivista trimestrale di diritto pubblico*. All three of these reviews are published by Giuffrè. The *Rassegna parlamentare* is monthly, and the others are quarterly. *Codici* on each major field of law are published by both houses. We have used Giuseppe Guarino and Leopoldo Elia's *Codice costituzionale* and Guido and Luciano Zanobini's *Codice delle leggi amministrativi*, both published by Giuffrè.

Government publications of particular importance besides the *Gazzetta ufficiale* include the *Annuario statistico italiano* and the *Annuario parlamentare*. The laws and national regulations appear in the *Gazzetta ufficiale*, and basic statistics in the *Annuario statistico*. The *Annuario parlamentare* is the Italian equivalent of the *United States Government Manual*. The Italian government also publishes an abridged *Annuario statistico* in English under the title *The Italian Statistical Yearbook*. The student of Italian constitutional law will also want to have available the many volumes of the *Atti dell'Assemblea costituente*.

La stampa (Turin), *Il corriere della sera* (Milan), and *Il giorno* (Milan) are considered the best Italian daily papers. We have generally preferred to use *La stampa* because of its greater degree of objectivity in political reporting. *Il sole* (Milan) and *Il globo* (Rome) are the leading economic dailies, which resemble the *Wall Street Journal*. The leading party papers in Italy are *Il popolo* (Christian Democrat), *L'unità* (Communist), *Avanti!* (Socialist) and *La voce repubblicana* (Republican). The lay left position is expounded in the weekly *L'Espresso*. The best of the monthlies is *Il ponte*, founded by Piero Calamandrei, an independent magazine with no party affiliation but socialist in outlook.

The frequent citations of newspaper articles for matters of opinion and judgment, particularly of articles in *La stampa*, are justified by the caliber of the authors. Among the regular contributors to this newspaper are the distinguished historian Luigi Salvatorelli, the economist Ferdinando Di Fenizio, and the jurist and historian Alessandro Galante Garrone, as well as the jurist Giovanni Conso. These are not ordinary reporters. They are men who have few peers in their various professions.

Many of the books that we cite are published either by Giulio Einaudi in Turin or by Giuseppe Laterza in Bari. Both these houses have unusually high standards and are rated in the field of general book publishing as high as Giuffrè and CEDAM in legal publishing. Their books deserve serious consideration.

INDEX

Abruzzi, 16–17, 22, 188, 189
Accursio, 26
ACLI (Associazione Cristiana dei lavoratori italiani), 156
Action Party. *See* P d'A
AFL (American Federation of Labor), 206–207
AGIP (Agenzia generale italiana petroli), 198
AGIP mineraria, 198
Agnelli, Giovanni, 195–196
agriculture, production, 189–191
Aimone I, King of Croatia, 8
Aleramo, Sibilla (pseudonym of Rina Faccio), 16
Alexander VI, 15
Alfieri, Vittorio, 12, 23
Alighieri, Dante, 15, 26, 27, 225
Allegri, Antonio (Correggio), 26
Alpini, 101
Alvaro, Corrado, 22
Ambrosini, Gaspare, 53
Amendola, Giorgio, 157, 158
Amendola, Giovanni, 21
Amministrazione autarchica non territoriale, 128
Amministrazione autonoma delle poste e dei telegrafi, 199
Amministrazione autonoma monopoli di stato, 199
amnesty, 150
ANAS (Azienda nazionale autonoma delle strade statali), 104, 200, 220–221
Anderlini, Luigi, 65
Andreotti, Giulio, 167
Angiolilli, Ugo, 184
ANIC (Agenzia nazionale idrogenazione combustibili), 198
ANMIL, 221
Antiquities and Fine Arts Council, 112
Antoniello da Messina, 21
Antonini, Luigi, 207
Ariosto, Ludovico, 26
Armed Forces, Council of, 112
army, 101
Arpinati, Learco, 12
ASFD (Azienda di stato per le foreste demaniali), 200
assegni familiari, 210
Assemblea regionale siciliana, 131
Associazione nazionale tra le vittime civili di guerra, 221
assoluzione per mancanza di prove, 148

attentato alla costituzione, 79
Avanti!, 240
Avvocatura dello stato, 128, 146
Azienda dei servizi telefonici, 200
Azienda di stato per l'intervento nel mercato agricolo, 200
Aziende autonome, 199, 200
Azzariti, Gaetano, 21

Bakunin, Mikhail, 159
Balbo, Cesare, 12
Balbo, Italo, 12, 26
Bartolo, 26
Basilicata, 21, 22, 176, 177, 189, 233
Basso, Lelio, 160
Beccaria, Marchese Cesare, 24, 148, 214
Belli, Giuseppe Gioacchino, 22
Bellini, Gentile, 25
Bellini, Giovanni, 25
Ben pensanti, 40
Benoist, Charles, 94
Bernini, Giovanni Lorenzo, 20
Bersaglieri, 101, 227
Besana, Mario, 216
Bissolati, Leonida, 38, 159
Boccaccio, Giovanni, 15, 27
bonifica, 104
Bonomi, Ivanhoe, 38, 52
Bonomi, Paolo, 190, 208–209
Bordiga, Armando, 159
Borgese, Giuseppe Antonio, 21, 43–44
Borja, Cesar, 15
Botticelli, Sandro, 27
braccianti, 191
Brancati, Vitaliano, 16
Briga and Tenda, 9
Brunelleschi, Filippo, 27
buon costume, 215
Buonarotti, Michelangelo, 20
Buozzi, Bruno, 205
bureaucracy, 114–117
Burns, John Horne, 22

Calabria, 17–18, 189, 195, 221, 233
Calamandrei, Piero, 27, 29, 52, 53, 56, 147, 160, 214, 232, 240
Calandrino, 15
camera (*pl.* camere) del lavoro, 204, 207
camera di commercio, industria, artigianato e agricoltura, 129
Camerata, 27
Campania, 12, 18, 19, 20, 22, 233
campanilismo, 25

"careers", civil service, 116–117
Carlo Alberto, King of Piedmont, 8, 46, 52
Carmagnola, Luigi, 206
Caruso, Enrico, 21
Casanova, Giacomo, 25
Cassa deposti e prestiti, 200
Cassa per il mezzogiorno (Cassa per gli interventi straordinarie nel mezzogiorno e nelle aree depresse del centronord), 88, 108, 194
Catholic Action, 152, 155
Cattaneo, Carlo, 12
Cavalli, Francesco, 25
Cavour, Camillo Benso, conte di, 8, 12, 23, 24, 162, 214
Cellini, Benvenuto, 27
Cesari, Vasco, 205–206
CGIL (Confederazione generale italiana del lavoro), 205–209
CGL (Confederazione generale del lavoro), 204, 205
Chabod, Federico, 10
Chamber of Deputies, 173–175
Chambers of Commerce, 129
charitable bodies, 128–129
Christian Democracy. See DC
Ciano, Conte Costanzo, 12
Ciano, Conte Gian Galeazzo, 12
CIL (Confederazione italiana del lavoro), 204, 205
CIO (Congress of Industrial Organizations), 206–207
CIP (Comitato interministeriale per i prezzi), 108
CIPE (Comitato interministeriale per la programmazione economica), 108–109
CIR (Comitato interministeriale per la ricostruzione), 109n
CISL (Confederazione italiana dei sindacati dei lavoratori), 155–156, 207, 208, 235
CISNAL (Confederazione italiana dei sindacati nazionali dei lavoratori), 207, 208
civil liberties, 214–231
civil service, 114–117
CLN (Comitati di liberazione nazionale), 205, 206
CNEL (Consiglio nazionale dell'economia e del lavoro), 55, 57, 65, 110–112, 207
CNEN (Contro nazionale per l'energia nucleare), 115
CNP (Comitato nazionale per la produttività), 108
codes: civil, 147, 151; criminal, 147–150, 151

Codignola, Tristano, 65, 162, 230
Colitto, Francesco, 184
collegi, 235
Colombo, Emilio, 21, 91, 154, 209, 213, 221
Colonnetti, Gustavo, 52
coltivatori diretti (Confederazione nazionale coltivatori diretti), 111, 190, 209
Comitato pel credito, 108
Comitato provinciale di assistenza e beneficenza pubblica, 127, 129
comizi, 182
commissario, 131–132
Commissario prefettizio, 121
commissioni permanti, 62
Committee of Eighteen, 53–54
Committee of Seventy-Five, 53–54, 82
committees, minor advisory, 127
Common Market (European Community), 73, 202, 213, 237
communes, 120–123
Communist Party. See PCI
compagnie, 105
conciliatore (pl. conciliatori), 134, 135, 141
confederazione (pl. confederazioni), 207
Confederazione generale dell'agricoltura italiana, 208
Confindustria (Confederazione italiana dell'industria), 196, 208
CONI (Comitato olimpico nazionale italiano), 107
Consiglio comunale, 121–122, 181
Consiglio di amministrazione, 117
Consiglio di giustizia amministrativa per la regione siciliana, 138
Consiglio di prefettura, 124, 127, 139
Consiglio di stato, 95, 108, 109–110, 137–139, 140
Consiglio nazionale delle ricerche, 112–113
Consiglio provinciale, 119, 127, 129, 179–181
Consiglio superiore della pubblica amministrazione, 112
Consiglio superiore per la magistratura, 54, 55, 65, 73, 79, 144–146
Consiglio supremo de difesa, 79, 108
Conso, Giovanni, 240
consorzio (pl. consorzi), 129
Consorzio autonomo per le opere del porto di Genova, 129
Constituent Assembly, 52–54, 56, 77, 80, 153
constitutional amendments, 71

Constitutional Court, 54, 55, 57, 73, 80–81, 95–99, 131, 136
Conti, Giovanni, 53
convitti, 235
Corelli, Archangelo, 26
corporate system, 46–47
corporazioni, 44, 46–47
Corriere della Sera, Il, 24, 216, 240
Corte dei conti, 95, 108, 113, 128, 137, 139–140
Corte di cassazione, 95, 136, 137, 140, 141, 144, 145, 147
Council of Agriculture and Forests, 112
Council of Europe, 73
Council of Ministers, 88–94
Court of Appeal, 135
Court of Assizes, 135, 141
courts: administrative, 137–140; Constitutional, 54, 55, 57, 73, 80–81, 95–99, 131, 136; High, for Sicily, 136; martial (tribunali militari), 140; officers, 141–144; ordinary, 134–136; special, 136–141
Covelli, Alfredo, 164
Crispi, Francesco, 21
Croce, Benedetto, 20, 52, 162
culture: history, 10–13; Mediterranean Italy, 14–22; European Italy, 22–28

Dal Monte, Toti, 25
D'Annunzio, Gabriele, 22, 41–44, 45
D'Aragona, Ludovico, 204
D'Azeglio, Marchese Massimo, 12, 30
DC (Democrazia cristiana), 52, 53, 86, 154–156, 157, 164–165, 167, 169–170, 174, 182, 183, 184, 190, 205, 206, 207, 208, 223n, 228, 229
De Caro, Raffaele, 184
De Filippo, Eduardo, 22
De Gasperi, Alcide, 91, 154, 206
De Gaulle, Charles, 9
De Luca, Giuseppe, 21
Democratic Socialist Party. See PSDI
De Nicola, Enrico, 21, 52, 78, 85
Di Pisis, Francesco, 25
De Sanctis, Francesco, 20
De Sica, Vittorio, 20
decree laws (decreti leggi), 92–93
decreti aventi valore di legge, 79
decreto legislativo (pl. decreti legislativi), 92–93
Del Canton, Maria Pia, 221
Deledda, Grazia, 22
Della Francesca, Piero, 27
demography, 1, 189
Di Fenizio, Ferdinando, 240

Di Giacomo, Salvatore, 21
Di Vittorio, Giuseppe, 21, 205, 206
Direzione generale della bonifica, 104
diritto casuale, 224
Discoteca dello stato, 108
disegni di legge, 66
Dolci, Danilo, 22, 30
Donatello (De' Bardi), 27
Donizetti, Gaetano, 24
Dossetti, Giuseppe, 52, 53, 228
Douglas, Norman, 22
Duse, Eleanora, 25

ECA (Ente comunale d'assistenza), 128
education, 232–236
Education, Council on, 112
Einaudi, Giulio, 23
Einaudi, Luigi, 23, 52, 78, 81, 82, 84, 85, 126, 162, 214
elections: cifre elettorali, 174; D'Hondt system, 176–177, 181; Hare system, 178; limited vote, 181; panachage, 181; preference votes, 181
elezioni amministrative, 182n
Emanuele Filiberto, 23
Emilia Romagna, 12, 22, 25–27, 190
ENEL (Ente nazionale elettricità), 200
ENI (Ente nazionale idrocarburi), 198–199, 216
Ente autonomo per l'acquedotto pugliese, 129
Enti di gestione, 199
esami di maturità, 234
L'Espresso, 240
European Italy, 22–28
Export-Import Bank, 100
exports, "hidden," 193

Fanfani, Amintore, 28, 68, 86, 91, 154, 161, 169–170, 220, 223n, 229
Farinacci, Roberto, 12
Farinelli (Carlo Bosco), 21
federazioni di categoria, 204, 207
Federazione italiana lavoratori poligrafici e cartai, 205
Federconsorzi, 64
fesso, 14, 15
Feste dell'Unità, 167
FFSS (Azienda autonoma delle ferrovie dello stato), 200
fiancheggiatori, 40
FIDAE (Federazione italiana dipendenti aziende elettriche), 205–206

FIL (Federazione italiana del lavoro), 207
FILP (Federazione italiana lavoratori dei porti), 205–206
Finmare (Società finanziaria marittima), 198
Finmeccanica, 198
Finsider (Società finanziaria siderurgica), 198, 199
FIOM (Federazione impiegati operai metallurgici), 205
Foa, Vittorio, 162
Foderaro, Salvatore, 184
Fogazzaro, Antonio, 12
Fortuna, Loris, 65, 173
Foscolo, Ugo, 12
Francesco, St., d'Assisi, 28, 29
frazione (*pl.* frazioni), 120, 129
Friuli-Venezia Giulia, 57, 130, 132, 173, 178, 181, 189
furbo, 14, 15, 29
Futurism, 41–42

Galante Garrone, Alessandro, 240
Galilei, Galileo, 27
gallismo, 15–16
Garibaldi, Giuseppe, 7, 8, 12, 29, 159
Gasparri, Pietro Cardinal, 227
Genoa, Republic of, 6
Gente del mare, 205–206
geography, 5; cultural, 10–11; economic, 188–189
Germi, Pietro, 22
Ghibellines, 225
Ghiberti, Lorenzo, 27
Ghidini, Gustavo, 53
Gianturco, Emanuele, 21
Gioberti, Vincenzo, 12
Giolitti, Giovanni, 23, 35, 37–38, 44, 153
Giorgione, 25
Giorno, Il, 216, 240
Giotto, 27, 28
giudice istruttore, 149
Giulietti, Giuseppe, 205–206
giunta comunale, 121, 122
giunta provinciale, 119, 221
giustizia ritenuta, 138
Gladstone, William, 7
Globo, Il, 240
Gobbi, Tito, 25
Gobetti, Piero, 23
Goldoni, Carlo, 25
governo (government), 88–92
GPA (giunta provinciale amministrativa [*pl.* giunte provinciali amministrative]), 124, 127, 173
Gramsci, Antonio, 30, 159
Grandi, Achille, 205

Grandi, Conte Dino, 12, 26, 147
Grassi, Giuseppe, 52, 53
Gronchi, Giovanni, 28, 82, 84, 85–86, 215
gruppo misto, 62
gruppi parlamentari, 61
guardia di finanza, 103
Guelphs, 225

High Court of Sicily, 136
High Judicial Council (Consiglio superiore per la magistratura), 54, 55, 65, 73, 79, 144–146
High Public Administration Council (Consiglio superiore della pubblica amministrazione), 112
hydroelectric power, 13, 188

Iacini, Conte Stefano, 12
idealisti, 40
IFITAS (Istituto finanziario delle industrie del tabacco e del sale), 199n
illiteracy, 233
impeachment, 83
INAIL (Istituto nazionale assistenza infortuni lavoro), 211, 212
INAM (Istituto nazionale per l'assicurazione contro le malattie), 211, 212, 213
indennità di contingenza, 210
indirizzo generale o constituzionale, 82
indirizzo politico, 82, 93
industry, 191–192
Ingrao, Pietro, 158
initiative, 65–66
INPS (Istituto nazionale per la previdenza sociale), 211–212, 213
intendente di finanza, 127
intendenza di finanza, 128
interesse legittimo (*pl.* interessi legittimi), 138, 139
International Monetary Fund, 100
interpellanza, 71–72
interrogazione, 71–72
IPA (Ispettorati provinciali agricoltura), 104
Ippolito, Prof. 115
IRI (Istituto per la ricostruzione industriale), 197–199
Irnerio, 26
irredentismo, 36–37
Istituto centrale di statistica, 108
Istituto di studi per la programmazione economica, 109
Istituto di sanità, 115
Istituto poligrafico dello stato, 200

Italian Democratic Party of Monarchist Unity. *See* PDIUM
Italian Socialist Party. *See PSI*
Italian Socialist Party of Proletarian Unity. *See* PSIUP
Italian Social Movement. *See* MSI
Italian Workers Socialist Party. *See* PSLI

John XXIII, 24, 170, 226, 227, 236
judges, 141–146

La Malfa, Ugo, 21, 117, 133, 162, 163
La Pira, Giorgio, 29, 228
La Tour du Pin Chambly de la Charce, René Charles Humbert, Marquis de, 46–47
Labor Democrat Party. *See* PDL
labor legislation, 209–211
Labour Party, British, 207
Labriola, Arturo, 159
Lateran Pacts, 49, 56, 173, 217, 228–229, 234
latifondi, 191
Lauro, Achille, 29, 164
Lazio, 233
LCGIL (Libera confederazione generale italiana dei lavoratori), 207
Lega lombarda, 11, 121
legal aid, 150
legal officers, 141–146
legal system, 146–150
legge truffa, 183
legislators, 61
Leonardo da Vinci, 24
Leone, Giovanni, 68, 86, 91, 154
Leopardi, Giacomo, 12, 27
Leopoldo, Grand Duke of Tuscany, 7, 8
Levi, Carlo, 15, 22
Liberal Party. *See* PLI
libero consorzio (*pl.* liberi consorzi), 120
Library Council, 112
liceo classico, 235
Liguria, 23, 188, 189, 191
Lizzadri, Oreste, 205
Lombardi, Riccardo, 21, 162
Lombardy, 12, 22, 24, 191
Longo, Luigi, 52
Lucca, Duchy of, 6

Machiavelli, Niccolò, 15, 27, 29
mafia, 18, 19, 231–232
Magnani, Anna, 20
Malagodi, Giovanni, 34, 162

Mancini, Giacomo, 220–221
mandamento giudiziario, 134–135
Manifesto, 158, 161
Manin, Daniele, 12
Manzoni, Alessandro, 12, 24
March on Rome, 32–33, 39
Marche, 27, 188, 190
Marchesi, Concetto, 52
Marconi, Marchese Guglielmo, 26
Maria José, Queen of Italy, 77
Maria Luisa, Duchess of Lucca, 6
Marinetti, Filippo Tommaso, 41, 43, 45
Mariotti, Luigi, 65
Marotta, Prof., 115
Marsilio of Padova, 121
Martinelli, Giovanni, 25
Marx, Karl, 159, 203
Masaccio (Tomaso Guidi), 27
Mattei, Enrico, 198, 198n
Matteotti, Giacomo, 46
Maxwell, Gavin, 22
mayor, 121, 122, 171
Mazzini, Giuseppe, 7, 12, 23, 29, 159, 163, 214
medico provinciale, 127
Merriam, Charles Edward, 78
Merzagora, Cesare, 86
Metastasio, Pietro (pseudonym of Pietro Trapassi), 20
Metternich-Winneburg, Prince Clemens Wenzel Lothar von, 6
mezzadria, 190
Ministry of:
    Agriculture and Forests, 89, 104–105, 112, 200
    Budget, 89, 102–103
    Defense, 89, 101, 219–220
    Education, 89, 103–104, 112, 235–236
    Finance, 89, 102, 103, 199
    Foreign Affairs, 89, 100–101
    Foreign Commerce, 89, 106
    Health, 89, 106–107, 112
    Industry and Commerce, 89, 105
    Interior, 89, 221
    Justice, 89, 145
    Labor and Social Security, 89, 209–213
    Merchant Marine, 89, 105–106
    Postal and Telegraphic Service, 89, 106, 199, 200
    Public Works, 89, 104, 200
    State-Controlled Enterprises, 89, 194, 200
    Tourism and Entertainment, 89, 107
    Transportation, 89, 106, 200
    Treasury, 89, 103, 200

Modena, Duchy of, 6, 7
Modigliani, Giovanni Emanuele, 38
Molise, 130–131, 176, 184, 188, 189
Monarchist Party. *See* PDIUM
Montale, Eugenio, 23
Monteverdi, Claudio, 24, 25
Moravia, Alberto, 22
Moro, Aldo, 21, 86, 91, 154, 170, 213, 230
Mortati, Constantino, 52, 53, 126
Mosca, Gaetano, 21, 74, 162, 223
motion, 70–71
MSI (Movimento sociale italiano), 163–164, 165, 166, 173, 174, 182, 208
municipal councils, 121–122, 181
Mussolini, Benito, 9, 12, 26, 29, 32–33, 39, 40–41, 45–50, 83, 95, 159, 197, 215, 227

Naples (region). *See* Campania
Naples, Kingdom of (also known as Kingdom of the Two Sicilies), 6, 7, 8
Napoleon III, 8
National Economic Council. *See* CNEL
National Health Council, 112
National Research Council, 112–113
Nazification, 49–50
Nenni, Pietro, 27, 160, 161, 170
Nievo, Ippolito, 12, 25
Nitti, Francesco Saverio, 21, 37, 52
norme precettive, 55
norme programmatiche, 55

Olivetti, Adriano, 196
ordinanze, 99
ordini o collegi professionali, 113–114
Orlando, Vittorio Emanuele, 21, 36, 52
L'Osservatore romano, 222–223, 226, 230
Ottaviani, Cardinal, 226
Ottieri, Ottiero, 22

P d'A (Partito d'azione), 53, 153, 162, 205, 228–229
Palazzo Madama, 69
Palazzo Montecitorio, 69
Palestrina, Pierluigi da, 20
Palladio, Antonio, 24
Papal States, 6, 7, 8, 19, 20, 22
Parliament procedure: in sede consultiva, 69; in sede deliberante, 66–68; in sede politica, 69; in sede redigente, 66, 68; in sede referente, 66–67

Parma, Duchy of, 6, 7
Parri, Ferruccio, 29–30, 52, 154, 162
Partito popolare, 21, 35, 38–39, 85, 152, 154
Partito socialista riformista, 159
partitocrazia, 168–169
party finance, 166–168
Pastore, Giulio, 86, 207
Paul VI, 24, 226–227
Pavelic, Ante, 8
Pavese, Cesare, 23
Pavolini, Alessandro, 12
PCI (Partito comunista italiano), 35, 38, 52, 64, 153, 154, 156–158, 164, 165, 166, 167, 169, 174, 182, 205, 206, 208, 223n, 228–229, 236
PDIUM (Partito democratico italiano di unità monarchica), 164, 174, 182
PDL (Partito democratico del lavoro), 52, 153, 205
peace conferences, Paris, 36
Pella, Giuseppe, 91, 154
Perassi, Tomaso, 52, 53
Pergolesi, Giovani Battista, 20, 21
Peri, Iacopo, 27
Perugino, 28
Petacci, Clara, 50
Petrarca, Francesco, 27
Petrolini, Ettore, 20
Piedmont (region), 12, 22, 23, 191
Piedmont, Kingdom of (also known as Kingdom of Sardinia), 6, 7, 8
Pietro Leopoldo, Grand Duke of Tuscany, 7
Pintor, Luigi, 158
Pinza, Ezio, 26
Pirandello, Luigi, 21
Pirelli, Leopoldo, 195–196
Pius IX, 7, 8, 34, 226, 227
Pius XI, 24, 39, 49, 226n, 227, 229
Pius XII, 227, 229
PLI (Partito liberale italiano), 34, 37, 52, 153, 162–163, 165, 169, 170, 174, 184, 205
PMP (Partito monarchio populare), 164
PNP (Partito nazionale monarchico), 164
Poerio, Carlo, 12
police, 128, 216, 223–224
Polo, Marco, 25
Ponte, Il, 240
Popolo, Il, 240
Prampolini, Camillo, 29, 38
prefect, 123–126, 224
Presidenza del Consiglio dei Ministri, 107–108, 112
pretore, 134–135, 141

PRI (Partito repubblicano italiano), 52, 86, 153, 163, 165, 166, 169, 170, 174, 205, 207, 208, 228–229
Primo presidente, 144
private member bill, 66
procuratore, 144
Procuratore generale, 144
professional associations, 113–114
progetti di legge, 66
proposte di legge, 66
prosecuting attorney, 144
provinces, 118–120, 179–181
Provveditorato generale dello stato, 103
Provveditori agli studi, 128
PSDI (Partito socialista democratico italiano), 86, 160, 161, 162, 165, 166, 169, 170, 174, 207, 208
PSI (Partito socialista italiano, formerly PSIUP), 34, 37–38, 52, 54, 86, 152, 153, 154, 158–162. 164, 166, 167, 169, 170, 174, 182, 205, 206, 208, 221, 228–229
PSIUP (Partito socialista italiano di unità proletaria): (1) former name of PSI, 160; (2) new party founded 1964, 158, 161–162, 165, 236
PSLI (Partito socialista dei lavoratori italiani, formerly PSDI), 160
PS(SIIS) (Partito socialista [Sezione italiana dell'internazionale socialista], formerly both PSI and PSDI), 159–160
PSU (Partito socialista unitario, formerly PSDI), 160, 161
Public Health Institute, 115
pubblico ministero, 144
Puglie, 12, 17, 22, 188

Quasimodo, Salvatore, 22
questore, 128, 217, 224
questura, 128

Raffaello, 28
Ragioneria generale dello stato, 103
ragioniere generale, 102
referenda, 55, 172–173
referendari, 109
regions, 54, 57, 130–133, 178–179
Regno lombardo-veneto, 6, 8
Renaissance (Rinascimento), 11, 214
Republican Party. See PRI
Resistenza, 11, 12, 13, 30, 153, 214
Ricasoli, Barone Bettino, 12, 28

ricorso straordinario al Presidente della repubblica, 79, 139
riforma agraria, 191
Rigola, Rinaldo, 204
Rinaldi, Giuseppe, 220–221
Risorgimento, 11–13, 29, 30, 33–34, 214, 227
Ristori, Adelaide, 25
Rocco, Alfredo, 46, 148
Roman Catholic Church, 155, 156, 193, 217, 224–231
Romano, Santi, 21
Rome, unique cultural position of, 19, 20
Rossanda, Rossanna, 158
Rossellini, Roberto, 20
Rossi, Ernesto, 218–219
Rossi-Doria, Manlio, 64
Rossini, Gioacchino, 27
Rossoni, Edmondo, 205
Royal Italian Senate, 60
Rubinacci, Leopoldo, 64
Ruggeri, Ruggero, 27
Ruini, Meuccio, 53
Rumor, Mariano, 91, 154

Salvatorelli, Luigi, 240
Salvemini, Gaetano, 21, 219
Saragat, Giuseppe, 23, 86–87, 160
Sardinia, 21, 22, 57, 130, 132, 172, 178, 179, 181, 189, 233
Scaglione, Pietro, 231
Scalfari, Eugenio, 65
Scarlatti, Alessandro, 20
Scelba, Mario, 21, 91, 126, 154, 223n
Schicchi, Gianni, 15
Schipa, Tito, 21
Sciascia, Leonardo, 22
Scoccimaro, Mauro, 223n
Scuola superiore della pubblica amministrazione, 117
Sephardic Jews, 225
Segni, Antonio, 21, 86, 91, 154
segretario comunale, 123
Senate, 176–178
sentenza (pl. sentenze), 99
serfdom, reestablishment of, 50
sex, obsession with, 16
Sforza, Carlo, 28, 44, 52
Sicily, 9, 18, 21–22, 57, 120, 130–133, 136, 138, 178–179, 181, 183, 189, 231–232
Silone, Ignazio (pseudonym of Secondo Tranquilli), 22
Simionato, Giulietta, 26
sindaco, 121, 122, 171
SNAM (Società nazionale metanodotti), 198
social security, 211–213

Social Democratic Party, Italian. *See* PSDI

Socialist Party, Italian. *See* PSI and PS(SIIS)

Socialist Party of Proletarian Unity. *See* PSIUP

Sole, Il, 240

South Tirol People's Party. *See* SV

Spaventa, Silvio, 12

squadristi, 40

Stabile, Mariano, 21

Stampa, La, 23, 216, 221, 240

state-church relations, 224–231

Statuto, 8, 46, 52, 54, 55, 95

Statuto dei lavoratori, 210

STET (società torinese esercizi telefonici), 197–198

Sturzo, Don Luigi, 21, 35, 85, 152

Supreme Council of Defense, 79, 108

SV (Südtiroler Volkspartei), 164–165, 176

Syllabus of Errors, 226

Tambroni, Fernando, 91, 154, 162, 216

tax courts, 140–141

Terracini, Umberto, 53, 223n

terza forza, 169–170

Tiepolo, Giovanni Battista, 25

Tintoretto (Iacopo Robusti), 25

Titian (Tiziano Vercelio), 25

Titta, Ruffo, 27

Togliatti, Palmiro, 53–54, 156, 157, 158, 159

Tomasi di Lampedusa, Prince Giuseppe, 21

Tommaseo, Niccolò, 12

Tosato, Egidio, 52, 53

Toscanini, Arturo, 26

tredicesima mensilità, 210

Tremelloni, Roberto, 64

Trentino-Alto Adige, 57, 130, 132, 164, 172, 176, 177, 178–179, 180–181, 183, 188, 189

Treves, Claudio, 38

tribuna politica, 182

tribunale, 135, 141

tribunali militari, 140

Tribunale regionale delle acque pubbliche, 135–136

Tribunale superiore delle acque pubbliche, 136

Tupini, Umberto, 53

Turati, Filippo, 29, 38, 152, 159

Tuscany (region), 12, 15, 22, 27–28, 190, 191

Tuscany, Grand duchy of, 6, 7

Uffici del genio civile, 128

Ufficio centrale nazionale, 175

UIL (Unione italiana del lavoro): (1) pre-Fascist union, 204–207; (2) post-Fascist union, 207–208

Umberto II, King of Italy, 77

Umbria, 28, 173, 176, 177, 188, 189, 190

unemployment benefits, 211–212

Union valdôtaine, 164–165

Unione socialista, 38

L'Unità, 167, 216, 240

Unità proletaria, 160

Unitary Socialist Party. *See* PSU

Unità socialista, 160

Università cattolica del sacro cuore, 103

Uomo Qualunque Party (Fronte nazionale dell'uomo qualunque), 184

USI (Unione sindacale italiana), 204–205

UV (Val d'Aosta Union), 9, 57, 130–131, 132, 164, 172, 175, 176, 177, 178, 183, 188

Vailland, Roger, 22

Val d'Aosta Union. *See* UV

Val padana, 11, 188

Veneto, 22, 24–25, 176, 188, 191

Venice, Republic of, 6

Verdi, Giuseppe, 12, 26

Verga, Giovanni, 21

Veronese, Paolo, 25

veterinario provinciale, 127

veto, presidential, 55, 79, 81–82

Vico, Giovambattista, 20

Vigorelli, Ezio, 64

vilipendio, 215–216

Vinci, Leonardo da, 24

Visconti, Luchino, 22

Vittorio Emanuele II, King of Italy, 9, 12, 227

Vittorio Emanuele III, King of Italy, 32, 77, 78

Vivaldi, Antonio, 25

Voce repubblicana, La, 216, 240

vote of confidence, 71, 72

voting in parliament: electric, 70–71; roll call, 70; secret, 70

wages, 210–211

Waldensians, 23, 225

World Bank, 100

Zacconi, Ermete, 26

Zoli, Adone, 91, 154